THE POLITICS OF
MIGRATION POLICIES

D1089560

THE POLITICS OF MIGRATION POLICIES

THE FIRST WORLD IN THE 1970s

edited by
Daniel Kubat
with
Ursula Merhländer & Ernst Gehmacher

1979
CENTER FOR MIGRATION STUDIES
NEW YORK

The Center for Migration Studies is an educational, non-profit institute founded in New York in 1964 to encourage and facilitate the study of sociological, demographic, historical, legislative and pastoral aspects of human migration and ethnic group relations. The opinions expressed in this work are those of the authors.

The Politics of Migration Policies
The First World in the 1970s

First Edition

Copyright © 1979 by
The Center for Migration Studies of New York, Inc.
All rights reserved. No part of this book may be reproduced without
written permission from the publisher.

Center for Migration Studies
209 Flagg Place
Staten Island, New York 10304

ISBN 0-913256-34-X
Library of Congress Catalog Card Number: 77-93185
Printed in the United States of America

Preface

THE need for a summary source of information on the development and state of policies pursued by countries to admit aliens for settlement, or employment, has been realized for quite some time. To meet this need, this volume offers a time series of data on the movements and characteristics of migrants, as well as a comparison of migration policies by which countries respond to their diverse demographic realities. That is, this volume represents a reference work offering standardized information on migration policies of some 22 countries of the West; it suggests analyses of the policies individual countries evolved to meet their migration needs, and it provides the data on which the analyses are based.

Juxtaposing the countries, one becomes aware of parallel trends in the countries concerned. It is also evident that they have similar problems and have attempted various solutions to the economic, demographic, social and cultural consequences of international migration. That most countries react to their respective situations in similar ways indicates not only that migration is producing common pressures but also that there is a growing interdependence among the countries concerned. Some of the interdependence has been institutionalized, as in the case of the European Communities who permit a free movement of labor by the nationals of the member states. In other cases the interdependence is subject to a much more rigid political and administrative control over the movement of population.

International labor migration is often followed by the migration of whole families and communities. Although relying heavily on the foreign workers during times of economic growth, advanced industrial countries are less sympathetic to migrants at times of recession. Migration may then be seen as threatening the economic welfare of their own nationals and even disturbing the political and social integration of the countries concerned. At the same time, those countries supplying workers suffer when migration serves as a substitute for economic growth at home, or when the demand for workers abroad declines with the consequent loss of remittances and increase in unemployment.

This book contains useful information on the treatment of alien workers in their host countries, the current migration policies, and offers valuable statistical data. *The Politics of Migration Policies* may be recommended to policymakers, scholars of migration and to all who are looking for an invaluable source of information on questions of international and regional migration. The authors of individual chapters are each reputed scholars of migration in their respective countries. The Research Committee on Migration of the International Sociological Association is proud to have been associated with the preparation of this text.

Anthony H. Richmond
President, Research Committee on Migration
International Sociological Association
and
York University, Canada

Acknowledgments

THE concept for this book was initiated at an International Conference on Migration Policies organized in Vienna by the Research Committee on Migration, International Sociological Association. The Conference, held in May, 1975, was hosted by Ernst Gehmacher, Director of the Institute for Empirical Social Research (IFES) in Vienna. Although the Conference participants supplied a framework for the book, the bulk of the contributors to this volume joined the project later.

At this point, I should like to praise the authors of this book for their willingness to be prodded into following a supplied syllabus. Furthermore, I owe all of them an apology for having behaved in a ruthless and Procrustean manner after they had graciously sent me their manuscripts. Not infrequently an elegant metaphor was lost when I attempted to impose a certain uniformity of style for the sake of comparability between the individual chapters. To the extent that I have not succeeded completely a stylistic diversity has been saved.

That the editorial work would not have proceeded so swiftly were it not for the valuable help of my collaborators Ernst Gehmacher and Ursula Mehrländer, need not be stressed. I wish to thank N.B. Kubat and E.M. Rideout for reading drafts of the manuscript and thus saving me from many a stylistic *faux pas*. My thanks also goes to Maggie Sullivan for her continuous efforts in the editorial process.

The kind persons who helped with typing were D. Lichtenegger and I. Strassner. Above all, my thanks go to Professors Kurt Freisitzer and Karl Acham, directors of the Institute for Sociology at the University of Graz, who kindly made the Institute's facilities available to me. In particular, I am thankful to Professor Freisitzer who invited me to Graz and made my stay at the Institute profitable to such an extreme, that doubts may be raised whether the Institute profited by my stay anywhere near so much as I have profited from staying there.

DANIEL KUBAT

May, 1977
Graz, Austria

Contents

List of Tables

Introduction

DANIEL KUBAT
University of Graz
and
University of Waterloo

Migrations, Politics and the Population Balance

THE countries of the First World[1] have possessed the institutions of self government perhaps longer than any other peoples. One well-developed trait of the democratic political system is the process that has become known as "muddling through"; a characteristic largely attributed to the political decision making procedure of the English speaking democracies, although not entirely unknown to the other members of the First World. This muddling through in politics is nothing other than *ad hoc* responses to social issues redefined as political issues. The responses may be couched in the rhetoric of long term goals and planning, but they are always accompanied by short term regulations. Actually, the householding of nations differs only in degree from the householding of individual families who face the problems of the day as they arise and who address exigencies as they happen. As there are differences between poor and well-to-do families, so there are differences between poor and well-to-do nations when it comes to defining the urgency of problems. That is, the well-to-do do not get their hand forced quite so often as the poor.

---

[1] A term used by implication only when referring to the Third World or the Fourth World countries and is synonymous with the Western World as so defined at the close of World War II.

The politics of migration policies then, are short term responses of nations and countries faced with the consequences of steps, taken only shortly before, to meet the needs for economic growth with their own supply of labor, to match their political aims with their population policies, and to accommodate the demographic pressures either from within or from outside the country. The traditionally immigration countries have discovered the supply of immigrants is greater while the need for them has all but disappeared and the countries of Northwest Europe have discovered that those guests invited to a dinner of economic prosperity show no signs of leaving.

Athough the migrations appear quite different on the surface, the *bona fide* migrants to North America and the English speaking Oceania, and the workers seeking temporary employment in the prosperous countries of Europe, have enough characteristics in common to be treated in a single volume. Not only do all the countries of in-migration belong to the same First World — a term practically forgotten as the Third World is not — but their responses to in-migration are essentially convergent. The term in-migration is used here advisedly in its generic meaning of population inflows. It is not easy to make a clear distinction between in-migration and immigration and their obverse, out-migration and emigration. Not only do agreements on the free movement of labor between countries blur the national boundaries of states otherwise fully sovereign, but the "last" settlement invariably remains uncertain: return migration from the New World to the Old is one case in point; another would be "foreigners" living for more than one generation in a country such as Switzerland; and, a third would consist of the professionals and highly skilled personnel moving from one country to another.[2] In general, however, one can still think of immigration to North America and Oceania, but in the case of Europe the probability of the naturalization of in-migrants varies from country to country. In case of doubt, the term in-migration remains the preferred term.

In the First World — and no doubt elsewhere as well — the realization has come that while there must be a demographic balance, or perhaps some growth of the population, the cyclical nature of economic development runs counter to the demographic stability of the resident population. Thus, the ultimate concern is expressed in the question of how to implement the cares of humanitarianism and how to face the question of the last man across the draw bridge. The authors in this volume seem to agree, and the data on migration policies bear them out, that both the traditionally immigration countries and the present in-migration countries of Europe have been forced to realize that in-migrations may have lost their justification. Those countries

---

[2] Anthony H. Richmond. "Sociology of Migration in Industrial and Post-Industrial Societies", *Migration*. A.J. Jackson, ed. Cambridge: Cambridge Univ. Press. 1969. Pp. 238-281.

supplying the migrants have also been forced to see that out-migration does not solve, but only postpones those problems which prompted it.

The year 1974 was declared World Population Year to dramatize the unfortunate demographic vigor of this planet. Ironically, the mid-1970s also saw a number of restrictive policies curbing international migrations. The restrictive policies followed either in the wake of reports by population commissions in the United States, in Canada, in Australia, in New Zealand and in the United Kingdom, or they followed on the heels of the oil embargo countries of Europe. In every case, the rationale to restrict in-migration was based on the syndicalist, that is, trade unionist principal of protecting one's own population, even though the various policies were couched in terms of humanitarianism and universalistic ethics, despite the fact that the pressure humanitarianism and universalistic ethics, despite the fact that the pressure of domestic unemployment, for instance, or the loud xenophobic sentiments, were surely taken into account by the politics of the day. Interestingly enough, as much as the restrictions of in-migration of labor were grounded in humanitarian concern lest the welfare of those in the country both the indigenous and the in-migrated be endangered, the same concern assured that the joining of families remained the priority of policy legislation on in-migration, thus enlarging the migrant inflow. Some of the policy guidelines had been set prior to the years when the closure, albeit tentative, of the borders went into effect. As such, the European Economic Community asserted in 1968 that there are rights to migration of whole families, even though the rights were extended, and still are extended, only to the nationals of member states.[3] Similarly, the International Labor Office endorsed, as late as 1973, the rights of families to be joined;[4] various international conferences and seminars kept stressing this point.[5] The immigration legislation of the overseas democracies reserved the preference categories to the next-of-kin of the resident population and, the United Kingdom, to sift the many potential immigrants to the Isles, has constituted a special category of "patrials". These would include those entitled to immigrate to the United Kingdom on the strength of their descent, but from a distance of not more than two generations of persons born there.

What the rejoining of families brought about at first was an increase in in-migration especially to those countries in Europe which, until 1973 or 1974, drew heavily on foreign labor for their economic well-being. The foreign labor force, once in the country, was supplemented by the next-of-kin,

[3] European Economic Community, Regulation No. 1612/68, Oct. 15, 1968.
[4] M.W.A. Dumon. "Family Migration and Family Reunion", *International Migrations*, 14:58-83. 1976.
[5] ICEM, International Committee for European Migrations. "Second Seminar on Adaptation and Integration of Permanent Immigrants. Geneva, November, 1975. Recommendations", *International Migrations*, 14:19-49. 1976.

The Politics of Migration Policies

confirming thus the observation that there are no labor migrations, but only people migrations.[6] The in-migration of whole families will make it unlikely that the proportion of foreign born population in Northwest Europe will decrease in the foreseeable future. The population of Switzerland consists of about 17 percent aliens, while France, Belgium and Sweden individually contain about 8 percent; Germany retains an alien population between 6 and 7 percent and the other countries trail behind with the exception of Luxembourg where aliens represent close to 20 percent of the population although the absolute numbers there, of course, are smaller.[7] Some out-migration movement began to take place in 1974. Switzerland, for example, had registered an outflow of some 300,000 foreign workers by December 1976, reducing her official unemployment count to under one percent.[8] Surprisingly, however, about 40 percent of the 110,000 aliens who left Switzerland during 1976 belonged in the preferred, domiciled category and were leaving not because their work or residence permits were in jeopardy.[9]

Experiences: The Immigration Countries

At this point, it becomes necessary to examine the experiences of various countries with immigration in the last ten or fifteen years and how these experiences have been translated into immigration policies. The experiences of the overseas English speaking democracies have been surprisingly parallel, given the divergent founding principles of each country. One can group Canada, Australia and New Zealand, all members of the British Commonwealth, together and compare them with the United States. The latter became independent of Britain too soon to let her immigration be mainly a resettlement scheme for the inhabitants of the British Isles, as was notably the case of Australia in particular. The United States attracted the type of immigrants classifiable in the Canadian immigration scheme as "independent". The overriding concern of all these countries, however, was to retain a population mix which would not be at variance with the population already there, even though both in the United States and in New Zealand substantial racial minorities were part of the settled population practically from the start. Different as the respective immigration histories were, by appointing the respective population commissions, all the countries felt compelled to ask whether or not they still had any business to remain immigration

[6] Alain Girard. "Postface", *Les Travailleurs Etrangers en Europe Occidentale*. P.J. Bernard, ed. Paris: Mouton. 1976. Pp. 407-414.
[7] Statistiches Bundesamt, The Federal Republic of Germany. "Wanderungen 1975", *Wirtschaft und Statistik*, 9:549-554. 1976; "Ausländer im Bundesgebiet", *Wirtschaft und Statistik*, 1:20-26. 1976.
[8] *Die Presse*, Jan. 28, 1977.
[9] *Süddeutsche Zeitung*, Feb. 2, 1977.

countries. All four came to the inevitable conclusion that the tradition of immigration must be reassessed in view of the new population growth realities. The policy to admit, for a compelling reason of compassion, those who have no other place to go, was never questioned. To keep admitting, however, those tired and poor who in times past huddled under the Statue of Liberty appears now a task to which even the most generous of immigration countries will not respond for long. Solutions are not easy: there is the problem of the Mexicans coming in droves and illegally into the United States; and there is the fear that the "underpopulated" Australia will be no match for the organized and large scale migrations forcing their way from neighboring Asia. Similarly, it is not easy to profess humanitarianism and racial tolerance and still feel that one must dissuade would-be entrants from coming to Canada because perfect conditions to receive them do not exist, or because their cultural heritage does not make them easily assimilable.

Indeed, it was only during the 1960s that the admission policies of the immigration countries became universalistic and that all of the racial exclusion clauses were removed from the immigration legislation. Shortly thereafter, however, recommendations to curb immigration severely were being openly entertained. The obvious, if not unexpected, dominance among the new admissions was of persons from the Third World and there was a corresponding decline of immigrants from the traditionally supply countries in Europe. The new immigrant mix made the difficulties of immigrant adjustment more visible just when the welfare state system was taking pride in that all residents were well taken care of. By the end of 1960s the population debate was won, so to speak, by those who came to it well armed with ecological arguments. Their recommendations to curb an unnecessary population inflow were based on the quality of life arguments and on the simple arithmetic of native born youth coming of age and needing jobs. With the population pressures from without thus under control, at least ideologically, a conscious policy of multiculturalism was able to get under way. Despite all of this development, some of which took place on a planning level only judging by the immigration figures still impressive during the 1970s, some old questions remain. The historical relationship between immigration and vigorous social change is still too well remembered to be dismissed lightly in the face of observations on isolationism and its consequent patriotic intolerance. Furthermore, in places where a large proportion of the population is not only foreign born but also enfranchised, as in some voting districts in Canada, creators of new immigration policies must walk a tightrope.

Experiences: The In-Migration Countries

The countries of Northwest Europe are in a seemingly better position "morally" *vis-à-vis* their immigrants. That is, they have never promised permanent settlement to their in-migrants. With only a few exceptions, these countries have barely ceased to be countries of emigration, their peoples having populated three continents, almost exclusively, and a fourth one at least partially, within a period of a few centuries, and more notably within the last one hundred years. Now these same countries are finding themselves hosts to about ten million aliens, mostly from the neighboring countries and not too distant places in the South of Europe. These *de facto* immigration countries, however, do not face, as the "true" immigration countries do, the potential issue of an immigration *triage*, to use the word perhaps too forcefully. Normally, triage refers to saving those men wounded in battle who have the best chances of getting well and returning to the fighting line. Applied to immigration policies, it would mean that those persons best suited to live in the country would receive a preferential admission even though the humanitarian and racially universalistic criteria would have to admit those to whom immigrant adaptation may not come so easily. The question, whether a country remains an immigration country or not, does not arise in the case of Northwest Europe. The countries define themselves as fully sovereign without any alien having the right, presumptive or precedential, to come and to settle, various older treaties to this effect notwithstanding as in the case of Switzerland. The irony is that the countries presume exportation of their own nationals to be a natural right and a meritorious gesture, whereas admission of other nationals to their country is not.

In any case, the countries of Northwest Europe seem to disclaim ever having been countries of settlement, despite historical data to the contrary. One need only recall that as recently as just prior to World War I there was a de facto free movement and settlement of persons; should one venture further back in history, large scale immigration settlements were not uncommon. Also, large population transfers took place as a result of most major wars, irredentism in various forms having brought about wholesale population transfers from one political jurisdiction to another.[10] In other words, migrations in Europe far outweigh, numerically, those populations resident in one place for generations.

The chapters in Part III deal individually with the in-migration receiving countries of Northwest Europe. Their authors offer incontrovertible proof of the argument that pressures of the in-migrant population, once arrived, will evoke similar policy responses despite the fact that in-migration policies of individual countries may have dissimilar roots. Take, for instance, the cases of France and of the Federal Republic of Germany. The first has a long

---

[10] G. Beijer. "Modern Pattern of International Migratory Movements", *Migration*. J.A. Jackson, ed. Cambridge: Cambridge Univ. Press. 1969.

tradition of immigration and the second has a long tradition of imported labor even though not always under the condition of free choice.

France: France presently maintains a population of 52 million. After World War II, the French policy on immigration continued to be liberal. France retains a long tradition of demographic self-concern. The Third Plan of economic development (1958-1961) indicated a renewed need for immigration: "To resort to immigration should be envisaged not as a palliative to overcome a certain temporary crisis but as a continuing increase of population and indispensable to the objectives of the III Plan".[11] Earlier, in 1947, the Ministry for Public Health and Population issued a directive favoring immigration of families. Over the years, there were fluctuations in French net immigration affected by economic cycles and the Algerian involvement. At the end of hostilities in 1962, about 100,000 Algerians claimed their French citizenship and immigrated. France first entered into bilateral agreements with her southern neighbors to regulate the inflow of labor, at first with Algeria in 1964. Prior to this there was a free movement of persons between the dependencies and the metropolis. Net immigration peaked around 1970, with about 150,000 migrants annually. This figure dropped well below 100,000, starting in 1974.

In 1973, the total number of foreigners in France was about four million. At the end of October, 1973, immigration "from within" was stopped. That meant that an alien could not become "regularized" if he found a job and then applied for work and residence permits while already in the country. Whereas in 1956 the "spontaneous" that is, de facto illegal in-migration to France, was about 20 percent of all immigration; in 1969 about 80 percent of all in-migrants were "spontaneous".[12] In July, 1974, France instituted a general immigration stop for admissions normally processed through the National Office of Immigration. As a result of the stop, more dependents than workers entered France for the first time since the end of World War II in addition to a new wave of illegal in-migrants.[13]

Germany: Germany presently maintains a population of 62 million. In-migration to Germany, on a large scale, developed only recently and has grown rapidly. Until the time of the Berlin Wall in 1961, Germany received

[11] Jeanne Singer-Kerel. "Conjoncture Economique et Politique Française d'Immigration 1952-1974", *Les Travailleurs Étrangers en Europe Occidentale.* P.J. Bernard, ed. Paris: Mouton. 1976. Pp. 23-63.

[12] Carmel Summut. "L'Immigration Clandestine en France Depuis les Circulaires Fontanet, Marcellin en Gorsé", *Les Travailleurs Étrangers en Europe Occidentale.* P.J. Bernard, ed. Paris: Mouton. 1976. Pp. 379-397.

[13] George Tapinos. *L'Immigration Étrangére en France.* Paris: Presses Universitaire de France. 1975. See also, "Les Migrations Internationales et la Conjoncture Presente", *L'Emigration du Basin Mediterranean vers l'Europe Industrialisée.* Franco Angelli, ed. Rome:' Univ. of Rome, Institute of Demography, 1976.

her major labor force supplements from East Germany. The millions of displaced persons and refugees in Germany at that time emigrated as soon as they were able. In 1961 there were about one-half million foreign workers in Germany and in 1972 about two million. During the peak years of in-migrations, the central register of foreigners showed over four million persons. Germany concluded labor recruitment agreements with most of the European Mediterranean countries and with Turkey. Turkey was a late-comer, but supplied about one-half million workers and, in 1975, there were one million Turks in Germany. Most of the in-migration was on an organized basis. The individual migration became restricted in 1972. A complete stop of labor recruitment went into effect in November, 1973. Since then, there has been a drop in the number of registered aliens, the count of September 30, 1975 totalling 3.7 million. Including new births to aliens and some recent upswing in the in-migration of European Community nationals, there were 3.9 million aliens in Germany at the end of 1976.[14] The year 1975 was also the first to register a net out-migration of dependents. In that same year, the proportion of single foreign workers has decreased to about 40 percent of the total. Three quarters of all foreigners have lived in Germany for more than three years as of 1975. The mean number of years of stay has increased by one year between 1973 and 1975.[15] The official German in-migration policy remains that Germany is not an immigration country. On the other hand, the Federal Government is exerting a powerful effort for a "temporary integration" of foreigners living there.

The number of foreign arrivals and the number of foreign residents may have diminished somewhat in both France and Germany. The fact remains, however, that most of the foreigners living now in the countries will remain and will not become naturalized citizens. The rapid naturalization process in France registers about 30,000 new Frenchmen annually. With the number of aliens at close to four million, most aliens will die before their turn comes in the naturalization court. In other words, substantial alien minorities will remain in the countries and will also remain beyond the pale of political patronage, disenfranchised as they are.

Experiences: The Out-Migration Countries

The countries of out-migration, dealt with in Part IV, are not likely to pressure their nationals to return even though it may have become clear that out-migration was not solving most of the problems it was expected to. The problems at home appear structural and their remedy is a long term proposition. On the whole, the first waves of out-migrants were those who

---

[14] *Süddeutsche Zeitung.* March 10, 1977.
[15] Statistiches Bundesamt. The Federal Republic of Germany, "Ausländer im Bundesgebiet", *Wirtschaft und Statistik,* 1:20-26. 1976.

independently sought work in Europe and who had substantial industrial skills to offer. The later, more organized waves of out-migration tapped the unused labor force from the countryside, whether it was in Portugal or Turkey.

The remittances sent home represented substantial hard currency transfers on the books; to most of the countries, these transfers became an important share of the foreign trade balance. However, most of the foreign currency earnings thus acquired were reexported through purchases of imported durable goods and the money brought home to be invested was used for real estate purchases, and made no impact on the industrial productivity of the country. Finally, the returning migrants appear to be only a questionable advantage since the conditions at home which encouraged them to leave, still exist. Having become politically articulate, the return migrants present problems of economic and political reintegration about which the present governments can do little.

As soon as a "tradition" of worker out-migration has become established,, the status quo will be considered as legitimate and the former "supplicants" will become demanding. The governments of the countries of labor out-migration seem to share the view that the industrial countries of Northwest Europe should be recruiting and then training only that labor force which is surplus to the sending countries, such as the young men and women from rural districts for whom there is no hope of employment at home. In some instances, the needs of the labor exporting and labor importing countries are complementary: Yugoslavia, for instance now encourages the out-migration of only the unskilled from the Northeast districts while Austria seems to prefer to import only unskilled labor.

The Migrants

When the in-migrants become fairly well established in their "host" countries and bring their families along and raise their children there, their interest in saving and sending remittances home wanes. Then, too, the interest of their governments in their welfare will cease to be justified and their return home may be awaited only with discomfort. On the other hand, their stay in their new country will remain legally tentative at best, and their children will be faced with a choice of where they belong. The choice is not easy for the children of in-migrants since their schooling is not geared fully to either country. Of course, seen from an historical perspective, successive waves of immigration have always been accompanied by social problems considered serious, but resolvable as long as the in-migrants and their host population did not differ too much from each other.[16] In any case, those willing to come

[16] Oscar Handlin. *The Newcomers*. Cambridge: Harvard Univ. Press. 1959.

and invest in their future were able to do so. That is, they were willing to sacrifice. The emergence of the new welfare state, now well-ingrained in Northwest Europe, has resulted in an insistence that all the resident population should live well. It is better, so the argument goes, not to come to a country unless all the advantages of an appropriate standard of living are obtainable. On the other hand, one may presume there are many potential in-migrants willing to forego some of the advantages, for the advantage of being able to forego them.

It was with the welfare of in-migrants in mind that the in-migration restrictions were announced. In general, three pressure groups were interested in the issue: the unions who, although not antagonistic to in-migrants, wanted to make sure that everybody was included in the "syndicalist" coverage; the welfare system officers who were appalled at the home conditions of many in-migrants; and, finally, the politicians hearing mumblings of discontent as to the visibility of the new minorities. The pressures applied by the governments were at first based on "the work to rule" principle. That is, the various labor recruitment agreements stipulated employment conditions, housing accomodations and welfare coverages including the language training of the aliens. By enforcing the provisions, the governments made it too costly for the employers to recruit labor from abroad. The pressures applied by the welfare authorities consisted of highlighting the ghettoization of the foreign minorities and their low standard of living. Much was made out of the worker exploitation issue by landlords. The unions were, as already indicated, willing for the indigenous workers to rise in the occupational structure, provided somebody else did the unpleasant jobs. At the same time, however, the unions jealously insisted that the foreigners did not work for lesser wages.

In most countries of Northwest Europe the foreign workers are in occupations and industries which either do not pay well, or which are unpleasant places in which to work. Given the skill levels of the workers from abroad — in most cases the issues are focused on workers from the Mediterranean basin — and given the choices they have, this should not be surprising. The reasons for in-migrating were not only economic in a general sense, as most migrations are, but also they were specific enough to inspire workers to send money home for particular wanted things. Given the wage differentials between the countries, the foreign workers, by holding their standard of living constant, soon accumulated income surpluses. Thus, it is not surprising that the standard of living of many foreign workers was markedly lower than that of their indigenous counterpart. However, the remittances sent home and the cash savings banked in the host country represented considerable sums. The savings were facilitated by the various welfare provisions as part of their work contract. In other words, the in-migrants to Northwest Europe behaved like the "classical" immigrants overseas who, by dint of their efforts, attempted to climb the social ladder in their newly found country even if it was not until the second generation that they succeeded. Even today, the Italian newcomers to Canada will purposefully "live like Italians" to save up money quickly. That means, they live with their kin and generally spend little money, save on the necessities of life. Such a way of life attracts the attention of social workers and others who are worried as to how their neighbors fare. Welfare dossiers in France, for instance, are full of reports on the visible poverty of in-migrants, particularly on those from Algeria and the former Subsaharan dependencies. All that these in-migrants are doing is trying to "live like Italians" while saving up money; they also maintain a tribal solidarity without which their undertakings would not succeed.[17] One often forgets that it is the foreign workers who control substantial cash savings and that, traditionally, immigrants surpass the native born in property ownership and entrepreneurial success. However, for reasons not difficult to guess, the visible poverty of in-migrants has served quite well as one of the rationales offered why in-migration should be curbed.

The United Kingdom

Migration flows to the countries of in-migration were unidirectional as were the outflows of migrants from the Mediterranean countries. Migrations to the United Kingdom, on the other hand, as described in Part II, were "unexpected". The United Kingdom was the country to set the immigration pattern for several continents, but it now found itself to be a country of immigration. It has not become a country of immigration because it is one of the better places to migrate to, but rather, because those flocking to its shores have few other places to go. The promise of a British passport to residents of the Commonwealth so generously extended earlier has been claimed, and the United Kingdom has now acquired a population of over one million of her own alien "British", in addition to at least as many bona fide aliens from other countries. The largest proportion of Britain's alien population are the non-patrials, that is, the British passport holders not connected to the United Kingdom through lines of immediate descent. They are the former residents of the New Commonwealth and represent England's racial and ethnic minorities. They are English speaking, but they are culturally distinct.

---

[17] Jacques Barou. "Role des Cultures d'Origine et Adaptation des Travailleurs Africains en Europe", *Les Travailleurs Étrangers en Europe Occidentale*. P.J. Bernard, ed. Paris: Mouton. 1976. Pp. 229-240.

The United Kingdom exemplifies the problems of a large scale immigration into a country with a well developed system of coverage of social services. The immigrants thus find themselves beneficiaries of provisions and services not easily obtainable elsewhere. The costs of extended welfare at home must eventually militate against a continued open admission policy, and it does so indeed in the case of the United Kingdom. This country, perhaps more than any other, had to adjust its immigration policies in view of the costs involved and the too visible decline in the well-being of its citizens. Other countries faced with similar problems have had only to cut off their recruitment of labor abroad. The United Kingdom has felt obliged to settle accounts outstanding left by the Empire. Even the principle of *noblesse oblige*, however, had eventually to be set aside. Through a redefinition of the British citizenship so that it extended to patrials only, the United Kingdom has been able to renege on the promissory notes of British passports to those once belonging to the Commonwealth.

A Sociological Lesson

This volume concentrates on issues connected with the recent and extensive migrations of labor into Northwest Europe. Descriptions of immigration policy responses in the traditionally immigration countries have been drawn on to point out the commonalities of problems. Descriptions of out-migration policies serve to illustrate the backgrounds from which the in-migrants to Northwest Europe came. The scenario of the new realities of migration policies in labor migrations, then, is simple enough:

> Young men leave their place of origin and are brought to another country to work. Their jobs are mostly low status, in factories and services. They often become the only individuals holding such jobs, which consequently discourages their integration in the host country. Should the extensive literature on social stratification not be wrong, persons with working class orientation are not going to mail remittances indefinitely. An occasional letter from home does not constitute a sufficient psychic income in exchange for the remittances sent. Either the worker returns, or, more likely, he sends for his family.
>
> At this juncture the sending country loses its remittances and the host country gains an ethnic or a racial minority. The principle of neighboring leads to ghettoization. The welfare agencies of the host country then enter with plans for the integration, and perhaps the assimilation, of the foreigners and the consular agencies of the sending countries become interested in a strengthening of nationalist sentiments. The children of in-migrants are caught in a cross-fire and are growing up to be "illiterates in two languages". There is a promise of increasing welfare costs, of

delinquency of the children of in-migrants, and of a general overloading of social services.

The host country tries to close the borders to additional in-migrants but allows the rejoining of families. This results in a new and increased influx of in-migrants. Also, illegal in-migration increases, at least temporarily. Deportation procedures are either undeveloped or an affront to the governments to which the illegal aliens are wards. The build-up of an alien population in the host country is perceived as critical. Attempts at an induced worker rotation meet with public disapproval or are dropped when the incentives prove too costly. Supranational organizations, like the International Labor Office, or the Council of Europe, or the Intergovernmental Committee for European Migrations are supported by labor unions and by governments of the sending countries both making sure that an exploitation of foreign workers is viewed as a moral offense. The forces of humanitarianism succeed in convincing governments that a simple economic utilization of foreign workers is not to be tolerated.[18] The unions in particular insist on equal rights for all workers. Finally, the occupational structure in Northwest Europe has changed sufficiently that without foreign workers most of the unpleasant jobs would not be manned.

The Politics

That the countries of Northwestern Europe have found themselves in an in-migration overrun is apparent. As in-migration squeeze occurs when a migratory influx has a run-away effect producing a pressure on the receiving country so that the country must accept more in-migrants than were originally planned. This becomes an acute political problem.

In the political responses to migrations in-migration has been considered only secondarily as a mechanism to restore a demographic balance in the host country. A conscious policy of settlement was abandoned by the immigration countries long ago. In Europe, France is perhaps the only country with a history of population policies. France has entertained immigrations for the sake of her population balance since the times of the mercantilist doctrine. On the other hand, immigration to Sweden has been a result of a humanitarian suasion that one just cannot import labor and then send it home when it is no longer needed. The Netherlands, however, have exported their population systematically until recently and only the shrinking of their overseas holdings has forced them to take in immigrants.

Primarily, political responses to in-migration have been those of accommodation, disregarding whether the migrants were already in the country and difficult to dispatch home or whether such accommodation was

---

[18] W.R. Böhning. "Migration of Workers as an Element in Employment Policy", *New Community*, 3:6-25. 1974.

informed by a benign concern for all the residents in the country. The internationalization of political action played, no doubt, a significant role in the arrangements now struck for the welfare of foreign workers in the host countries. The large countries, like France and Germany with their many millions of foreigners, cannot but remain circumspect in handling the issue of aliens in their midst. France avows her hospitality to foreigners, and Germany goes to great extremes for a "temporary integration" of her aliens even though a temporary integration sounds too much like a political slogan. The small countries cannot but follow the lead, especially as many international agencies issue more and more directives and recommendations to safeguard the welfare of all. Ultimately, however, the issue of in-migration is subject to a "syndicalist" solution to protect those already there, and to exclude others who came too late to partake in the feast.

In a democracy, the politics of migration policies are either a response to pressure for more workers, or a response to pressure to preserve the national identity by limiting in-migration. In any case, migration policies will remain a matter of waiting to see what will happen next while issuing ad hoc regulations. As far as migrants are concerned, it remains difficult to discredit the observation that people migrate from bad to good. Thus far, it appears, an enlargement of the realm of universalism in human interface may have come about through migrations.

Part I

Countries of Settlement:
Immigration Policies of the
Overseas Anglo-Saxon Democracies

Part I

Countries of Settlement:
Immigration Policies of the
Overseas Anglo-Saxon Democracies

1

Australia

CHARLES PRICE
Australian National University

Historical Overview

EVER since the British occupation in 1788, immigration has been a major force in Australian life and development. Fully aware of their remoteness from the motherland, suspicious of the imperial ambitions of various European and Asian powers, conscious of their smallness in relation to the size of their continent, and aware of their wealth in natural resources, the youthful Australian colonies soon embarked on policies of rapid population growth, by encouraging large-scale immigration. Here, they realized their disadvantage in gaining British and European settlers, compared with Canada and the U.S., in that North America had been longer settled and was easier to reach both in terms of time and cost. Gradually, they evolved procedures for using public monies and land to assist suitable families with passage costs, accommodations and jobs. Such families were sometimes selected by government recruiting agents and sometimes recommended for public assistance by business firms, voluntary societies, relatives, or other private sponsors. Additionally, persons, such as businessmen, tourists, goldminers and the like, coming for short periods only, were encouraged to stay permanently by easy schemes for obtaining land, acquiring British nationality and other similar incentives. Australian policy, even to the present, has always stressed permanent settlement and, except for programs helping foreign students to obtain higher education, has rarely encouraged schemes for short term migration, and has never encouraged schemes for recruiting short term laborers such as seasonal or "guest" workers.

After federation in 1901, when the new commonwealth government assumed responsibility for immigration, the commonwealth and colonies (now called states) operated these schemes in cooperation. In the period from 1788 to 1939, Australia received some 2.5 million settlers, nearly half of whom arrived with government assistance.

Alongside this positive policy of recruitment there developed a negative policy of restriction, partly directed against pauper, criminal, lunatic, diseased and politically suspect persons, but also against persons who were considered difficult or impossible to "assimilate", that is, persons from countries other than Britain (the "motherland") and the nations of North-western Europe. These last were considered sufficiently similar to Britain in culture, customs and history to enable the growth of a homogeneous British-like people in Australia. Also there was fear of being overwhelmed by large numbers of settlers, especially from Asia, with characteristics, cultures, histories and political systems far removed from those of Britain and Northwestern Europe. Hence the well-known "White Australia Policy", by which non-Europeans could come to Australia only for business visits and education (though in fact some merchants and others, by continual renewal of temporary permits, did gain a de facto permanent residence), and the less well-known policy of restricting the intake of southern and eastern European settlers to a few thousand a year. These restrictions, unlike the U.S. quota laws, did not operate through specified statutory quotas, but rather, through administrative powers to accept or reject, without giving reasons, such numbers of any particular class, race, or nation as seemed good to the government of the day.

In accordance with this restrictive policy, assistance with passage costs was rarely granted to Asians, southern Europeans or eastern Europeans, but was occasionally granted to western Europeans; over the years 1788-1939 some 95 percent of assisted immigrants were of British ethnic origin. Similarly, British settlers had considerable advantages over alien settlers with respect to civil rights, ownership of land, position in the public service, and so on, while non-Europeans labored under even greater disadvantages than white aliens as they were barred from various occupations, such as mining, and from social welfare benefits such as old age or widows' pensions. Similarly, British nationals of British ethnic origin received considerable advantages in temporary movement: they could normally enter without visa requirements, could transfer to permanent status relatively easily, were eligible for most social benefits and had all the rights of native Australians, such as voting in elections. For other persons seeking temporary admission, visa procedures varied: northern Europeans received them fairly easily; southern and eastern Europeans had more difficulty; and non-Europeans received entry permits only after searching enquiries into previous record, financial status, family connections in Australia, and so on. The reason here was the government's determination to refuse a temporary entry permit to anyone who, not being approved for permanent settlement, might enter as a visitor, stay on illegally and, with the help of friends in Australia, elude discovery for lengthy periods (In this essay the words "permanent" and "temporary" have their natural meaning, not the artificial meaning given by some migration statisticians and officials to distinguish between migrations of more or less than a year.).

In practice, with inadequate statistics, it is difficult to estimate how many visitors did stay on permanently and how many of those coming to settle permanently later changed their minds and remigrated. There were clearly considerable numbers in both categories, some estimates of settler loss for southern Europeans being over one-third that of the arrivals. In net terms, however, the outcome of Australia's prewar migration policy — both positive and negative — was a total population of some 7,620,000 in 1947 (including an estimate for 85,000 or so Aborigines) divided ethnically somewhat as follows: British 87.8 percent; Northwestern Europeans 7.2 percent; southern Europeans 1.7 percent; eastern Europeans 0.8 percent; other white persons 1.2 percent; non-white 1.3 percent (0.9 percent being full blood and mixed blood Aborigine).

Though generally supported in the long term these immigration policies and programs were sometimes opposed in the short term. In particular, the laboring classes sometimes resisted the recruiting policy, notably during the great recessions of the 1890s and 1930s, on the grounds that immigration was simply a capitalist device to enlarge domestic markets, keep down wages and replenish the reserve of unemployed. Even during the 1920s, when economic conditions were relatively good, the Labor Party frequently attacked non-Labor governments for allowing too many immigrants in for settlement. Partly because of this, and partly because governments and private persons and organizations tended to postpone migration decisions and operations in recession, immigration to Australia, both permanent and temporary, tended to soar in economic booms and slump in depressions. Recession also tended to change the sex and age composition: single men seeking employment tended to remigrate or stay away, but husbands and fiancés well settled in Australia continued to sponsor their wives, fiancées and children, even in times of economic difficulty.

World War II and After

With World War II there came some important changes. First, the Japanese offensive revealed that the Australian population was too small to defend itself. Second, the country felt that the best answer to the international plea to open its land and resources to Asia's crowded millions, was to populate the continent, and develop its resources, with as many white persons as possible. Third, politicians suddenly became aware that the birth rate had fallen so low during the 1930s that the number of young persons now entering the work force was actually declining, and endangering the development program. Fourth, the Labor government (1941-1949) was confident from its experience in wartime administration that it could successfully combine large scale immigration with a policy of full employment; it therefore set about persuading the Trade Union movement to agree with it and by 1945 had largely succeeded. The Liberal-Country Party opposition, representing interests that had long favored immigration, naturally gave this policy full support.

In 1945, then, the Labor government launched a program designed to increase the population by two percent a year. Because roughly one percent was already coming from natural increase, the other one percent had to come from net immigration, i.e. about 70,000 a year in 1945, or 134,000 a year at present. Labor refused, however, to change traditional ethnic priorities, administering the White Australia Policy with great rigor (refusing to let Australian soldiers bring their Japanese wives back with them and ordering Asian refugees who had settled in Australia during the war to leave, even if married to Australians) and endeavoring to maintain a British proportion of 10:1. Later, however, when it became clear that Britain could not supply 90 percent of Australia's requirement, and that in the camps of the I.R.O. (International Refugee Organization) there existed many thousands of suitable settlers, Labor changed its policy and began to assist European refugees. Later, Labor, and its Liberal-Country Party successor (1949-1972), made migration arrangements with Germany, the Netherlands, Austria, Belgium and the Scandinavian countries, and also with southern and eastern European countries such as Yugoslavia, Malta, Italy, Greece and Spain; sometimes these were bilateral migration agreements or treaties, but sometimes they were arrangements reached under the auspices of international migration agencies such as I.C.E.M. (Intergovernmental Committee for European Migration). No government was willing, however, to give immigrants from continental Europe such favorable conditions of assistance as were granted British immigrants and it took many years of diplomatic pressure — including a temporary suspension by Italy of the Australian-Italian migration agreement — before the Liberal government granted all continental Europeans equal assistance with passage costs and settlement benefits (1967-1970). Even then, the Liberals maintained the practice of favoring British temporary immigrants against visitors from other countries.

The Liberal government also agreed, although somewhat slowly and reluctantly, to follow the example of New Zealand, Canada and the U.S. and gradually to dismantle the restrictive immigration policy. First, they allowed wartime refugees to stay (1949) and those Chinese in Australia under temporary permits who argued they could not return to China once the Communists were established there. Eventually, in 1956, the Liberals agreed to give such persons, and other non-Europeans who had been many years in Australia on successive temporary residence permits, the right to "permanent residence", to become naturalized, and to bring in wives, children and aged parents. Second, they opened the door a little to regular non-European migration by allowing a few "highly qualified and distinguished" persons in for settlement (1956), later expanding these categories to include skilled technicians and other educated persons such as teachers (1966). Third, in 1964, they eased restrictions on the entry of part-Europeans. Fourth, they inaugurated a small scheme of assisting selected families from Turkey (some 13,000 from 1968-1973) apparently to attract as settlers to Australia some of the Turks moving as guest workers to western Europe. Here, the argument seemed to be that the peoples of the Middle East — Anatolian Turks, Lebanese, Armenians, Assyrians and others — were close to being Europeans and did not raise the same difficulties as the peoples east of Baghdad or from Africa proper. Fifth, they quietly set about abolishing the old discriminatory legislation which denied non-Europeans benefit of commonwealth pensions, and encouraged the states to repeal discriminatory laws restricting non-Europeans with respect to mining and other occupations. As a result the existing non-European population of Australia became more stable and permanent, while the intake of new non-European settlers rose from a mere handful in 1946-1949, to approximately 12,000 a year in 1969-1972.

Certain things, however, the Liberals would not do for persons of non-European race: grant them assisted passages, even if qualified on all grounds other than race; grant them equality in naturalization, the residential period for them remaining five years after that for Europeans had been reduced to three; extend to them, unless they were New Zealand citizens of Maori origin, the no visa system operating between Australia and New Zealand; grant to non-European students an automatic right to stay in Australia after completing their course, even if they were acceptable in terms of language, social intermixture and a secure job; or extend to non-European refugees, such as the Ugandan Asians, the same easy entry and post-settlement benefits granted to European refugees such as the White Russians from China or the Czechoslovaks fleeing the 1968 Russian invasion.

Migration Policy and the Labor Government

These relics of racial discrimination, plus Australia's occasional support of South Africa in the United Nations, or of assisting the U.S. in Southeast

Asia, fostered, in some countries overseas, the notion that Australians were a white imperialist people with a racist immigration policy designed to consolidate white supremacy in the southwestern Pacific. The new Labor Party of the late 1960s, headed by Gough Whitlam, therefore decided to create a "new public image", by repudiating much of the old American Australian cooperation and by abolishing what was left of racial discrimination in immigration policy. They abandoned the White Australia policies of earlier Labor governments, announced an immigration policy based on the "avoidance of discrimination on any grounds of race, color of skin, or nationality", and soon after taking office in late 1972, abolished the remaining discriminations. They also introduced a points system of selection closer to those of Canada and the U.S., stressing family reunion and education. As a result, non-European settler intake rose slightly, to 13,500 or so a year, in 1973/1974.

Additionally, in July, 1973, the Labor government introduced an easy visa system whereby tourists and other short term visitors from non-European countries, or from European countries hitherto closely supervised, could obtain visas without the careful checks heretofore prevailing, simply by producing a prepaid return ticket, a valid passport, a declaration that they had enough funds to support their stay and a promise not to take jobs while in Australia. Some senior officials warned that many visitors would probably stay on illegally when their visitor permits expired, but the government, anxious to soothe the Filipinos, Fijians and others who had been strongly protesting about the racist discrimination in Australia's temporary entry procedures, decided to go ahead. The warnings proved realistic and eighteen months later, with somewhere between 30,000 and 50,000 illegal immigrants in the country, the government suspended the easy visa scheme. It has been left to the new Liberal-National government (1975-) to tidy up the situation by declaring an amnesty to all visitors overstaying their permitted time; all but criminals and similar undesirables have been granted permission to settle permanently, the government declaring that this was a final arrangement and would not recur as the easy visa system would stay abolished.

Skilled Immigrants

The new Labor government was less innovative concerning skilled migration. The points system did, in fact, favor the admission of educated persons, but the increase in the proportion of immigrants with professional, technical and administrative training was not startling; the proportion did increase but simply in line with the prevailing trend upwards. In fact, it had been a long established policy to encourage the immigration of skilled persons through the assisted passage scheme, through recruiting special officers

TABLE 1:1

Percent Distribution of Male Settlers[a] in Australia by Intended Occupations, Since 1949

Category	Years						
	1949-1952	1952-1954	1954-1960	1960-1963	1963-1970	1970-1972	1972-1974
Professional and Technical	4.2	4.8	5.7	7.2	9.1	13.1	15.3
Executive and Administrative	1.9	2.6	2.4	3.1	4.5	5.4	6.4
Skilled Tradesmen	33.0	27.6	30.1	37.5	38.4	39.7	39.1
Unskilled Laborers[b]	12.7	17.8	13.0	19.1	16.9	14.2	11.6
Others	43.2	43.3	42.4	26.2	24.4	20.2	21.3
Not Stated	5.0	3.9	6.4	6.9	6.7	7.4	6.3
TOTAL	100.0	100.0	100.0	100.0	100.0	100.0	100.0
N	245,439	67,940	272,998	106,120	369,182	101,507	70,306

Notes: [a] Changes in occupational categories, and a switch from permanent and long term arrivals (those coming to stay more than a year) to settler arrivals (those coming to settle permanently), make the statistics for 1949-60 strictly incomparable with those for 1960-74. The strict incomparability, however, does not conceal the general trend. Estimated population for Australia in 1974 was 13,338,500.
[b] The unskilled proportion is too low as many persons — farm workers, transport workers, caretakers, etc. — are included in 'Others' with clerical, sales, rural, mining and service occupations. Alternative statistics suggest that for 1967-73 the true unskilled proportion averaged some 24 percent.
Sources: Statistical Bulletins of the Department of Immigration, Canberra.

trained to handle professional enquiries and applications, and through continued pressure on the professional organizations of Australia to recognize foreign qualifications. As a result, though there has been some drain away from Australia to North America and the United Kingdom of certain categories of skill such as dentists, nurses, teachers and scientists, there has been a more than compensating inflow of skilled persons (doctors, engineers, geologists, accountants, electronics experts and many others) not only from India and other parts of Asia, but also from North America, the United Kingdom and New Zealand. Easing of the discriminatory procedures since 1966, however, has meant that an increasing proportion of the professional and technical intake has been non-European.

Nor was the new Labor government particularly innovative in the migration policy of refugees. The Liberal government of 1949-1972, on the whole, maintained Labor's 1947-1949 policy which sponsored physically well refugees from the I.R.O. camps, and permitted some Jewish, Yugoslav and other refugees to enter privately if sponsored by relatives and friends already established. It continued these arrangements when U.N.H.C.R. (United Nations High Commissioner for Refugees) and I.C.E.M. succeeded to I.R.O.'s functions in 1951, taking additional "refugees" from Yugoslavia, numerous families fleeing from the ravages of the Greek civil war, several thousand White Russians leaving China after 1949 and numbers of other European refugees. It also accepted a few Armenians, Assyrians and other refugees from the Middle East. Later it moved quickly to sponsor 15,000 of the Hungarian refugees of 1956-1957 and about 5,500 Czechs of the 1968 crisis. It was most reluctant, however, to take refugees of non-European origin (apart from those from the Middle East), and only with much hesitation agreed to accept 200 or so Indians expelled from Uganda in 1972. Moreover, it was just as strict in matters of health, age and family composition as had been the Labor government in 1947-1949 and it concentrated on assisting physically fit refugees who were young, or middle aged, and had smallish families. During World Refugee Year it made a small gesture towards resettling refugee families with aged or physically handicapped members (fewer than 100 all told), but for the most part did no more than to allow various voluntary agencies to sponsor a number of handicapped refugees, the agencies being responsible for all the special care and accommodation (On occasion, though, the government did help U.N.H.C.R. and the agencies by making available temporary accommodation in government hostels, special grants for a few refugee old peoples homes, and normal pension rights for the aged). In these ways, by the end of the twenty-three years of Liberal rule, Australia had accepted about 375,000 refugees (16,000 a year on average), some two-thirds being sponsored and assisted by the government and the remainder by relatives, friends or voluntary agencies. Because of declining refugee numbers in Europe this intake averaged only 8,000 a year over the period 1970-1972.

To this system, the Whitlam Labor government made a few changes. First, in line with its non-discriminatory race policy, it announced its willingness to accept a few more Indian refugees from Uganda early in 1973 and in 1975 accepted 500 or so Vietnamese refugees from Southeast Asia; the new Liberal government is continuing this policy, slightly broadening the somewhat narrow admission categories imposed by the Labor government and making preparations for another 800 or so Vietnamese. The Labor government was somewhat slower, however, than the Liberals in dealing with refugee crises. Whereas the Liberals had moved with great speed in the Hungarian and the Czech crises, the Labor government took some time to make up its mind on the Chilean revolution of September, 1973. Later, after the main crisis was over, it strengthened its migration staff in Chile and eventually admitted some 2,500 Chilean settlers in 1974, over 90 percent with government assistance; but it did all this far more through normal immigrant intake categories and procedures than through special arrangements for refugees.

Similarly the Labor administration weakened the special consideration given by the Liberal administration to refugees sponsored by the voluntary agencies; throughout 1973-1974 the voluntary agencies were becoming increasingly concerned that Labor's general admission criteria were bearing almost as heavily on refugees as on normal immigrants and that their guarantees about jobs and accommodation, accepted by the Liberal administration with little query, seemed to count for less and less; they were also concerned about the government's slowness to act in the Chile crisis. After a special meeting in March, 1974, where the agencies asked for a refugee intake over and above the ordinary new settler target and for better procedures for handling refugees in emergencies, the Labor administration became a little easier on refugee applications for entry, but the basic questions of refugee policy have still to be worked out. Also to be worked out is Australia's novel position as a country of first asylum for refugees from Timor — about 1,300 are still in Australia awaiting the outcome of events in their island home.

Over the first two years of Labor government (1973-1974) some 3,000 refugees were admitted to Australia for settlement as refugees, and maybe another 7,000 or so Chileans, Cypriots and others, although virtually all refugees, were admitted as normal immigrants at an annual average of some 5,000 a year. In addition, several thousand Timorese were admitted as refugees in temporary asylum.

Nationalism and Migration Policy

Some of these changes by the Labor Party to Australia's restrictive and refugee immigration policy rose partly from its desire, first, to break free from the precedents and habits of the 23 years of Liberal Country Party government and, second, to assert much more strongly than before the independent character of Australian nationalism against its natural imperial mother, Great Britain, and its adopted imperial father, the United States. Hence, all the moves to vote more with the unaligned members of the United Nations and the much stronger stance against South African apartheid were initiated. In matters of immigration this more self-conscious, almost brash, Australian nationalism expressed itself in several ways. It led, for instance, to Australia's withdrawal from I.C.E.M. because Whitlam and others felt, it seems, partly that I.C.E.M. was too much under the U.S. influence and partly that it was more efficient for Australia to conduct its migration arrangements by direct bilateral agreements rather than through an international migration organization which sometimes duplicated selection procedures and had to take account of the interests of other member countries.

Independent Australian nationalism also expressed itself in the abolition of British preferences in visa procedures and naturalization. In November, 1974, the Whitlam government put British and Irish nationals on the same basis as aliens with respect to visas, reentry permits, naturalization procedures and, eventually, local privileges such as voting. After some dismay by traditional British supporters, the system has settled down, with little decrease in numbers travelling. The main effect has been to encourage more Britons to apply for Australian citizenship, a practice made easier by the recent recognition of dual citizenship. The effects are visible in the rapid growth of applications for citizenship, many being due to the extra British demand: 1972 — 47,000; 1973 — 52,000; 1974 — 115,000; 1975 about 133,000. The old British Australian feeling so strong in earlier Liberal-Country Party governments, that historic ties with "Mother Country" and "Empire" deserved some special mark in migration policy and procedure, clearly weighed little with the Labor government.

Additionally, to emphasize the importance of Australian citizenship and also as compensation for the failure of the easy visa system, the Labor government, in 1975, decided to tighten up control over all temporary movements both British and alien. Visitor visas were administered quite strictly and even residents found themselves under stricter controls. Persons of non-Australian citizenship, even if well established and resident many years, and hitherto able to leave and return quite easily, were advised to obtain reentry permits before leaving Australia for a short visit overseas lest they found reentry denied them. Although this had little effect on the volume of temporary movements, which had been rapidly rising from some 75,000 arrivals in 1951 to nearly 220,000 in 1961, to over 900,000 in 1971 and nearly 1,400,000 in 1974, approximately half being residents and half visitors, it annoyed many residents and was speedily abolished by the new Liberal government early in 1976.

The rapid increase of the temporary movement took place, largely in fewer than three months, substantially up to two years and finally trailing away to almost nothing by five years. This movement had little to do with short term labor schemes, although some of the longer durations represent the migration of engineers, executives, diplomats and others coming to Australia for business or government for two years or more. The increase basically represents the rapid growth of Australia's postwar immigrant population, now well over three million in number, and their desire to make short visits to their country of origin, or to have relatives visit them in Australia. It also represents the rapid expansion of overseas travel facilities

TABLE 1:2

Migrant Arrivals and Departures, Australia, Since 1969

	Arrivals					Departures				Net
Year	Settlers Total	(Assisted)	Visitors Entering	Residents Returning	Total	Settlers Loss	Australian Born Loss	Other Residents and Visitors	Total	Gain
1969	183416	(125958)	388144	327298	898858	35808	17499	716505	769812	129046
1970	185325	(134428)	447322	394028	1026675	40102	21121	842578	903801	122874
1971	155525	(103811)	462893	460380	1078798	50735	19076	924382	994193	84605
1972	112468	(63710)	452962	545240	1110670	61375	22470	998979	1082824	27846
1973	105003	(49822)	499494	685863	1290360	41750	22064	1186128	1249942	40418
1974	121324	(52194)	559667	815538	1496529	18524	14560	1376324	1409408	87121

Notes: Settlers arriving have permits for permanent residence while visitors have temporary entry permits.

Settler arrival statistics above are from official sources unmodified for visitors converting to settlers and the return of second time settlers; the text statistics have been so modified.

Settler loss refers to foreign born persons only and is the deficit figure, i.e. the extent to which the net gain of foreign born persons falls short of the total of foreign born settler arrivals; this estimate of loss differs somewhat from the text estimates which work with modified totals of settler arrivals and also make allowance for time lag in the movements of foreign born residents and visitors. Australian born loss is the extent to which Australian born returners fall short of Australian born departures; no allowance is here made for time lag.

The two losses together represent the total of permanent departures for which settler arrivals have to compensate before there is a net gain.

Sources: Statistical Bulletins of the Department of Immigration, Canberra.

and Australia's growing attraction to the tourist trade.

Short Term Migration

So far, when speaking of diminishing racial discrimination, of encouraging the professional and skilled, of admitting refugees, of changing controls over temporary movements of visitors and residents, we have been discussing matters of long term policy rather than short term changes in new settler targets arising from the ups and downs of economic conditions. Nevertheless, there is a close connection. First, even for those categories benefiting from removal of restrictions, the immigration officials slowed down the issue of entry permits in times of economic difficulty — but not for short term visitors when their entry was important both to the tourist industry and foreign currency earnings. Second, although administrators might, in terms of policy, keep the permanent and temporary movements quite separate in practice, these were indissolubly connected: many persons arriving as temporary visitors eventually decided to stay permanently while many residents leaving for temporary visits abroad later decided, especially if originally from overseas, to stay away permanently. Although precise statistics are lacking, estimates suggest that over the period 1971-1974 visitors becoming settlers (including a proportion of easy visa overstays) averaged about 10,000 a year and residents failing to return, about 20,000 a year. These last, if born abroad, belong to the general category of former settlers departing permanently which, after deducting those who reverse their decision and come back to Australia as "second time" settlers, is the equivalent of settler loss or settler wastage. This loss averaged about 30,000 a year in 1967-1969, 50,000 a year in 1970-1972 and 30,000 a year in 1973-1974. Loss of native Australians, some of whom are the Australian born children of former settlers departing, for the same periods averaged some 14,500, 21,000 and 18,000 a year. Intake of new settlers minus settler and Australian born loss gives the net migration total, the measure against which immigration policy can be assessed.

It should be noted that the movements in settler and native Australian loss do not correlate so closely with economic cycles as does settler intake. With native Australian loss, Australian born children of settler parents going "home" to avoid recession in Australia are to some extent counter-balanced by native Australians returning home to avoid recession abroad. With settler loss, however, there is considerable response to economic conditions and there is also the tendency of many discontented settlers to return home two to three years after arrival, irrespective of economic conditions; hence the reason why the rise and fall in settler loss lags about three years behind the rise and fall in settler intake.

It should also be noted that large scale settler loss has caused much public and government unease, has produced numerous statements about the loss of public funds involved in assisting settlers when a quarter or more return home again, has occasioned several governmental enquiries into the scale and causes of loss, and attempts to improve conditions for newcomers, provide better welfare and interpreter services, making housing and education easier. These policies persist while the various political parties criticize each other for failing to do as much as possible to help newcomers settle happily. This again reveals Australia's concentration on permanent settlement and shows how far it is from accepting the notion that the short term immigration of workers as distinct from students, tourists and visitors, is desirable and useful.

With the settler movement itself, the arrival peaks occurred in 1949-1950 (158,000 a year), in 1955-1956 (115,000 a year) and in 1969-1970 (180,000 a year) while troughs occurred in the economic downturn of 1952-1953 (68,000 new settlers in 1953 and 43,000 net gain), in the credit squeeze recession of 1961-1962 (90,000 new settlers and 62,000 net gain in 1962), in 1972-1973 (110,000 new settlers and 34,000 net gain a year), and in 1975 (about 53,000 new settlers and a 6,000 net loss).

In these movements, government policy was of great importance. Not only could it reduce unassisted migration by slowing down the issue of entry permits but it could also cut back the assisted passage program, and vice versa. So, by 1953, it had cut back the 1950 new settler target of 200,000 to 80,000 and assisted arrivals from 119,000 to 27,000, by which time assisted arrivals were 40 percent of new settlers instead of 74 percent as in 1950. Similarly, by 1974, it had progressively cut the 1970 target from 175,000 new settlers a year to 80,000 and assisted passages from 134,000 to 50,000, by which time assisted arrivals were 46 percent of new settlers instead of 74 percent as in 1970. In short, even allowing for the fact that unassisted migration of its own accord came down during recession and rose again in prosperity, the government stimulated or depressed immigration largely through its control of the assisted passage scheme.

It is important to note here that in the 1961-1962 recession the Liberal government did not cut the target of 125,000 a year, although it did reduce assisted passages from 68,000 to 45,000, largely because the cuts of 1952-1953 had annoyed countries with which Australia had recently concluded migration agreements. To avoid another international rebuke, and to overcome the difficulty of getting migration programs going again after severe cutting, the government kept migration as high as possible, but counterbalanced the effects of new migrants arriving in conditions of unemployment by decreasing the proportion of male workers and increasing the proportion of dependents. Thus, the number of male settlers fell from 61,000 in 1960-1961 to 40,200 in 1961-1962 but female settlers fell from 47,200 to 45,700 only; which meant the sex ratio falling from 129 to 88 males per 100 females (much as it happened in the 1930s but at the initiative of the migrants themselves). Likewise, while the immigration of working age male settlers dropped from 41,300 in 1960-1961 to 23,300 in 1961-1962, that of boys and older men fell only from 19,800 to 16,800.

By 1971-1972, however, conditions were different. There had been occasional criticism of large scale immigration during the 1952-1953 and 1961-1962 recessions, mainly from those economists who felt that immigration was inflationary in its effects and should be substantially reduced. In the early seventies these critics were joined by others: persons involved in immigrant welfare who felt that public welfare, health, educational and housing resources were lagging further and further behind; persons concerned at the rapid growth of Italian, Greek and other "ghettoes" in major Australian cities and at the problems of "assimilation" so arising; persons worried about environmental and pollution control who felt immigration was a major element in the uncontrolled growth of Australia's metropolitan centers (in fact immigration was responsible for nearly 60 percent of such growth, 1947-1971); and persons influenced by notions of zero population growth and who could not see any sense in a policy of increasing population at the rate of 2 percent a year. The Liberal government noted these views and, partly as a consequence, met the 1971 recession by reducing the 1970 settler target of 170,000 to 140,000 but it was reluctant to reduce it further. The new Labor government, however, was much more influenced by notions of zero population and environmental control, and was little bothered about opinions in those countries with migration agreements with Australia. In any case, it knew that the traditional source countries of Europe felt differently about migration in 1972 than in 1952, the European economies being so much more active, and skilled persons so much more in demand. It, therefore, had no hesitation in cutting the target to 110,000 in 1973 and then to 80,000 in 1974; still later, in the budget of mid-1975, it announced that there would be no target at all and provision for only 20,000 assisted settlers. With serious refugee problems in the Middle East, and easier entry for non-Europeans, however, the number of unassisted settlers remained higher than expected producing, for 1974, a settler intake of some 126,000 (counting some easy visa overstays) with an assisted element of 52,000. This partly explains why, in this particular migration cutback, the sex and dependency ratios in settler intake changed less than during 1961-1962, the sex ratio lowering slightly only from 116 in 1969-1970 to 104 in 1973-1974 and the dependency ratio (children aged 0-14 and adults aged 60 and over) rising slightly from 34.4 percent in 1969-1970 to 35.1 percent in 1973-1974. In 1975 the cutback became more effective, with a settler intake of little more than 50,000.

Before the Labor government could make its next migration decision it suffered electoral defeat in late 1975. The new Liberal government has already announced that it hopes to increase immigration by 1977, to reduce the pressure of cost-inflation, increase the size of home markets and to encourage private business to expand factories, equipment and production. It has not yet, however, produced a precise statement on targets for settlers or assisted passages.

Demographic Impact

In demographic terms these ups and downs in net migration, and changes in sex ratios and dependency proportions, have had little effect on the character of population growth. Models suggest that the long term effects on the sex and age composition, and size, of the population are similar to the effects of a steady net migration of one percent a year with constant age and sex distribution. The effects of the migration itself on total population, however, have been considerable, particularly as the natural increase of the immigrant population has been noticeably higher than that of the native born, mainly because most immigrants undergo medical checks before receiving an entry permit while the selection procedures for assisted migrants favor the age groups 15-44. This gives the immigrants a lower crude mortality and higher crude fertility than the native born. As a consequence, the Australian population has increased from 7.6 million in mid-1947 to 13.6 million in mid-1976, about 60 percent of this 5.9 million increase being due to postwar immigrants and their children (41 percent due to the immigrants and 19 percent to their Australian born children). As a result, nearly 30 percent of the Australian population is either a postwar immigrant, or the child of one. In terms of the original two percent target, this means that the Australian population between mid-1947 and mid-1975 increased at an average annual rate of 2.1 percent, about 1.0 percent from the population increase of the 1947 population and about 1.4 percent from the postwar immigrants and their children. In this sense, the "one percent" policy has been successful and, even in terms of net migration alone, taking no account of immigrant children born in Australia, averaged 0.9 percent over the period 1947-1972. Additionally, the age and sex composition of the immigrants has been largely responsible for changing Australia from a country with a slowly increasing population of low fertility and low mortality, as it was prewar, to a faster increasing population with larger proportions in the younger ages; for instance, the proportion aged 10-29 in 1947 was 30.8 percent compared with 34.9 percent in 1973. This difference will, of course, diminish if Australia continues to follow North American and western European trends to lower fertility, as it now appears to be doing.

Conclusions

Australia has been, and still is, in a different migration position from the countries of western Europe and, to some extent, of North America. In postwar Australia, although short term economic cycles have influenced the volume of settler immigration, and the volume of settler loss and net migration, this has been in the context of a firm policy, agreed to by all major political parties from 1945-1972, to maintain, over the long term, a high level of settler immigration for purposes of population building and development. The Labor government of 1972-1975 moved toward a lower level of settler immigration, but even so, and in spite of economic recession, saw net migration averaging about 40,000 a year during its terms of office; in the past this was due to Labor's own policy of easing restrictions on non-European immigration, both permanent and temporary. The new Liberal government is now moving back toward earlier attitudes and policies and hopes to raise settler arrivals and net immigration by at least 50 percent.

In demographic terms, although the migration of single adults, particularly males, has reflected the current needs of the labor market the immigration of women and dependents has been much steadier, reflecting the fact that family reunion is slowed much less by economic recession than is worker immigration. Over all, Australia has been little affected by problems of labor specifically recruited for short periods, as is the case with many seasonal and "guest" workers elsewhere in the world. In Australia, the great emphasis has been on the permanent immigration of settler workers and their families and on the temporary immigration of students, tourists and visitors not seeking employment. Australian immigration policies, in terms of recruiting, occupations, housing and welfare, have always been geared to the permanent settler and his family.

2

Canada

DANIEL KUBAT*
University of Waterloo

Overview

CANADA, with her 23 million inhabitants of today has but a short population history.[1] Canada's numbers have increased-sixfold during the last one hundred years. Prior to that, the growth of Canadian population had been slow. The history of immigration to Canada, although some three hundred years in duration, became a history of mass immigration only since the time of Confederation. Before then, the distance and the discomforts attending a transatlantic journey were a strong barrier to going to a land which did not have the mystique of "true" America, the United States. Canada's unique immigration history is due to her geographical position north of the United States, her image abroad as a country of severe winters, as well as to her open immigration policy aided by a systematic recruitment abroad.

The years of heavy transoceanic migrations preceding World War I were also years of heavy out-migrations from Canada, mostly to the United States. It was as if Canada were a central railway station for the immigrant masses who somehow missed the boat to the U.S. seaports. Since Confederation in 1867, Canada has received close to ten million immigrants.

* The author extends his thanks to A.H. Richmond and J.L.Elliott for their help in securing sources.

[1] Daniel Kubat and David Thornton. *A Statistical Profile of Canadian Society*. Toronto: McGraw-Hill Ryerson. 1974. Passim.

Had they all stayed, thus adding to the hefty natural surplus of births over deaths, Canada's population of today would be twice its size. It is estimated that prior to World War II about six million persons left Canada.

Now, however, Canada is retaining most of her immigrants and also receiving U.S. emigrants in large numbers. Only twice before have Americans migrated in considerable numbers to Canada: the Loyalists after the American Revolution in 1776 and the farmers seeking open land in the southern sections of the Canadian prairies after the turn of the century.

Population Growth and Immigration

In 1871 there were over 3.5 million Canadians; during that decade, an additional ten percent of the population was added by immigration, but there were also 1.5 million births registered during the same period. In the first decade of this century, Canada received 1.8 million immigrants and showed at least as many births to add to the 5 million population enumerated in 1901. The following two decades show immigration continuing, but severely reduced, during World War I and the Great Depression. It was not until 1946 that immigration to Canada resumed its heavy flow. By 1951 Canada had 14 million inhabitants. Another 1.5 million were added during that decade through immigration, and Canada registered close to 4.5 million births. The early 1960s saw immigration reduced in numbers, well under 100,000 annually. By 1966, immigrants to Canada were again numbering close to 200,000, decreasing somewhat thereafter but reaching a new peak of 218,000 in 1974. From now on, one must reckon with an immigration much more curtailed. In 1976, there were about 149,000 immigrants.

The Immigrant Mix

The traditional type of an economically motivated immigrant and settler was joined by an immigrant with no country of his own: the displaced person and the refugee. There is no doubt that the new mix of immigrants was responsible for the decrease in out-migration, for the postwar immigrants came to Canada as the country of their first choice.

More recent years saw another change in the mix of immigrants: the Mediterranean populations and the Third World countries showed a heavy increase in response to the new universalistic criteria of immigrant admission to Canada. The traditional dominance of Europeans from the northwestern part of the continent as well as the settlers from the British Isles lost their numerical weight in the immigration figures. The pattern and mix, however, of the Canadian population have been set. To change the mold would take more than a few years of today's composition of immigrants. The two

TABLE 2:1

Immigration to Canada by Country or Geographical Area of Last Permanent Residence, Since 1946

Source country or area	Years									
	1946-1967[a]	1968	1969	1970	1971	1972	1973	1974	1975	1976
	Percent									
Britain	26.5	18.4	17.8	16.0	11.7	14.9	14.6	17.6	18.6	14.4
Other Europe	55.9	47.2	36.9	35.2	31.0	27.1	24.4	23.0	20.2	19.0
Africa	1.0	2.8	2.0	2.0	2.3	6.8	4.5	4.8	5.2	5.2
Asia	3.9	11.8	14.4	14.3	18.2	19.1	23.4	23.2	25.2	29.7
Australasia[b]	1.4	2.6	2.7	3.0	2.4	1.8	1.5	1.2	1.2	1.3
United States	6.6	9.3	11.9	14.1	17.0	18.5	13.8	12.1	10.7	11.6
Other North and Central America[c]	3.2	6.2	10.8	11.5	12.6	7.6	11.2	11.6	10.4	10.8
South America	1.1	1.5	3.0	3.4	4.2	3.5	6.0	5.7	7.1	7.1
Oceania and Other Islands	0.4	0.2	0.4	0.6	0.7	0.7	0.6	0.8	1.4	1.0
	100.0	100.0	100.0	100.0	100.0	100.0	100.0	100.0	100.0	100.0
Number (000s)	132.8[a]	184.0	161.5	147.7	121.9	122.0	184.2	218.5	187.9	149.4

Notes: Population of Canada at 1976 Census was 22.6 million.
[a] Annual averages; [b] Australia, New Zealand and related; [c] Includes Caribbean Islands.

Sources: Department of Manpower and Immigration: Annual Statistical Reports; Department of Manpower and Immigration: 1975 Immigration Statistics, Table 3; Immigration Canada, Department of Manpower and Immigration. Immigration 1976-Fourth Quarter. Ottawa, 1977.

nations, the British and the French, chartered by the British North America Act remain dominant: the British succeeded to anglicize most of the immigrants; the French retained, until recently, their one-third proportion in the population by what has been called the *revanche des berceaux*. Now that the expansionist philosophy of Canadian immigration policy is gone the population mix can change only slowly through natural increase of births over deaths.[2] The ethnic and racial differences in these basic demographic processes have become but slight.

The proportion of foreign born at any given census remains at about one-tenth of the population. The concentration of the foreign born in some provinces, primarily Ontario, and in some cities, primarily Toronto, is also traditional. One-half of all foreign born in Canada are registered in Ontario in 1971 the same as in 1901; the city of Toronto shows about 40 percent of her inhabitants to be foreign born. In 1971, 1.7 million out of the 3.2 million foreign born in Canada were in Ontario.

Such concentrations produce a great visibility of immigrants, especially if the national composition changes, as it has in the recent years. They become, then, easy scapegoats for the problems of urbanization and the concommitant ills of megalopolises.

History of Canadian Immigration Policies

On February 3, 1975, Robert Andras, Minister of Manpower and Immigration tabled a report in the Parliament. The report is known as the Green Paper, a vehicle by which the government indicates the intent of a policy.[3] The Green Paper summarizes the previous immigration policies and offers four new alternatives for the future: no change, linking immigration closely to the manpower needs, and two options of a numerical limitation on immigrants. It represents a major departure from the previous immigration policy which was expansionist as set down in the White Paper on Immigration.[4]

Section 95, of the British North America Act, 1867, assigns responsibility for immigration jointly to the Federal and Provincial governments. The latter takes care of settlement and the Federal government handles admission and selection. However, Ontario has its own recruitment offices abroad and

[2] Anthony H. Richmond. "Immigration, Population and the Canadian Future", *Sociological Focus*, 9:125-136. 1976.

[3] Department of Manpower and Immigration. *Immigration Policy Perspectives*, Vol. 1; *The Immigration Program*, Vol. 2; *Immigration and Population Statistics*, Vol. 3; *Three Years in Canada*. Ottawa: Information Canada.

[4] Department of Manpower and Immigration. *Canadian Immigration Policy* (The White Paper). Ottawa: Queen's Printer. 1966.

Quebec signed an agreement with Ottawa in 1971 to have a provincial representation officer in some of the Canadian immigration offices abroad.

Immigration into the country was basically free until 1895. During the free period, only about 1.5 million immigrants came to Canada. Promotion activities were allowed only in the British Isles assuring a flow of immigrants of uniform stock. Assisted passage and cheap land were the chief inducements to come.

Ad hoc immigration regulations kept enlarging the prohibited classes of immigrants. The restrictions were directed at those whose physical or mental capacities were believed to make them public charges or whose moral character was believed unwelcome. In addition, those persons deemed unassimilable were discouraged. By 1885 there was a head tax of 50 dollars on Chinese immigrants. They were effectively barred from immigrating to Canada until 1947.

Massive settlement programs began during the incumbency in the Ministry of the Interior of Clifton Sifton, 1896 to 1914. The settling of the west was done in an orderly fashion, settlers being preceded by land surveyors and the Royal Canadian Mounted Police. By 1914 the "open frontier" closed in Canada, some years later than in the United States. Faced with a heavy influx of immigrants from southern and eastern Europe, Canada began to encourage "positive" immigration from the United Kingdom. This was Canada's response to the same situation that produced pressure for a policy of quota on ethnic groups in the United States.

The period until the end of World War II saw additional restrictions on immigration. One was the introduction of visas obtainable only from consular offices abroad. The other important addition to the Canadian immigration policy was the introduction of sponsored classes of immigrants, allowing family reunification in Canada.

Major Rulings on Immigration

As most countries of Anglo-Saxon jurisprudence, Canada handles matters of immigration not so much by promulgating Acts but, rather, by issuing various Orders in Council, regulations and amendments of regulations.

Four preferred classes of immigrants were stipulated by Order of Council of March 21, 1931:[5] British subjects with sufficient means from United Kingdom, Ireland, Newfoundland, New Zealand, Australia and South Africa; United States citizens; dependents of Canadian residents; and agriculturalists with sufficient means.

After the last world war, Canadian immigration policy started to change

[5] Privy Council 695.

rapidly. Speaking before the Parliament, Prime Minister Mackenzie King summarized the past and outlined the future immigration policy.[6] Canada remained committed to growth; upper limits to immigration were set only by the "absorptive capacity" of the country. Chinese prohibition was repealed and the admission of displaced persons and refugees encouraged. The prohibition of enemy aliens from the war time was repealed. However, blacks remained inadmissible unless they belonged to the preferred classes. Nor was there a general repeal of the prohibition of Asiatic immigration. The preference for the British, French and American citizens remained. "Assimilability" was the criterion which has survived from previous policies. Enterpreneurs and professionals, domestics and nurses' aides, those sponsored by their future employers were the new classes of admissible immigrants, indicating a new responsiveness to the changed conditions in Canada: not settling on the land, but working in the cities.

New Immigration Regulations issued in 1962 increased the emphasis on educational training and occupational skills, partly to counteract the flow of unskilled immigrants coming to Canada as sponsored immigrants or specifically as domestics from the Caribbean, and partly to match immigration and the needs of an advanced industrial nation. During that year, 100 Chinese refugees were admitted, effectively ending the Asiatic ban.

A press release accompanying the new Regulations stated: "The most important provision of the new Regulations is Section 31 which is in fact the core of Canada's immigration policy...[It] lays primary stress on education, training and skills as the main condition of admissibility, regardless of the country of origin of the applicant..."[7]

A universalistic immigration policy was laid down on October 1, 1967. One year earlier, the White Paper on Immigration stated: "We do not have a frontier open to new agricultural settlement...Despite its low population density, Canada has become a highly complex industrialized and urbanized society. And such a society is increasingly demanding of the quality of its work force".[8]

In spite of her determination to gear immigration to her needs of manpower, Canada's image abroad and her foreign born political constituents at home dictate admission of immigrants not destined for the labor force. Apart from the sponsored classes, Canada has admitted major groups of refugees.

Admission by special programs included about 38,000 Hungarians in the period 1956 and 1957, about 12,000 Czechoslovak refugees in 1968 and

[6] Order in Council, May 1, 1947, P.C. 1734.

[7] Freda Hawkins. *Canada and Immigration: Public Policy and Public Concern.* Montreal: McGill-Queens Univ. Press. 1972.

[8] Department of Manpower and Immigration. *Canadian Immigration Policy* (The White Paper). Ottawa: Queen's Printer. 1966.

1969, 228 Tibetans in 1970, about 5,600 Ugandan Asians in 1972 and 1973 and about 1,200 Chileans during the years 1973 and 1974.[9] All in all, about 10 percent of all postwar immigrants were refugees.[10] By 1976, 7,000 Chileans were admitted. Refugees entering Canada in 1976 numbered about 10,000.

With regard to admitting unsponsored handicapped persons, Canada's record is meager. During 1973 and 1974 combined, only four handicapped refugees were admitted.[11] The problem lies, at least partially in the administrative system of immigration whereby the Provinces are responsible for settlement and maintenance of immigrants and the Federal government for their admission which, in turn is dependent on the settlement provisions.[12]

Immigration Regulations in Force

Admission to Canada is determined by the Immigration Act of 1952 as amended in subsequent years and as stipulated in Immigration Regulations of 1967,[13] and as amended. The Minister of Manpower and Immigration has powers to amend the Act by Order in Council. Persons admitted as immigrants must pass a health check and they may not belong to any of the twenty prohibited classes (physical and mental disabilities, criminal record, subversive activities and similar). However, Americans fleeing draft at home were not denied admission.

There are three classes of admissible immigrants: independent immigrants, sponsored dependents and nominated relatives. Independent applicants are those expected to become self-supporting in Canada. They must meet a number of criteria based on skills, education and an estimate of suitability for life in Canada as determined by the admission officer. They must secure at least 50 of the possible 100 points. Normally, they may bring their families, that is their spouses and unmarried children under 21 years of age. There are, altogether, nine criteria against which the independent applicants are assessed (see Table 2:2), in addition to which a modest sum between 200 and 1,000 dollars is expected to be in their possession to tide them over the first few days of stay.[14]

[9] Department of Manpower and Immigration. *The Immigration Program*. Vol. 2. Ottawa: Information Canada. 1974; Anthony H. Richmond. "Canadian Immigration: Recent Development and Future Prospects", *International Migration*, 13:163-180. 1975.

[10] Department of Manpower and Immigration. *Immigration Policy Perspectives*. Vol. 1. Ottawa: Information Canada. 1974.

[11] Anthony H. Richmond. "Canadian Immigration: Recent Developments and Future Prospects", *International Migration*, 13:163-180. 1975.

[12] Freda Hawkins. *Canada and Immigration: Public Policy and Public Concern*. Montreal: McGill-Queens Univ. Press. 1972.

[13] Privy Council 1967:1616.

[14] Department of Manpower and Immigration. *The Immigration Program*. Vol. 2. Ottawa: Information Canada. 1974.

TABLE 2:2
Selection Criteria for Immigrant Admission to
Canada, Immigration Regulations, 1967

Independent Applicants

Long Term Factors	Range of Units of Assessment that May Be Awarded	Short Term Factors	Range of Units of Assessment that May Be Awarded
Education and Training	0-20	Arranged Employment/Designated Occupation	0-10
Personal Qualities	0-15		
Occupational Demand	0-15	Knowledge of English and/or French	0-10
Occupational Skill	1-10		
Age	0-10	Relative in Canada	0 or 3 or 5
		Area of Destination	0-5
		Potential maximum	100

Nominated Relatives		Sponsored Dependents	
Long Term Factors (as for independent applicants)	1-70	Close Relative in Canada Willing to Take Responsibility for Care and Maintenance	Units of Assessment not required
Short Term Settlement Arrangements Provided by Relative in Canada	15,20,25 or 30		
Potential Maximum	100		

Notes: Independent Applicants and Nominated Relatives, to qualify for selection, must normally earn 50 or more of the potential 100 units of assessment. In addition they must have received at least one unit for the occupational demand factor or be destined to arranged employment or a designated occupation.

In unusual cases, selection officers may accept or reject an Independent Applicant for Nominated Relative notwithstanding the actual number of units of assessment awarded.

Entrepreneurs are assessed in the same way as Independent Applicants except that they receive automatically 25 units of assessment in lieu of any units they might have received for the occupational demand and occupational skill factors.

A change in the regulations was made in October, 1974. The regulations now stipulate that, from the total points awarded either an independent or nominated applicant, 10 are deducted unless the applicant shows evidence of bona fide arranged employment, or is going to a job where persistent regional shortages are known to exist (i.e. a "designated occupation"). The applicant will receive credit for arranged employment only when it has been established that no Canadian citizen or permanent resident is available to fill the vacancy.

Source: Department of Manpower and Immigration, 1974b:59-60.

Sponsored dependents must be close relatives of Canadian citizens or residents: spouses, affianced, unmarried children under 21 years of age, parents or grandparents over 60 years of age, younger if widowed or disabled; an orphan sibling; nephew, niece or grandchild less than 18 years of age; an unmarried adopted child under 21 years of age provided adoption occurred prior to his turning 18; or an orphaned or abandoned child under 13 years whom the sponsor intends to adopt. Finally, a person without close relatives in Canada or abroad may, once only, sponsor one relative of any degree to come to Canada as his companion, heir, or similar. Apart from the health requirements stipulated in the prohibited classes, sponsored dependents need not meet other criteria provided the sponsor is at least 18 years of age and capable of supporting his wards.

Nominated relatives are credited with up to 30 units of assessment. In other respects, their eligibility is that of the independent immigrants. The nominating person must be at least 18 years of age and, in principle, be able to sustain the nominated wards for a period of up to five years to forestall their becoming wards of the state and public charges. However, the welfare provisions in force make such a requirement largely superfluous. It is this class of immigrants which least fits the new policy of immigration to reward skills and training.[15]

The immigration priorities are in order of listing: sponsored dependents; independent immigrants and nominated relatives; enterpreneurs; and others. The last two categories refer to those who will provide jobs for others and those whose admission is at the discretion of the Minister of Immigration.[16]

A normal procedure to apply for immigration to Canada is through a consular office, or an immigration office abroad. Historically, offices were located only in England. After the last war, a number of immigration offices opened, primarily in the British Isles and Northwestern Europe. In 1950 there were only two offices out of a total of 15 which took care of Southern Europe and Asia. By 1973, on the other hand, there were 55 offices in operation abroad, 17 of which were in Southern Europe and the areas of the Third World and 12 of which were in the United States.[17]

Sponsors, or nominators, of immigrants thus far have seldom failed in their efforts to bring persons to Canada. On the other hand, the proportion of successful independent applicants has been at 50 percent since about 1960, and somewhat higher prior to that time.[18]

---

[15] Anthony H. Richmond. "Canadian Immigration: Recent Development and Future Prospects", *International Migration*, 12:163-180. 1975; Department of Manpower and Immigration. *Immigration and Population Statistics.* Vol. 3. Ottawa: Information Canada. 1974.

[16] Department of Manpower and Immigration. *The Immigrant Program.* Vol. 2. Ottawa: Information Canada. 1974.

[17] Freda Hawkins. *Canada and Immigration: Public Policy and Public Concern.* Montreal: McGill-Queens Univ. Press. 1972; Louis Parai. "Canada's Immigration Policy, 1962-1964", *International Migration Review*, 9(4):449-477. 1975.

[18] Department of Manpower and Immigration. *The Immigration Program.* Vol. 2. Ottawa:

Successful applicants for immigration may be eligible for an Assisted Passage Loan; immigrants receive information and counselling abroad. In Canada, they are eligible for emergency medical assistance and their children up to 18 years of age receive family allowance payments, provided one of the parents is subject to Canadian taxes on income. Independent immigrants are also eligible for emergency financial assistance. All immigrants are covered by an Interim Health Program. There are language and skill retraining classes available through Manpower services and living expenses are paid for up to six weeks to avail oneself of such services.

The current Immigration Regulations were supplemented by the Immigration Appeal Board Act of August 15, 1973. The new Act was brought down to simplify the existing appeal procedures and to clear the decks of the accumulated cases. What was being dealt with was the result of a provision allowing visitors to Canada to apply for landed immigrant status from within the country. Between 1967, when this provision entered in force, until 1973, about one-third (in the last year of the provision) of all applicants availed themselves of such an advantage. The inequality of such an arrangement became obvious.[19] Since a substantial number of applicants from within did not meet the criteria for admission but were allowed to appeal their cases, by 1973 about 17,000 appeals were pending and their resolution proceeded at a rate of 1,200 annually.[20]

In summary judgment, most appeals were upheld and an amnesty was declared for those who entered Canada as visitors prior to November 30, 1972. Such persons were to report to the respective immigration offices and become admitted as landed immigrants on relaxed criteria. They were given until October 15, 1973. Close to 50,000 persons availed themselves of this amnesty, a number well under the estimate of illegal immigrants in Canada.[21]

Immigration Act 1976

On July 25, 1977 the House of Commons of Canada passed Bill C-24, embodying the new immigration policy for Canada. The Bill was proclaimed law on April 4, 1978. In essence, the Immigration Act of 1976 articulates an immigration policy as evolved through previous legislation but which is now closely tied to a population policy for Canada. Whereas the Immigration Act of 1952 was essentially expansionist but particularistic in the selection

---

Information Canada. 1974.

[19] Anthony H. Richmond. "Canadian Immigration: Recent Development and Future Prospects", *International Migration*, 13:163-180. 1975.

[20] Louis Parai. "Canada's Immigration Policy, 1962-1974", *International Migration Review*, 9(4):449-477. 1975.

[21] *Ibid.*

of immigrants on the basis of race and ethnicity, the new Act is designed to ensure a demographic stabilization but is universalistic in the admissibility of immigrants.

Under the new Act the Government of Canada reserves the right to establish demographic targets for immigration, to be implemented by the Minister of Manpower and Immigration setting annual guidelines as to the composition and size of immigration; this policy is not dissimilar in its intent to the U.S. policy of immigration ceilings. The multiculturalism policy is expressly stated as to a desirability of an ethnic and racial mix of immigrants. Of first importance, however, the new immigration policy is fully geared to facilitate family reunions. Similarly, Canada's obligations in settling refugees is affirmed explicitly for the first time in the history of Canadian immigration policies.

The selection criteria for admission of immigrants remain largely those of the preceding legislation, but the class of nominated relatives has been removed. An explicit interdependence between the admission of immigrants and the settling of immigrants in different provinces or localities has been accepted and anchored in the legislation. The classification of inadmissible immigrants has been modified by dropping now controllable diseases, e.g. epilepsy, from the prohibited list, and by expanding the list of persons inadmissible for essentially political reasons, e.g. known or probable subversives and terrorists. Residents in Canada who are not citizens of the country must demonstrate having maintained viable ties to Canada if they have been out of the country for more than six months and are seeking reentry.[22]

Naturalization Policy

Canada's naturalization policies were always liberal. Once a person became admitted as a landed immigrant, all that stood between him and the Canadian citizenship was a waiting period, usually five years and his willingness to apply. A short "examination" of his knowledge about Canada preceded his confirmation as a suitable citizen. The conferring of citizenship was done with less ceremonials than is the case, for instance, in the United States. The waiting period in Canada has been now shortened to three years. The new Citizenship Act went into force on February 15, 1977. The new Citizenship Act corresponds to the new immigration policies in that it has become explicitly universalistic. The changes which took place are, in particular, the

[22] The House of Commons of Canada, C-24, 2nd Session, 30th Parliament. An Act Respecting Immigration to Canada. July 25, 1977; Department of Manpower and Immigration. The Immigration Bill Explanatory Notes. Ottawa, November, 1976.

removal of status difference between men and women, disregarding their marital status when applying for citizenship and the age of majority has been lowered to 18 years of age. Applicants are now treated equally disregarding their ethnic or racial background.

The new Act was preceded by the realization that the immigrants to Canada make little use of their rights to become citizens. Immigrants representing major immigration countries from Europe took, on the average, at least ten years before applying for citizenship.[23]

Employment Visa

As of January 1, 1973, Canada offered employment visas for workers to pursue a temporary employment for a period of up to twelve months. Prior to this date, persons from the United States could obtain a work permit at the border also for a period of one year. It was renewable provided they had employment in Canada but were domiciled in the United States.

The new visa regulations are intended to solve the labor market condition in Canada without a recourse to immigration. Over 80,000 visas were issued by the end of 1973, one-third of which went to Americans. Only a small number were actually issued to the commuters from the United States and about as many visas were issued again in 1974.[24] A substantial proportion of visa holders are in the travel and entertainment industry and in the management and scientific fields.

Canada has entered into bilateral agreements with a number of Caribbean countries and, in June, 1974, with Mexico, to import seasonal workers for agriculture. The Caribbean Seasonal Workers Program as well as the Mexican program bring several thousand agricultural workers to Canada annually to do work for which there are no Canadians available.

Thus, Canadian immigration policy is becoming increasingly closely linked with the labor force needs. Starting with 1974, the Department of Manpower through its employment services must certify that the position an alien is applying for from without Canada cannot be manned by a Canadian citizen or resident (See Table 2:2).[25]

[23] Daniel Kubat et al. *German Nationals in Canada: Their Intentions to Naturalize.* Report to the Secretary of State. Waterloo: Univ. of Waterloo, Dept. of Sociology. 1976.

[24] Department of Manpower and Immigration. *The Immigration Program.* Vol. 2. Ottawa: Information Canada. 1974; Anthony H. Richmond. "The Green Paper — Reflections on the Canadian Immigration and Population Study", *Canadian Ethnic Studies,* 7:5-21. 1975.

[25] Louis Parai. "Canada's Immigration Policy, 1962-1974", *International Migration Review,* 9(4):449-477. 1975.

TABLE 2:3

Immigrants to Canada by Class of Admission and by Proportion Destined for Labor Force, Since 1946

Year	All Immigrants N	Percent Workers	Proportion of Workers by Class of Admission Sponsored	Nominated	Independent
1946-50	430,389	48	—	—	—
1951-55	791,750	54			
1956-60	782,911	53	36		64
1961	71,689	49	37		59
1962	74,586	49	33		62
1963	93,151	49	31		63
1964	112,606	50	35		60
1965	149,758	51	35		60
1966	194,743	51	35		59
1967	222,876	54	35		63
1968	183,974	52	17	54	64
1969	161,531	52	20	56	63
1970	147,713	53	20	56	64
1971	121,900	50	22	57	63
1972	122,006	49	23	57	59
1973	184,200	50	21	54	61
1974	218,465	50	21	52	55
1975	187,881	43	21	52	55
1976	149,429	41	27	52	51

Note: — indicates data not available.

Sources: Department of Manpower and Immigration, Annual Reports; Department of Manpower and Immigration, 1974b, Tables 3.6, 5.3, 5.5; Parai, 1975, Table 7.5; Department of Immigration and Manpower: 1975 Immigration Statistics; Immigration Canada, Department of Manpower and Immigration. Immigration 1976-Fourth Quarter. Ottawa, 1977. Office of the Minister of Manpower and Immigration, Press Release, April 13, 1977.

Immigration of Professionals

The typical immigrants to Canada were agriculturalists and craftsmen when the prevalent source countries were those of the British Isles and Northwestern Europe. During the years of heavy immigration until World War I, the average skills levels declined. However, the heavy expansion of urban centers in Canada could well use unskilled hands for the building of roads, canals, service facilities and the like.

After World War II, a new supply of skilled immigrants became available in the ranks of displaced persons and refugees, and the new emphasis on education and training in the selection criteria of independent applicants. A recent decline in the skills levels, attributed to the class of immigration on the basis of kinship relatedness, has been noted and commented upon.[26] Nonetheless, the proportion of those immigrating to Canada and intending to work in professional and technical occupations has remained above 20 percent during the last 15 years.

Around the year 1970 there was a noticeable influx to Canada of professionals in the high status categories, primarily of university teachers, medical doctors and the like. University teachers, in particular, were, largely Americans, who have always considered Canada as their domain. Since the Canadian universities actively advertised for staff and publicized considerable tax savings available, the ensuing "Americanization" of Canadian universities is easily understood.

In response to the temporary, as it was the trend in immigration of professionals, the traditionally modal category of immigrants destined for manufacturing has changed to that of professional and technical occupations. In the longer run, however, the occupational profile of immigrants to Canada will again return to the dominance of skilled workers and trades. That is particularly so since a traditional outlet for Canadian residents to migrate to the United States has been all but closed by the recent American immigration restrictions. Fortunately, the emergent nationalism in Canada makes the loss of opportunities abroad a virtue at home.

Immigration and the Future of Canadian Population

Statistics Canada, the agency responsible for population statistics, estimated Canada's population at 23.1 million on May 1, 1976. The count of the 1976 Census on June 1, 1976 shows 22.6 million.[27]

The only weak link in the equation for estimation of population is in the estimate of emigration. Emigration has been variously estimated to converge to 50,000 persons annually for the years 1955 to 1965, it then increased somewhat and now, during the 1970s it has decreased. Components of emigration statistics come from the immigration counts in the United States and in Britain. About 20,000 persons are presumed to go elsewhere in any given year. France, for instance, does not include return migrants as immigrants. The American figures are not likely to include their own returning nationals. A dispersal of some of the illegal immigrants intercepted

---

[26] *Ibid.;* Monica Boyd. "Immigration Policies and Trends: A Comparison of Canada and the United States", *Demography*, 18:83-104. 1976; Department of Manpower and Immigration. *The Immigration Program.* Vol. 2. Ottawa: Information Canada. 1974.

[27] *Financial Post*, Nov. 6, 1976.

TABLE 2:4

Occupational Distribution of Immigrant Labor Force for Selected Periods Since 1946 and Occupational Distribution of Native Born Labor Force, Canada, in 1967

| | Average Values | | | | | | | | Native Born 1967[a] |
| | Years, Immigrant Labor Force in Percent | | | | | | | | |
Occupations	1946-50	1951-57	1958-61	1962-67	1968-73	1974	1975	1976	
Managerial, professional, technical	7.7	12.7	21.7	25.8	32.0	26.6	31.5	32.6	22.7
Clerical, sales	11.4	14.8	15.8	16.8	18.5	18.6	18.6	19.5	22.1
Service, recreation	10.9	14.9	18.9	10.5	10.8	10.1	8.9	9.4	17.8
Manufacturing, mechanical[b]	31.6	30.9	23.2	23.3	21.6	24.6	23.2	21.1	24.8
Construction[b]	–	–	–	8.8	7.0	10.3	9.4	6.5	
Primary industries	25.4	9.6	7.2	4.1	3.7	3.0	2.3	2.3	8.8
Laborers[b]	9.2	14.0	11.5	8.3	2.5	0.6	0.6	–	–
Other	3.9	3.1	1.9	2.4	3.9	6.2	5.5	8.6	3.8
	100.0	100.0	100.0	100.0	100.0	100.0	100.0	100.0	100.0

Notes:

[a] Based on Dominion Bureau of Statistics Labor Force Survey, February, 1967; categories not completely comparable. – indicates no data available; source: Kubat and Thornton, 1974:169.

[b] For 1974 through 1976 categories more inclusive with the exception of Laborers who became defined very narrowly.

Sources: Department of Manpower and Immigration, *The Immigration Program*, 1974, Table 3.8; Department of Manpower and Immigration:1974 Immigration Statistics, Table 14; 1975 Immigration Statistics Table 14; Immigration Canada, Department of Manpower and Immigration. Immigration 1976-Fourth Quarter. Ottawa, 1977.

TABLE 2:5

Immigrants to Canada by Intended Professional and Technical Occupations, by High Status Professional Occupations by Country of Last Residence, Since 1962

Year	Immigrants Intended for Labor Force N	% Prof. and Techn.	Surgeons, Physicians, Professors, Principals Country of Last Residence			
			Britain	U.S.	Other	Total
1962	36,748	22	225	271	424	920
1963	45,866	21	380	351	495	1226
1964	56,190	21	438	328	575	1340
1965	74,195	23	552	519	805	1876
1966	99,210	24	708	673	1024	2405
1967	119,539	26	814	922	1673	3099
1968	95,449	31	923	1092	1542	3557
1969	84,349	32	908	1129	1698	3745
1970	77,723	29	634	1005	1360	2999
1971	61,282	27	434	880	1021	2345
1972	59,432	26	429	651	938	2019
1973	92,228	21	493	823	1335	2651
1974	109,232	26	499	674	1008	2181
1975	81,189	31	486	460	626	1572
1976	61,461	23	229	365	1609	1015

Sources: Department of Manpower and Immigration, Annual Reports; Department of Immigration and Manpower: 1975 and 1976 Immigration Statistics; Immigration Canada, Department of Manpower and Immigration: Immigration 1976- Fourth Quarter.

TABLE 2:6

Emigration from Canada (country of last permanent residence)
to the United States, by Proportion of Dependents and
by Proportion of Professional and Technical Occupations
Among Those Intended for the Labor Force, from 1952

Years[a]	All Emigrants	Dependents in Percent	Professional, Technical, as % of All Workers
1952-60	352,072	49	—
1961	47,270	49	—
1962	42,272	47	20
1963	50,509	50	21
1964	51,114	50	21
1965	50,035	50	22
1966	37,273	54	36
1967	34,768	57	33
1968	41,716	54	31
1969	29,303	54	32
1970	26,849	53	33
1971	22,707	54	39
1972	18,596	54	36
1973	14,800	56	—
1974	12,301	55[b]	—
1975	11,215	56	—

Notes:
[a] to June 30, each year.
[b] This figure calculated on the base of 11,385 emigrants to the U.S.; this number represented "selected" occupations.

Sources: Department of Manpower and Immigration, 1974, Table 7.2; Immigration and Naturalization Service, annual reports; *Canada Manpower and Immigration Review*, 9(3). 1976, Table 7; *Canada Manpower and Immigration Review*, 8(4):14. 1975.

in the 1971 Census but not taking advantage of the Immigration Appeal Board amnesty in 1973 may have also played a role in the current "undercount". The sex ratio remained favorable to men in the 1971 Census even though the mortality patterns and the sex balanced immigration patterns did not warrant a male favored sex ratio. Either by self-enumeration, or by being enumerated, the illegal immigrants found a quasi-legalization of their stay. The 1971 Census may have accounted for a considerable number of persons not calculated into the estimates. The economic recession and the "scare" of the amnesty may have sent home additional persons.

Population projections prepared for the Canadian Immigration and Population Study confirm the demographic power of immigration. Assuming only a self-replacement fertility, but variable immigration (net immigration, after subtracting estimated emigrants), today's labor force of about 9 million will close to double in the year 2001 should the net rate of growth by net immigration alone be about one-half of one percent. The demographic structure of Canadian population contains enough momentum to increase the size of its labor force by about 46 percent by the year 2001 even with net annual immigration remaining at zero.[28]

Considering the Canadian immigration policy, which is to gear immigration to the labor force needs, and considering the growth potential of her own population, Canadian immigration policy makers face, indeed, a trilemma: there is the immigration tradition and Canada's image as a vast country. The fact that the vastness is mostly wasteland, is seldom mentioned in promotional literature on Canada.

There is the sociological probability that any large influx of persons is self-sustaining short of a drastic closing of the border. When the immigrants are coming from areas where want is great, invoking of kinship obligations becomes particularly frequent.

There is enough demographic momentum in Canada's young population even at the self-replacement level that a shortage of manpower in the foreseeable future is unlikely. It remains doubtful that there will be a match between jobs and inclinations to work. In case the match does not obtain, immigration will always be the answer.

[28] Warren E. Kalbach. *The Effect of Immigration on Population.* Ottawa: Information Canada. 1975.

3

New Zealand

JEAN LEONARD ELLIOTT*
Dalhousie University

The Context of Immigration

THROUGHOUT New Zealand's history, immigration to New Zealand has reflected the broader economic, cultural and foreign policy concerns of the country. The settlement era which actively favored immigration from Britain came to an end in 1974. Prior to this, British born citizens of European background were granted more or less, unrestricted access to New Zealand.[1]

New Zealand revised its immigration policy regarding Britain for a number of reasons, many of which were economic. With the entry of Britain into the European Community New Zealand's reliance upon the British market for dairy products exports became questionable. New Zealand was forced to search for new markets and is expanding now in the Pacific, Middle East and Eastern Europe. Trading uncertainty, coupled with inflation and an adverse balance of payments, brought along import restrictions and a drive toward domestic self-sufficiency. The country has geothermal energy and hydroelectric power, but it is heavily dependent on the importation of fossil fuels.

In the past, New Zealand was offering assisted immigration schemes to recruit labor for the domestic market even though skilled labor was trained

* This research was supported, in part, by Canada Council Leave Fellowship W74 0170, 1974-75. The support is gratefully acknowledged.

[1] Immigration Advisory Council. *Review of Immigration Policy.* Wellington: Government Printing Office. 1974.

at home whenever possible, rather than recruited from abroad. The country prides itself on a full employment economy and her immigration policy is formulated with this goal in mind.

Between 1968 and 1970 New Zealand registered a net migration loss. Unemployment then was at its highest since the depression of the 1930s. It also became apparent that immigration had to be more tightly controlled. Immigrants were seen as placing a strain on the economy, in such areas as housing, schools, and social services. To restrict the British immigrants, who were the most numerous, seemed a natural first step toward bringing down the number of immigrants to a more manageable level.

The Maori Culture

The reassessment of New Zealand's historical ties with Britain occurred at a time when New Zealand had come increasingly to see its own destiny firmly linked with the other Pacific nations. A noticeable strengthening of *Maoritanga* (Maori culture) in New Zealand is observable among the European as well as the Polynesian population. Maori culture is an integral part of New Zealand society in spite of the "Maori Wars" which were really disputes centered upon the control and ownership of land.[2] The resurgence of interest in the New Zealand Maori heritage is witnessed by the creation of Maori studies curricula at the university level, and Maori language training for secondary level students. In 1976 there were 127 secondary schools teaching Maori to 11,255 students. During the last thirty years, the government has been subsidizing the construction of *Maraes*. A Marae is a complex of buildings and grounds of a sacred nature where *tangihanga* (death ceremonials) and *manaaki i te manuhiri* (caring for visitors) are practiced among other ritual and community activities.

Asiatic Exclusion

New Zealand has had racially exclusive immigration policies, particularly with respect to Asians. Nevertheless, the first Chinese Immigration Act of 1881 was hotly debated.[3] All in all, it would be grossly amiss to label New Zealand a thoroughly racist society. Indeed, quite the contrary is the case.[4]

[2] Keith Sinclair. *A History of New Zealand.* London: Penguin. 1959.

[3] W.T. Roy. "Immigration Policy and Legislation", *Immigrants in New Zealand.* K.W. Thompson and A.D. Trilin, eds. Palmerston North: Massey Univ. Pp. 15-24; W. David McIntyre and W.J. Gardner, eds. *Speeches and Documents on New Zealand History.* Oxford: Clarendon. 1971.

[4] Keith Sinclair. "Why Are Race Relations in New Zealand Better Than in South Africa, South Australia or South Dakota?" *New Zealand Journal of History*, 5:121-127. 1971.

Currently the 1974 Immigration Policy goes a long way toward righting an historic anti-Asian bias. Until 1974 "no persons other than a person of British birth and parentage shall (except as by this Act is specially provided) enter into New Zealand unless he is in possession of a permit to enter . . . The Minister of Customs . . . may, in his discretion, grant or refuse to the applicant a permit to enter New Zealand".[5] In spite of the liberal reforms evident in the 1974 policy, it is clear that New Zealand is not willing to open the door to "anyone from anywhere". This caution stems from the realization that New Zealand is not the answer to Asian overpopulation and poverty. The new immigration policy is restrictive rather than exclusive in emphasis.

The South Pacific Community

Many of the islands in the South Pacific tend to fall within New Zealand's sphere of influence. New Zealand citizenship is granted the inhabitants of Nuie, Tokelau, and the Cook Islands. Western Samoa occupies a special status vis à vis New Zealand because of her former status as a trust territory. Not counting Australia, these islands and Fiji and Tonga contribute the lion's share of immigration to New Zealand from the South Pacific.[6]

The 1974 Immigration Policy is integrated with foreign policy objectives. Foreign aid is dispensed by New Zealand to various South Pacific islands in the hope of correcting adverse economic conditions constraining their population to out-migrate. As a part of its foreign aid program New Zealand trains foreign students in its universities. Students from as far as Malaysia are financially supported by New Zealand. In 1972, there were about 3,000 foreign students in New Zealand.

Population Growth

New Zealand passed the three million population mark in 1973. Its first million was reached in 1908, 68 years after the founding of New Zealand as a nation. The second million was reached in 1952. Whereas immigration was responsible for the early growth of the New Zealand population, starting in the late 1870s natural increase became the chief contributor to the population growth of the nation. The census of 1881 tipped the population balance in favor of the native born recorded as 50.2 percent of the total. The native born population increased to 85.6 percent in 1971. Even though the surplus of births over deaths was the chief component of the population

[5] *New Zealand Statutes*, 23(11):78-83. 1920.
[6] *New Zealand Official Yearbook*. 1975.

TABLE 3:1

Recent Growth of New Zealand Population and Components of Population Change, Since 1970

Year	Population	Net difference of females	Annual Percent Increase	Natural Increase N	Increase Per 1,000 Population	Net Migration[a]
1970	2,852,137	+1,267	1.7	37,210	13.20	−2,997
1971	2,899,067	+2,169	1.6	40,151	14.01	1,212
1972	2,960,996	+ 702	2.1	38,414	13.17	7,553
1973	3,026,930	+ 522	2.2	35,415	11.89	19,168
1974	3,094,700	−3,100	2.2	34,075	11.19	27,477
1975	3,148,400	+ 600	1.7	31,526	10.16	22,439
1976						5,300

Notes:

a Period ending March 31.

b Provisional

Sources: Department of Statistics. *Monthly Abstract of Statistics*, Oct., 1975, pp. 5, 11; July, 1976, T.1, p. 7 and March, 1977, T.1, p. 7 and T.10, p. 13; *New Zealand Official Yearbook* 1975. Pp. 58, 87; 1976, pp. 57, 86.

growth, there was also a steady immigration interrupted only occasionally when the economic situation was significantly adverse. In 1974, natural increase exceeded net immigration by about 6,500 persons, the overall population increase registering about 61,000 persons in that year.

New Zealand registered a net increase in the total number of migrants in the period between 1971 and 1973, but there was a shortfall for both sexes in the 20 to 24 age group despite the leap from 7,553 in 1971 to 19,168 in 1972 in the net balance of migration. However, the sex ratio of migrants remained more or less stable. The negative migration balance for the age category of 20 to 24 testifies perhaps more to the venturesomeness of the young New Zealanders than to the unattractiveness of the country for immigrants.

Occupational Structure

An increase in the labor participation rate has kept pace with the overall population growth. Within the occupational structure, the service sector experienced the fastest growth, from 49 percent of the labor force in 1961 to 53 percent in 1971. The secondary sector employment remained stationary with about 35 percent of the labor force while the primary sector declined by about 3 percent.

New Zealand has a favorable net immigration of professionals. In any given year, however, a particular professional group may register a net migration loss. Thus, for instance during the administrative year of 1971/1972 there were minor net losses among physical scientists (-6), dentists (-13), and accountants (-42); on the other hand, physicians, engineers, architects, agronomists and teachers showed a net gain. Female teachers, however, showed net loss (-204).

New Zealand has a tradition of assisted immigration. The "subsidy scheme" shows a recent peak in the administrative year 1971/1972 (April/ March 31) when 21 percent of all permanent new arrivals were covered with a full travel subsidy and a guarantee of housing and employment. For the most part, the subsidized immigrants were from Britain, Western Europe and the United States. Another subsidy scheme was geared specifically to immigrants from Britain. Persons belonging in preferred occupation categories as approved by the New Zealand Secretary of Labor could apply for the "assisted passage" subsidy. The scheme was terminated in April, 1975. During 1974, 450 immigrants arrived under this scheme. They represented, however, only one percent of that year's total of permanent arrivals.

TABLE 3:2

Distribution of New Zealand's Immigrants and Emigrants by Age and Sex
Since 1971

Year[a] and Category		-15	15 - 19	Age Groups 20 - 24	25 - 44	45 +	Total
1971-72							
Immigrants	N	10,139	3,784	10,257	15,470	5,449	45,009
	SR[b]	107	79	95	128	89	106
Emigrants	N	6,699	4,201	12,334	10,703	3,609	37,546
	SR	105	80	106	134	86	107
Net Migrants		3,440	-417	-2,077	4,767	1,840	7,553
1972-73							
Immigrants	N	13,186	4,329	11,080	19,631	6,425	54,651
	SR	107	81	93	126	91	106
Emigrants	N	6,213	3,732	11,512	10,642	3,384	35,483
	SR	104	73	98	134	89	105
Net Migrants	SR	6,973	597	-432	8,989	3,041	19,168

TABLE 3:2 (continued)

Distribution of New Zealand's Immigrants and Emigrants by Age and Sex Since 1971

Year[a] and Category		Age Groups					Total
		-15	15 - 19	20 - 24	25 - 44	45 +	
1973-74[c]							
Immigrants	N	17,652	5,712	13,248	23,192	10,011	69,815
	SR	108	82	97	125	108	108
Emigrants	N						
	SR	100	78	110	144	106	110
Net Migrants		10,039	507	-300	12,087	5,371	27,477
1974-75							
Immigrants	N	16,017	5,868	13,624	24,220	6,171	65,900
	SR	108	78	100	126	99	109
Emigrants	N	7,597	4,940	13,529	13,675	3,720	43,461
	SR	105	73	109	141	108	112
Net Migrants		8,420	928	95	10,545	2,451	22,439

Notes: [a]From April 1 to March 31; [b] Sex Ratio; [c] For 1973-1974 breakdown by age differs.

Source: Department of Statistics. *New Zealand Population and Migration.* 1974. T. 19, 20; *New Zealand Official Yearbook.* 1973, 1975, 1976; *Population and Migration. Part B.* Wellington: Department of Statistics, 1976. Table 26, 27.

TABLE 3:3

Immigrants to New Zealand by Class of Immigration, Since 1970

Year[a]	New Permanent Arrivals								Long Term Arrivals[d]		
	Assisted[b]		Subsidized[c]		Others		Total		Returning Residents	Visitors	All Immigrants
	N	%	N	%	N	%	N	%			
1970-71	538	3.0	3,182	17.9	14,015	79.0	17,735	100	12,236	9,406	39,377
1971-72	438	2.4	4,183	20.6	15,640	77.0	20,261	100	14,578	10,260	45,099
1972-73	506	1.9	3,036	11.4	23,124	86.7	26,666	100	16,694	11,291	54,651
1973-74	450	1.0	4,836	12.7	32,835	86.1	38,121	100	17,123	14,571	69,815
1974-75	437	1.3	7,670	22.5	26,035	76.2	34,142	100	17,566	14,192	65,900
1975-76											48,460

Notes: [a] April 1 to March 31.

[b] Only from Britain and limited to 500 persons per year, aged 18-45, skills in designated occupations by the Secretary of Labour. Began in 1947, terminated April, 1975.

[c] Passage paid one-quarter by the employer, three-quarters by the government. Between 1970 and 1975, immigrants other than British were Dutch (1,999), German (32), Swiss (147), American (163), and Other (153).

[d] After an absence of, or intending to stay for 12 months or more.

Sources: Department of Statistics. *New Zealand Official Yearbook*. 1875, 1976; *Monthly Abstract of Statistics*, October, 1975. T. 10, and March, 1977, T. 10.

Labor Mobility

New Zealand's labor force statistics on immigrants include new permanent arrivals and long term arrivals as two categories of immigrants. The latter comprises both visitors who intend to stay longer than 12 months and New Zealand residents returning after a stay overseas of more than one year. While it may be assumed that the new permanent arrivals will bolster the labor force in the long run, the long term arrivals make the "true" labor situation somewhat problematic to gauge. The insular nature of professional training in New Zealand informally compels many professionals to acquire overseas experience as part of their certification. Upon return, they are counted as immigrants.

On the other hand, when Islanders, for instance, from Fiji, Tonga or Western Samoa are issued work permits, their movement to and from New Zealand is tabulated with other short term visitors and tourists. In the early 1970s, the work permits for Islanders were for 3 or 6 months. The National Party came to power in November, 1975, and its platform included the reduction of immigration from all sources. Consequently, the work permits were immediately cut back to one month which, in effect, closed the program of imported short term labor.

The right of access to New Zealand enjoyed by inhabitants of the Cook Islands and Nuie has not been affected by the new measures since the Islanders are New Zealand citizens. Likewise, movement across the Tasman Sea to Australia remains also unrestricted for citizens from both countries. There is, however, a provision dating to 1971 governing migration from the Cook Islands to New Zealand. As of April, 1976, the migrants must have a job, housing and must prove that the dependents left behind are being cared for. Orientation courses to familiarize the Islanders with New Zealand life, previously voluntary, are now mandatory.[7]

It is the current policy of the New Zealand government not to accept as immigrants skilled workers from developing countries. Immigration from countries like Fiji, however, may proceed on kin and humanitarian grounds. It is the goal of the governing National Party to replace immigration with a detailed work permit scheme.

The cutbacks in work permits are swelling the number of illegal immigrants. In the spring of 1976, an attempt to register overstayers with an inducement of an extended permit or perhaps a permanent residence in New Zealand resulted in 3,382 people coming forth; 95 percent of them were from Tonga and Samoa. The deportation figures of some 250 persons annually are no indication of the extent of illegal immigration. In most instances, however, the work permit overstayers are being asked to leave voluntarily to save themselves the stigma of deportation.[8]

[7] *New Zealand Herald*, Feb. 12, 1976. [8] *Ibid.* June 26, 1976.

Ethnic Composition

Numerically, the impact of immigration on the ethnic mix of New Zealand population is not dramatic. In a qualitative sense, however, the non-European population in New Zealand has been affected significantly by immigration. The key, in part, to understanding the impact of ethnic immigration lies in the regional distribution of the non-Europeans. Polynesians settling in New Zealand have favored the North Island because of its subtropical climate. The 1971 census lists 94 percent of all Maoris as living on the North Island. Not only is the Island an ancestral home of the Maoris, it is also preferred by immigrants. One in ten New Zealanders has a non-European ethnic origin. The Polynesians constitute 9.6 percent of the total population, the Fijians .1 percent, the Chinese .4, the Indians .3 and all other non-Europeans .2 percent of the total population.[9]

The Polynesian component of the New Zealand population is bound to grow. Natural increase among Maoris has been more than double that of the total population. Their population pyramid is wide at the base and narrow at the top. In 1971, 49 percent of the Maoris were under fifteen years of age as compared to 32 percent of the general population. Their crude death rate is low, 6.2 per thousand, as compared to the 8.7 per thousand for non-Maoris. Only about 11 percent of Maoris are older than 45 years of age, compared with the corresponding 28 percent for non-Maoris. For statistical purposes, a child with one Maori parent is counted as Maori.[10]

Naturalization

The countries of last residence most frequently listed by immigrants to New Zealand between 1970 and 1975 were the United Kingdom and Australia; the United States was third and Canada usually fourth. With the exception of the United Kingdom, the country of last residence does not match the country of birth.

Who are the New Zealanders? In 1974, the countries contributing most of the new citizens, in addition to Britain, were: the Netherlands with 8.6 percent, India with 5.4 percent, Western Samoa with 5.4 percent, Fiji with 4.5 percent and China with 4.4 percent. Asian and Pacific countries, not counting Australia, contributed at least 24 percent of the new citizens in 1974 and their proportions are not likely to diminish in the future.

[9] *New Zealand Official Yearbook.* 1974. Pp. 59, 68.
[10] *Ibid.* 1974. P. 85.

TABLE 3:4

Distribution of Citizenship Granted to Immigrants
in New Zealand by Country of Birth, Since 1970

Year (ending March 31)

Country of Birth	1971		1972		1973		1974		1975	
	N	%	N	%	N	%	N	%	N	%
Australia	16	1.1	15	0.9	52	1.9	25	1.1	65	1.3
Asia										
China	84	5.9	83	5.1	197	7.2	104	4.4	77	1.6
Hong Kong	21	1.4	25	1.5	49	1.8	19	0.8	36	0.7
India	100	6.7	103	6.3	145	5.3	128	5.4	111	2.3
Indonesia	21	1.4	19	1.2	24	0.9	20	0.8	10	0.2
Malaysia	10	0.7	20	1.2	21	0.8	36	1.5	41	0.8
Europe										
Denmark	25	1.7	9	0.6	23	0.8	8	0.3	10	0.2
Germany	27	1.8	46	2.8	45	1.6	33	1.4	31	0.6
Greece	21	1.4	40	2.4	90	3.3	53	2.3	36	0.7
Hungary	20	1.3	31	1.9	37	1.4	31	1.3	29	0.6
The Netherlands	271	18.1	317	19.4	391	14.3	202	8.6	298	6.2
Poland	35	2.3	47	2.9	51	1.9	30	1.3	25	0.5
Yugoslavia	50	3.3	92	5.6	111	4.1	92	3.9	67	1.4
Other	66	4.4	66	4.1	125	4.6	77	3.3	181	3.7

TABLE 3:4 (continued)

Distribution of Citizenship Granted to Immigrants
in New Zealand by Country of Birth, Since 1970

Country of Birth	Year (ending March 31)									
	1971		1972		1973		1974		1975	
	N	%	N	%	N	%	N	%	N	%
Pacific Island										
Fiji	48	3.2	110	6.7	130	4.7	107	4.5	103	2.1
Western Samoa	94	6.3	96	5.9	165	6.0	126	5.4	115	2.4
Tonga	8	0.5	27	1.7	43	1.6	19	0.8	21	0.4
South Africa	47	3.1	40	2.4	64	2.3	80	3.4	57	1.2
United Kingdom	379	25.3	246	15.1	702	25.6	891	37.9	3,228	66.7
United States	13	0.9	29	1.8	26	0.9	19	0.8	27	0.6
Other Countries	142	9.4	172	10.5	246	8.9	253	10.7	271	5.6
Total N	1,498		1,633		2,737		2,353		4,857	
Percent		100.0		100.0		100.0		100.0		100.0

Source: Department of Statistics. *New Zealand Official Yearbook.* 1974, p. 75; 1975, p. 77; 1976, p. 76. *New Zealand Population and Migration.* 1971-1972. 1974, p. 10.

Conclusion

A major settlement phase in New Zealand's immigration history concluded with the termination of the assisted passage scheme in April, 1975. In November, 1975, the National Party was elected with its pledge to curtail immigration from all sources. Prior to the election of the National Party, the Labor Government's 1974 Immigration Policy eliminated the unrestricted special status enjoyed by Britain. The new universalistic guidelines for immigration selection recognize the multiracial basis of New Zealand society as well as its membership in the larger South Pacific community.

The White New Zealand policy is gone.[11] Now "migrants may be drawn from a wider range of countries than at present".[12] There is concern, however, that settlement should proceed "harmoniously". Specifically:

> One important element for permanent entry to New Zealand should be the likelihood that applicants will settle harmoniously within the country over a reasonable period of time... The objective of harmonious settlement should not stand in the way of orderly change in the ethnic composition of the population, but to avoid the creation of racial tensions, the rate of change should be within the limits of community tolerance.[13]

Some might argue that harmonious settlement to date among ethnic groups in New Zealand stems from full employment and the absence of a permanent underclass. Inasmuch as ethnic minorities are visible scapegoats in times of economic downturns, which are bound to occur, hostilities may surface should, for instance, unemployment rise.

New Zealand may stand or fall on its response to the Maori minority. Now the country is affluent and harbors a vigorous multiracial population. The romantic mythology of New Zealand is replete with accounts of an interdependence and mutual respect between Maori and *Pakeha* (Europeans). However, as elsewhere, the pressure of numbers and the situation abroad rather than the egalitarian ideology at home may influence New Zealand's future. New Zealand's size and history place it at a distinct advantage over other countries with longer immigration histories such as Canada or the United States. It has a clear sense of how many immigrants are needed and how many can be accommodated. The modest immigration quota of 5,000 per year will assure that sudden changes in the racial composition will not occur. In any case, New Zealand has ceased to be an indiscriminate receiving ground for British immigrants. While remaining essentially British, it is also a multiracial South Pacific nation come of age.

[11] P.S. O'Connor. "Keeping New Zealand White, 1908-1920", *New Zealand Journal of History*, 2:41-65. 1968.

[12] Immigration Advisory Council. *Review of Immigration Policy*. Wellington: Government Printing Office. 1974. P. 20.

[13] *Ibid.* 1974. P. 28.

4

The United States of America*

CHARLES B. KEELY
Center for Policy Studies
The Population Council

UNITED States immigration policy is often characterized as being restrictive. The historical record presents a different picture as does contemporary practice relative to other countries. To be sure, the history of U.S. policy is not unblemished and the openness to immigration, however wide or narrow during different periods, was not only based on altruistic motives. Nevertheless, the numbers of immigrants, their absorption and subsequent contributions are a source of pride for the United States and for the immigrants and their descendants who have built the nation.

Between 1790 and 1970, immigration accounted for about 50 percent of the population growth.[1] The federal effort to keep statistics on immigration began in 1820. In 1825, recorded immigration surpassed 10,000 for the first time. In 1842, 100,000 were registered at ports of entry and by 1881, the half million mark was exceeded. The level of one million immigrants in a single year was reached in 1905 and that level was exceeded six times in the following decade. This decade before World War I was the peak period of

---

* Sections of this paper are based on a paper presented at the Smithsonian Institution, Research Institute on Immigration and Ethnic Studies, Conference on the "New Immigration: Implications for American Society and the International Community", held November 15-17, 1976.

[1] C. Gibson. "The Contribution of Immigration to the United States Population Growth: 1790-1970", *International Migration Review*, 9(2):151-177. Summer, 1975.

immigration to the United States.[2]

It was against this numerical background, with all its implications for economic and industrial growth, urbanization, ethnic pluralism and politics, that U.S. immigration policy was shaped. Until a Supreme Court ruling in 1876, regulation of immigration was handled by state governments.[3] The court ruled that immigration was a federal prerogative under the Constitution. In 1875, Congress excluded criminals and prostitutes from admission as immigrants and entrusted collectors of the ports with responsibility for immigrant inspection. There followed a series of Acts which expanded the excludable classes. In essence, these intermittent pieces of legislation were an attempt to define minimal qualitative criteria regarding the health and moral character required of immigrants.

However, in this early period a more important policy line was developed beginning in 1882 with Chinese exclusion. The barring of Chinese was bound up with the question of labor competition and fanned by racial fears about the "Yellow Peril". However, the legislation excluded a group on the basis of nationality (and obviously racial criteria).

It was also during this period that the growth in immigration volume and the change in the origin of European immigrants from the northern and western to the southern and eastern countries (the "new immigrants") led American nativists to pay attention again to immigration. The focus was the newly developing federal policies for controlling and regulating immigration. Based on the theories of "scientific racism", nativists called for a reduction in immigration of "inferior races" who were coming in larger numbers. The major tool proposed was a literacy test which would supposedly sharply cut back on the number of "new immigrants", thus reducing volume and providing a better quality of immigrant by the racial standards then in vogue. It should be noted in passing that exceptions to literacy tests were provided for close relatives of immigrants in the country, thus establishing a family reunion motif which is important in subsequent legislation. Congress passed literacy test legislation four times and it was vetoed each time by the President in office — in 1897 by Cleveland, in 1913 by Taft and in 1915 and 1917 by Wilson. Congress overrode Wilson's second veto. This bill represents the first legislation aimed at reducing volume, even though the mechanism, the literacy test, was to do so indirectly.

The 1917 bill also further expanded Asian exclusion by creating the Asiatic barred zone and prohibiting immigration by persons from the barred

---

[2] United States Bureau of the Census. *The Statistical History of the United States.* New York: Basic Books, 1976.

[3] E.J. Harper. *Immigration Laws of the U.S.* Indianapolis and New York: The Bobbs-Merril Co., 1975. 3rd Edition. p. 5. *See* Harper for a more detailed account of individual legislation summarized here.

zone to the United States.

Thus, the federal legislation until the end of World War I had three major thrusts: quality control in terms of individual criteria for minimal health and moral character; ethnic and racial exclusion, specifically aimed at Asians and indirectly at the new immigrants by means of literacy tests; and numerical limitation, again by the indirect effects of literacy tests.

National Origins Quota Legislation

The anti-immigrant feeling which led to the literacy test legislation was augmented by the isolationist mood after World War I. This led to the national quota acts during the 1920s. These acts firmly established the principles of numerical limitation and national origin discrimination. Each country of the Eastern Hemisphere, excluding the Asiatic barred zone, had a proportion of 150,000 immigrant visas reserved; a number which was determined by the ratio of people of that national origin to the total U.S. white population. The total authorized visas was slightly over the 150,000 figure since each country had a minimum of 100 visas. The greatest share of visas were reserved for northern and western European countries with smaller quotas or minimum quotas for southern and eastern Europe and independent countries of Africa. The Western Hemisphere was excluded from the quota system. This was not due to a lack of fear by restrictionists about the "back door" but was justified on the basis of labor needs, particularly continuation of essentially temporary movement from Mexico, and on the basis of Good Neighbor rhetoric. It was pointed out that administrative control and limitation of Western Hemisphere movement was possible without quota limitations by using qualitative criteria (including public charge criteria) and because Caribbean movement was limited since colonies were given a small sub-quota of the mother country.

There was opposition to the quota concept as a policy criterion since its inception. The exclusion of Asians was an embarrassment, to say the least, when China was an ally during World War II. The refugee movements after the War also made it clear that the quota system was, in fact, not producing the national origins mix envisioned by the framers of the quota mechanism. This led to a general review of immigration legislation beginning in 1948 and resulting in codification of immigration law in the Immigration and Nationality Act of 1952, the McCarran-Walter Act, which is still the basic immigration statute. The McCarran-Walter Act reaffirmed the national origins quota system as a major selection mechanism. The opposition to this reaffirmation was great. In fact, the Act was passed over President Truman's veto. He subsequently formed a Presidential Commission to review the new law which issued a report, *Whom We Shall Welcome*,[4] which criticized the maintenance of the national quota principle.

The new law gave prominance to another feature of earlier immigration legislation, the preference system. The preference system reserved portions of each country's quota for specified groups, namely the highly skilled and close family members of citizens and permanent residents (See Chart 1). The 1952 Act abandoned the Asiatic barred zone and provided quotas, usually a minimum of 100 to Asian nations. Nevertheless, racism was still integral to the law. Persons of Asian ancestry were not counted against the quota of country of birth, as was the case for all others, but against the quota of the country of Asian forebears. If a person were more than one-half Asian but of mixed nationality background (e.g., a combination of Cambodian, Vietnamese and French), that person was counted against a special Asian-Pacific Triangle quota of 100 created precisely for those cases. The racism imbedded in the McCarran-Walter Act is also clear from the fact that quotas assigned to Asia totalled 2,990 and to Africa 1,400 visas. Europe's quota was 149,667.[5]

Immigration Reform: The End of the Quota System

Between 1820 and 1925, more than 35 million immigrants were registered at the ports of entry and land border crossings. This figure is probably an undercount since border crossing counts began only in this century and port registration was not universal. The immigration legislation of the 1920s and 1952 was meant to limit immigration and regulate the ethnic and racial mix. Between 1925 and 1965, about 7.3 million immigrants entered the United States. This number exceeded the quota allotments due to Western Hemisphere movement, exempt family relations, and special refugee allotments, despite the fact that many visas allotted to high quota countries went unused each year.

Many of the opponents to the quota reaffirmation in 1952, including ethnic and religious groups, voluntary agencies and organized labor, continued to agitate for immigration reform. In addition, opposition to the quota policy was expressed in presidential platforms of both parties in the intervening election years. With the election of John F. Kennedy, the new administration was committed to immigration policy change. The legislative process to alter the law began in the Kennedy years culminating in the 1965 Immigration Act signed by President Lyndon B. Johnson on October 3, 1965.

[4] President's Commission on Immigration and Naturalization. *Whom We Shall Welcome.* Washington, D.C.: GPO, 1953.

[5] U.S. Dept. of Commerce. *Statistical Abstract of the United States.* Washington, D.C.: GPO, 1957. p. 91.

The 1965 Immigration Act introduced four basic policy changes: 1) the abolition of the national origins quota system; 2) the introduction of a new preference system; 3) the institution of individual labor clearance procedures; and 4) the imposition of a ceiling on Western Hemisphere immigration.

1) The 1965 Act abolished the national quota system which applied to Eastern Hemisphere nations.[6] This was accomplished over a 31 month period, December, 1965 to June, 1968, during which the quota system remained in effect. However, during the transition, any visa numbers not used by undersubscribed countries were put into a visa pool for use by preference immigrants from nations with a waiting list. Provisions which discriminated against persons of Asian ancestry were immediately abolished. Beginning with fiscal year 1969 (July, 1968), immigrant visas were distributed without regard to country of birth in the Eastern Hemisphere, except for colonies which remained credited to their mother country. Natives of Eastern Hemisphere countries, however, could not receive more than 20,000 visas a year and the total number of Eastern Hemisphere visas were limited to 170,000 per year.

2) The second change in immigration policy contained in the 1965 Act was the greater emphasis placed on family relationships as a basis for selection of immigrants. This change was accomplished in two ways. First, parents of United States citizens over the age of 21 were added to the list of immigrants not subject to numerical limitations of any sort. Second, the preference system was altered so that family reunification rather than labor force needs, was emphasized (See Chart 1). The preference system applied again only to the Eastern Hemisphere countries.

Of the seven preference categories in the new immigration legislation, labor market considerations were moved from the first to the third and the sixth preference, while the other categories specify admissible relatives. The overall annual ceiling from the preceding legislation remained at 158,261 until the end of the transition period, June 30, 1968; after that time, the annual quota was set at 170,000 for the Eastern Hemisphere. Under the 1965 Act, the new preference system was applied during the transition period to the quota of each country and to the visa pool for those immigrants from oversubscribed countries. After July 1, 1968, the new preference system was applied to the 170,000 ceiling for the natives of the Eastern Hemisphere, regardless of the country of origin of the immigrant, but limiting the total visas granted to individuals from any one country to 20,000 per year.

---

[6] For immigration purposes, the world is divided into two hemispheres: the Western Hemisphere which includes all of North and South America and the Caribbean and the Eastern Hemisphere which includes all other countries. *See* Charles B. Keely. "Effects of the Immigration Act of 1965 on Selected Population Characteristics of Immigrants to the United States", *Demography*, 8(2):157-169. May, 1971.

Chart 1
Preference Systems

Immigration and Nationality Act of 1952 (McCarran-Walter Act)

First preference: Highly skilled immigrants whose services are urgently needed in the United States and the spouse and children of such immigrants. 50 percent plus any not required for second and third preferences.

Second preference: Parents of United States citizens over the age of 21 and unmarried sons and daughters of United States citizens. 30 percent plus any not required for first and third preferences.

Third preference: Spouse and unmarried sons and daughters of an alien lawfully admitted for permanent residence. 20 percent plus any not required for first or second preferences.

Fourth preference: Brothers, sisters, married sons and daughters of United States citizens and an accompanying spouse and children. 50 percent of numbers not required for first and third preferences.

Nonpreference: Applicants not entitled to one of the above preferences. 50 percent of numbers not required for first three preferences, plus any not required for fourth preference.

Immigration Act of 1965

First preference: Unmarried sons and daughters of United States citizens. Not more than 20 percent.

Second preference: Spouse and unmarried sons and daughters of an alien lawfully admitted for permanent residence. 20 percent plus any not required for first preference.

Third preference: Members of the professions and scientists and artists of exceptional ability. Not more than 10 percent.

Fourth preference: Married sons and daughters of United States citizens. 10 percent plus any not required for first three preferences.

Fifth preference: Brothers and sisters of United States citizens. 24 percent plus any not required for first four preferences.

Sixth preference: Skilled and unskilled workers in occupations for which labor is in short supply in the United States. Not more than 10 percent.

Seventh preference: Refugees to whom conditional entry or adjustment of status may be granted. Not more than 6 percent.

Nonpreference: Any applicant not entitled to one of the above preferences. Any numbers not required for preference applicants.

Immigration Act of 1976

Same as 1965 wih the following changes:
Third, sixth and nonpreference all require a job offer — no blanket certifications.

Fifth preference: The petitioning United States citizen brother or sister must be over 21 years of age.

3) The third major policy change included in the 1965 legislation was the introduction of a requirement for employment clearances for certain intending immigrants. Prior to 1965 the Secretary of Labor was empowered to certify that certain occupational categories were not needed. The 1965 Act specified that no worker was to enter the United States unless the Secretary of Labor certified that there are not sufficient, able and qualified workers in the United States and that the alien would not adversely affect wages and working conditions. In effect, these clearance procedures reversed previous practices and placed the burden of proving no adverse effect upon the applying alien. Elaborate administrative procedures were introduced in the Department of Labor to provide these clearances. Labor certification was required for the third and sixth preference applicants as well as for non-preference applicants for the Eastern Hemisphere. It also applied to all natives of the Western Hemisphere except the parents, spouses and children of United States citizens and resident aliens. Of course, immigration of professionals to the United States did not diminish because of the legislative restrictions, although the source countries of professionals did change.

4) The fourth innovation in the 1965 Act was actually a series of changes aimed at maintaining Western Hemisphere immigration at levels similar to experience in the early 1960s. The basic regulators were an annual ceiling of 120,000 visas for the Hemisphere and labor certification requirements for all immigrants except immediate relatives of United States citizens and permanent resident aliens. Both House and Senate wanted to change the policy of numerically open immigration from the Western Hemisphere for all who met the health, criminal record and self-support requirements. The House sought to do this by the labor certification requirements alone, without resorting to an overall ceiling. Thus, as with literacy tests in an earlier era, the effort to control volume was to rest on an indirect means in the House version of the bill. Without a ceiling, there was no need for a preference system and so the preference system for the Western Hemisphere was not in the House version. The purpose of omitting the ceiling was to avoid foreign policy implications of a ceiling imposition for the first time. The Senate version contained a ceiling and the Senate conferees were adamant on this point in the House-Senate conference on the final version of the bill. The final version of the bill included a ceiling of 120,000 to begin in 1969 after the transition period. However, there was no country ceiling of 20,000 and no preference system provisions in the bill that emerged from conference. The bill did contain language requiring labor certification (except for the close relatives of citizens and resident aliens as already cited) for applicants from the Western Hemisphere.

A final important difference in treatment of the two Hemispheres in the 1965 Act was the availability of adjustment of status. This process allows someone in the United States with certain types of nonimmigrant visas to apply for and receive an immigrant visa without applying at a consulate overseas, assuming all other requirements are met and a visa number is available. This gives obvious advantages in such areas as employment opportunity and job experience to persons already in the country. The 1965 Act prohibits natives of the Western Hemisphere to apply for adjustment of status. For the Eastern Hemisphere, this process was eased in 1970 when nonimmigrant visa categories eligible to adjust status were expanded to include many exchange visitors and temporary workers.

A special note should be made of the status of "dependent areas" (colonies) of other countries. Under the 1965 Act, all colonies were permitted 200 visas to be counted against the country ceiling of 20,000 and the hemisphere ceiling of the mother country. The intent and impact of this continuation of previous policy was to check the volume from colonies in the Caribbean and high demand places such as Hong Kong.

The 1965 Immigration Act ended the 40 year policy of national origins quotas and special discrimination toward Asian countries. The new law emphasized family reunion and protection of American labor. However, immigration of highly skilled persons from developing countries was facilitated by the abolition of the quota system and labor certification procedures. Although the Congressional debate on the bill emphasized that there was no intent to encourage a brain drain, the new found opportunities for immigration from previously low quota countries, and for Asians particularly, resulted in the proportion of professionals among all immigrants rising above previous levels, and the source countries decidedly shifting to developing areas.

Further, the reform movement resulting in the 1965 Act was not focused on the hemisphere. The Western Hemisphere provisions were seen by the supporters of national origins quota abolition as a price of passage. The rather strange combination of Western Hemisphere provisions — the ceiling of 120,000, no country ceiling, no preference system and labor certification for all but immediate family — was extremely unsatisfactory. Cuban refugees, who by special legislation were permitted to adjust status, used up a large proportion of the ceiling. A two and one-half year waiting period resulted. These variables plus the unilateral termination by the U.S. of the temporary worker (Bracero) program with Mexico in 1964 have contributed to the undocumented movement which dominates U.S. immigration policy discussion currently.

The Immigration Act of 1976

On October 20, 1976, President Ford signed Public Law 94-571. Under this set of amendments to the Immigration and Nationality Act, the provisions of a slightly revised preference system, individual labor certification and adjustment of status apply to both hemispheres. Each hemisphere retains its quota, 170,000 for the Eastern and 120,000 for the Western Hemisphere. All countries now have a 20,000 per country limit. Colonies can now use up to 600 visas but these are counted against the hemisphere ceiling of the colony's location. The new legislation incorporates an administrative rule not to count Cuban refugees in the United States against the 120,000 Western Hemisphere limitation. The preference system in this bill remains basically the same. However, the third, sixth and non-preference categories all require a job offer; there are no blanket certifications. Further, to obtain a fifth preference, the petitioning United States brother or sister must be over 21 years old. Adjustment of status is available to natives of both hemispheres. In short, the bill creates two parallel immigration systems, one for each hemisphere differentiated only by the separate hemisphere ceilings.

No doubt, more questions have been opened by the new legislation than can be answered. For example, we do not know the effect that permitting adjustment of status to Western Hemisphere natives will have on the characteristics of the immigrant streams from those countries. Furthermore, the per country limitation of 20,000 will prove difficult in the case of Mexico, for instance, from where great numbers have been arriving both legally and illegally.[7]

Chart 2 summarizes the provisions of the three major pieces of immigration legislation. It is clear that the major lines of policy developments have been abolition of quotas; the greater importance of the preference system for immigrant selection, particularly for family reunion; labor protection; expanding availability of adjustment of status; and the greater regulation of the Western Hemisphere immigration, starting with overall numerical controls and developing to the current situation of two parallel systems. The next step in this evolution is the creation of a single worldwide system combining the two hemispheres. Such a proposal is the objective of a bill currently pending (June, 1978) in the House of Representatives.

Changes in the Immigrant Mix

The legislative summary presented, highlights current law and passes over a great deal of detail that affects the process of granting visas. Tremendous changes in the composition of the immigrant stream have resulted from the 1965 Act. We do not yet have enough experience with the 1976 Act to study its effects on immigration composition trends. To profile the effects of the

[7] E.R. Stoddard. "A Conceptual Analysis of the 'Alien Invasion:' Institutionalized Support of Illegal Mexican Aliens in the U.S.", *International Migration Review*, 10(2):157-189. Summer, 1976.

Chart 2

Major Provisions of Immigration Laws of 1952, 1965, 1976
by Hemisphere

Provision	Eastern Hemisphere	Western Hemisphere
Ceiling		
1952	158,561[a]	None
1965		
Transition	158,261[b]	None
Post-1968	170,000	120,000
1976	170,000	120,000
National Origins Quotas		
1952	Proportional to 1920 U.S. ethnic composition	None
1965	None	None
1976	None	None
Per Country Limit		
1952	Appropriate Quota	None
1965	20,000	None
1976	20,000	20,000
Preference System[c]		
1952	4 Preferences	None
1965	7 Preferences	None
1976	7 Preferences	7 Preferences
Labor Certification		
1952	On complaint or 25 petitions by an employer	On complaint or 25 petitions by an employer
1965	3rd, 6th and non-preference	All except immediate family of citizens and resident aliens
1976	3rd, 6th and non-preference	3rd, 6th and non-preference
Adjustment of Status		
1952	—	—
1965	Permitted, with certain visa holders excluded	Prohibited
1976	Permitted except crew members and persons en route	Permitted except crew members and persons en route
Colonies		
1952	100-attributed to quota of mother country	100-attributed to quota of mother country
1965	200-attributed to country and hemisphere ceilings of mother country	200-attributed to country and hemisphere ceilings of mother country

Chart 2 continued

Provision	Eastern Hemisphere	Western Hemisphere
1976	600-attributed to ceiling of mother country but hemi-sphere ceiling of place of colony	600-attributed to ceiling of mother country but hemi-sphere ceiling of place of colony

Notes:
[a] as of 1965.
[b] quota of 100 eliminated for Asia and Pacific Islands, Jamaica and Trinidad and Tobago.
[c] See Chart 1.

1965 Act, the last five years of the McCarran-Walter Act and the first five years under the full provisions of the 1965 Act are compared, the first series reflecting the McCarran-Walter immigration pattern and the second series reflecting the new immigration.[8]

Volume: Between the two periods of these Acts, the volume of immigration increased about 30 percent, from 1,450,000 to about 1,887,000 immigrants. Secondly, the source countries of immigration shifted. The Eastern Hemisphere contributed a greater share in 1969-1973 than it had in the 1961-1965 period (57.3 percent versus 50.8 percent of all immigrants). Similarly, there were important shifts in source countries within the Eastern Hemisphere. The European share of total immigration dropped from 41.9 to 27.3 percent. Asia overtook Europe as the chief source of Eastern Hemisphere immigration moving from 7.6 to 27.4 percent of the volume. Within Europe, southern and eastern countries took the lead as the number of immigrants from northern countries declined. Guaranteed large quotas were no longer available to natives of these countries and they had to compete, including obtaining labor certification with all other potential immigrants from the entire hemisphere. The natives of many Asian countries benefited greatly under the new law, notably those from India, the Philippines, and China. The Western Hemisphere share of total immigration declined and there was also a decided shift away from Canada as a sending country. Caribbean countries increased in their proportions and Latin countries generally declined.

Labor: The shifts in the distribution of the immigrant labor force were equally dramatic, even though labor force data from immigration statistics

[8] Keely, *op cit. See also,* Charles B. Keely. "Immigration Composition and Population Policy". *Science,* 185 (4151):587-593. Aug. 16, 1974 and Charles B. Keely, "Effects of U.S. Immigration on Manpower Characteristics". *Demography,* 12 (2):172-191, May, 1975.

present many problems of accuracy and interpretation.[9] Between 1961-1965 and 1969-1973, the proportion of the number of immigrants who stated an occupation declined from 45.6 to 41.3 percent. The average annual number of immigrants for the two periods was about 290,000 and 377,000 respectively. However, the proportion who listed a professional occupation increased from 19.8 to 28.9 percent. This proportion was over 60 percent from Asia and Africa. It should be noted, however, that the proportion of professionals declined for North and South America. Apparently one of the effects of the peculiar Western Hemisphere provisions of the 1965 Act was that they did not encourage large increases in professional immigration to the U.S.

These data highlight the different effects of the 1965 Act for various countries and regions. Nontraditional sources of immigration during the quota period became more prominent and produced the "new- new immigration" from Asian and Caribbean countries. Secondly, the brain drain has increased, but not universally so. As noted, the brain drain from the Western Hemisphere has not been notably exacerbated. "The proportionally smaller contribution to the work force of Europe and the Americas were also contributions of less skilled workers. The converse was true for Asia, Africa and Oceania. Their proportional contributions to the work force were greater, and they were of a higher occupational level."[10]

Population Growth and Immigration: A Redefinition

Recently, the role of immigration in the population dynamics of the United States has again become the object of demographic analysis and policy debate. Thus, recent fertility declines and the increased immigration following the 1965 Act have led to discussions of an increased importance of immigration for population growth.[11] Some of these discussions have led to misleading conclusions resting solely on the increasing proportion of immigration as a component of population growth. As fertility and births decline, a steady stream of immigrants necessarily becomes an increasing proportion of growth. In a zero natural increase situation, one migrant accounts for 100 percent of growth. In addition, not enough attention has been paid to the volume of emigration from the U.S. of natives and foreign born persons. However, given this increased role of immigration, two topics

[9] S.M. Tomasi and C.B. Keely. *Whom Have We Welcomed?* New York: Center for Migration Studies, 1976. Chapter 5.

[10] *See* Charles B. Keely. "Effects of U.S. Immigration Law on Manpower Characteristics", *Demography*, 12(2):188. May, 1975.

[11] U.S. Commission on Population Growth and the American Future. *Population and the American Future*. Washington, D.C.: GPO, 1972.

became the center of the population debate: the impact of immigration on future growth and the effects of immigration on the path to characteristics of a stationary population, that is, zero population growth.[12]

Future Growth: Most projections of the effects of immigration assume net immigration to remain at a level of 400,000. However, other estimates put the emigration of foreign born persons from the United States between 1960 and 1970 at over one million persons.[13] Native born emigration has been running at over 50,000 persons per year, judging from the immigration statistics of other countries. Further, the 400,000 figure often cited and used in immigration and population projections includes other than alien immigrants such as United States citizens born abroad, net Puerto Rican movement, and federal civilian employees.

Projections of American population growth using Series II assumptions from the Census Bureau estimate the effects of net alien immigration at recent rates to be lower than Census Bureau estimates.[14] Instead of assuming 400,000 immigrants with the age-sex structure used by the Census Bureau, a net alien immigration and age-sex structure resulted from using the average annual alien immigration of 1969 to 1973 minus the estimated alien emigration. These estimates put net alien migration to the United States in recent years at about 264,000 rather than the 400,000 persons.[15] The lower estimate would result in almost 700,000 fewer people added to the population between 1975 and 1980; 3.8 million fewer within 25 years or, by the year 2000; and 13.6 million fewer over 75 years, by the year 2050. These reductions would be subtracted from the Census Bureau projections of total U.S. population of 222 million in 1980, 263 million in 2000 and 320 million in 2050.[16]

Zero Growth: The second question related to the population issue is what adjustment in native fertility would be necessary for the United States to achieve zero growth and also to continue immigration levels. This question was analyzed in a research paper for the U.S. Population Commission, by

[12] A.J. Coale. "Alternative Paths to a Stationary Population". In U.S. Commission on Population Growth and the American Future. *Demographic and Social Aspects of Population Growth.* C.F. Westoff and R.E. Parke, Jr., eds. Vol. I of the Commission Research Reports. Washington, D.C.: GPO, 1972. pp. 591-603.

[13] R. Warren and J. Peck. "Emigration from the United States: 1960-1970". Paper presented at the annual meeting of the Population Association of America. Seattle, April, 1975.

[14] The Capital Series II projections assume the "most realistic" trend in fertility which are intermediate to other projected fertility trends used in the Census Bureau series. Series II projections which include immigration assume an annual level of 400,000 net immigration and an age-sex distribution based on a recent year's alien immigration.

[15] Warren and Peck, *op. cit.*

[16] C.B. Keely and E.P. Kraly. "Recent Net Alien Immigration to the United States: Its Impact on Population Growth and Native Fertility", *Demography*, 15(3):267-283. August, 1978.

Ansley Coale.[17] A similar analysis, replicating Coale's work but substituting estimates of recent net alien immigration volume and age-sex structure rather than the 400,000 figure and the corresponding age-sex structrue he used, resulted in a less severe need for native fertility reductions. Whereas the results of the Population Commission study estimated that the net reproduction rate and total fertility rate necessary to accommodate immigration at the 400,000 level would have to decline from 1.0 and 2.11 to .934 and 1.971 respectively, the new estimates require a fertility decline to .948 and 2.0 respectively; that represents a drop in fertility of 5.2 percent. The ultimate size of such a stationary population would be about 8.4 percent larger for having accommodated immigration at the figure of 400,000 annually and about 5.8 percent larger by accommodating immigration at a figure of 264,000 annually. In either case, given current fertility experience in the U.S., the requirements of no growth population need not call for a curtailment of immigration.

These estimates and projections are not predictions. They are benchmarks that are only as reasonable as are the assumptions about mortality, fertility, migration and population structure on which they are based. The projections reveal that an immediate cessation of immigration would not substantially affect the transition to a no growth population in the United States.

The effect of estimated current size and age structure of net immigration on the future of American population ought to blunt the arguments used in the past to play on xenophobia. Blatant forms of these arguments probably will not emerge or will be dismissed if they do. More subtle forms of the arguments may appear, especially given the change in the countries of origin of recent immigrants.

Immigration policy obviously is directly tied into the image of the United States as a pluralistic society. A continual infusion of persons of foreign culture is viewed both with alarm and as a needed and continuous revitalization that had brought benefits in the past. It is not clear whether recent declines in foreign born and the foreign stock will continue or be reversed. It is by no means clear that the fear of non-Western cultures is a thing of the past or that the U.S. population will accept and integrate the new immigrant groups created by the 1965 Act. Balancing the generally agreed upon need for opportunity for United States minorities and women and the high proportion of professionals among immigrants and the relationship between unemployment and undocumented workers are hotly debated but hardly solved. The questions and the conflicts continue.

[17] Coale, *op. cit.*

Part II

Migration Policies of an Empire

5

The United Kingdom

TOM REES
The Runnymede Trust

Immigration Policies

THE history of immigration into the United Kingdom is a history of the unexpected. Although the United Kingdom has primarily considered itself a country of emigration, at least twice within the last one hundred years, it has been the recipient of large net population inflows. To understand immigration into the United Kingdom in the years following World War II and the legal and social framework within which changes in migration policies in the postwar years have taken place, it is necessary to delve into the period preceding World War I.

The main lines of British policy toward immigration, both in respect to control and in respect to social policies toward immigrants, have traditionally been *laissez-faire*. Changes in the direction of immigration regulation and positive provision, or negative exclusion, have largely come about under the pressure of events, external to Great Britain rather than as the outcome of the country's anticipation, and purposeful planning. The natural bias of the system, therefore, has consistently been not to interfere with existing arrangements, with the result that the pattern of immigration has often been conditioned by historical circumstances several years precedent to the immigration itself.

TABLE 5:1

Overseas Born Population of Great Britain, 1971

Country of Birth	Resident in Great Britain
Total Ireland	709,235
Irish Republic	615,820
Ireland (part not stated)	93,415
Total New Commonwealth Countries	1,151,090
Nigeria	28,565
Barbados	27,055
Guyana	21,070
Jamaica	171,775
Trinidad and Tobago	17,135
Cyprus	73,295
Hong Kong	29,520
India	321,995
Pakistan	139,935
Malta and Gozo	33,840
Total European Countries	632,770
Germany	157,680
Italy	108,980
Poland	110,925
Spain	49,470
Total Other Countries	979,990
America	131,540
China	13,495
USSR	48,095
Turkey	6,615

Note: Estimated population of the United Kingdom in 1976 was 57,000,000.

Source: Census 1971, Great Britain, Country of Birth Tables.

Early Determinants of Immigration Policy: The Irish

The largest group of immigrants to England during the nineteenth century was the Irish. The rapid growth of population and sporadic bad harvests in Ireland precipitated an enormous movement of population from Ireland to the United States and Britain. By 1841 there were more than 400,000 Irish living in England, Scotland and Wales, and the 1851 Census showed that there were 727,326 Irish immigrants in Britain, constituting 2.9 percent of the population of England and Wales, and 7.2 percent of the population of

Scotland.[1] This immigration had the character of an internal migration. Ireland was, at the time, part of the United Kingdom and the doctrine of laissez-faire economics could be applied no less to movements of population than to movements of capital. In any event, the social costs of absorbing Irish in-migration were not striking.[2] By-and-large the group has been absorbed with relative ease into the British society. No calculation exists of the proportion of the present British population which is of Irish descent. The 1971 Census depicted, for the first time, the various groups of people in the United Kingdom, according to the country of birth of their parents. There were 361,800 persons resident in England, Scotland and Wales both of whose parents had been born in the Republic of Ireland, and 893,195 persons one of whose parents had been born there. The actual Irish born population in England, Scotland and Wales in 1971 numbered 681,110.[3] Given that since 1851 the actual Irish born population of Great Britain has never fallen below 360,000, and in the majority of decades has been over 500,000, it seems legitimate to infer that the population in Britain of relatively recent Irish descent may approach 10 percent. Thus, it is easily understood that the arrangements for regulating immigration from Ireland have always been almost totally unrestricted.

Finally, the other distinctive aspect of Irish migration to Britain has always been that much of it has been rather short term. "The short distances involved and the economic, political, social and cultural ties between the different parts of the British Isles have always served to produce a large scale to-and-fro movement of migratory workers, harvesters, navvies and vagrants, in addition to those who made a more permanent settlement."[4] Flows between the two countries are rather difficult to estimate, but in the 1950-1961 period, migration figures were running about three-quarters of one million people in each direction annually. The net annual flow from the Republic of Ireland fell normally into the range of 30,000 to 40,000 persons.[5]

Early Determinants of Immigration Policy: The Jews

Britain experienced a wave of Jewish immigration in the decades preceding World War I. It has been estimated that the Jewish population, which in 1880 numbered about 60,000 persons, had within the next forty years

---

[1] J.A. Jackson. *The Irish in Britain.* London: Routledge and Kegan Paul. 1963.

[2] E.P. Thompson. *The Making of the English Working Class.* London: Gollancz. 1965.

[3] *1971Census of Great Britain. See* Country of Birth Tables. These are all conservative figures: excluded are persons shown as born in Ireland but without specifying which part in Ireland.

[4] J.A. Jackson. *The Irish in Britain.* London: Routledge and Kegan Paul. 1963.

[5] *Ibid.* P. 194.

approximately quintupled. Actual immigration of Jews into Britain over this period was substantially lower, around 120,000, natural increase accounting for the remainder of the growth.[6] The Jewish immigration was unprecedented in that it was largely composed of people who spoke no English; who were poor; and whose occupation had been those of small artisans and traders in essentially agricultural societies. Furthermore, the Jews arrived in a society which had no particular need for their labor. Yet, "the Jews were not peasants or illiterates; the cultural baggage which they carried contained folklore, but was basically a conscious historic culture; and migrations were a common experience, if not in their own lives, then in the historic experience of the Jewish people...they were...a town-dwelling people".[7]

Jewish immigrants displayed a number of characteristics which later waves of immigrants were to follow. First, they colonized a relatively small area of London relatively densely. Jewish immigrants had almost exclusively settled to the East End of London where population densities were reputed to have reached 600 persons per acre. To the surprise of some of their older established coreligionists many of these migrants were reluctant to disperse from their principal areas of settlement. The reasons for this were multiple. Largely, however, these newcomers sought the support and insulation against the outside world, provided by a large body of other Jewish immigrants; and relief from the fear of linguistic and cultural decay and the insidious effect of British morals on Jewish youth. In addition, Jews met resistance from the indigenous British in other potential areas of settlement; and, within their group there were strong economic incentives to remain in those trades in which Jewish immigrants managed to obtain a foothold, such as the garment industry, boot and shoe making, furs, walking sticks and canes, cabinet making and tobacco.[8] Even today, the highest concentrations of Jewish populations in London may still be found in the East End.

The presence of Jewish immigrants in the garment industry, particularly their presence in the sweatshops of the East End, provided much of the ammunition for the political campaign against alien immigration. Initially, the campaign was slow to get off the ground. Yet, it survived a Parliamentary Select Committee investigation into the desirability of immigration control, which recommended against immigration control in a report of 1889. It also

---

[6] Lloyd P. Gartner. *The Jewish Immigrant in England.* 1 870-1 914. London: Allen and Unwin 1960. *See also,* John A. Garrard. *The English and Immigration.* London: Oxford University Press (for the Institute of Race Relations). 1971.

The statistical records for this movement are extremely unsatisfactory. Many more Jewish immigrants stopped briefly on their way to the United States, giving the false impression of a rather large immigration flow to England.

[7] Lloyd P. Gartner. *The Jewish Immigrant in England, 1870-1914.* London: Allen and Unwin. 1960. P. 27.

[8] E. Krausz. *Ethnic Minorities in Britain.* London: Paladin. 1972.

survived a report in the same year by the House of Lords Committee on "Sweating" (the habit of employing workers at low wages, for long hours, or under other unfavorable conditions) which effectively concluded that sweating was not a distinctive feature of trades in which foreign workers were concentrated, and indeed existed in trades "which do not appear to be affected by foreign immigration". Partly in consequence, partly because of the ascendancy of the Liberal Party, but most of all because of relatively low unemployment and emigration and war overseas, pressure for control of immigration momentarily subsided.

The lull was not to last long. In the first years of this century the Boer War ended and agitation against "alien" immigration mounted, both inside and outside Parliament. A Royal Commission under Lord James was appointed to enquire into the desirability of legislation and sat for thirteen months before reporting in 1903 in favor of limited restriction on immigration and the prohibition of certain areas to new immigrants.

The Conservative Government, in its last year of office after a twenty year term, passed the Aliens Act in 1905 to regulate the inflow of foreigners.[9] The new Act was limited in scope. It gave powers to control "undesirable and destitute aliens". Aliens were defined, however, as only those foreigners who came as steerage passengers, and only those aliens travelling in ships which carried twenty or more aliens were covered. The Act was administered in a far from oppressive way by the new Liberal Government. "The Liberals probably did about as much as was possible to soften its effect without actually amending or repealing it."[10]

The significance of the 1905 Act lay in the breach with the principle of the previous eighty years that Britain should be freely open to immigration from overseas for motives of both economic self-interest and humanitarian concerns. Its introduction spelt not only a declining faith in the virtues of the free movement of labor paralleled by the contemporary political demand for protectionism in trade, but it also spelt a movement away from the belief that Britain was a place of unquestioning refuge and tolerance.

The antecedents of the 1905 Act were significant in that much of the anti-alien agitation was profoundly racist in character. The proponents of immigration control were at pains to dissociate themselves from any suggestion of anti-semitism. Their argument was conducted along general eugenic lines. Yet, ultimately, there was no doubt in the public mind as to the composition of the immigrant inflow of the period: it was comprised of Jews. "The very fact that the immigrants were Jews and that the agitators

[9] Paul Foot. *Immigrants and Race in British Politics*. London: Penguin. 1965.

[10] Lloyd P. Gartner. *The Jewish Immigrant in England, 1870-1914*. London: Allen and Unwin. 1960. P. 109.

were further exploiting an already universal scapegoat dominated the discussion and exercised a considerable influence on the course of events."[11]

The Aliens Restriction Acts of 1914 and 1919

In 1914, with war close, more Draconian immigration legislation was enacted and the relatively mild provisions of the 1905 Act were swept away. The long and contested prelude to the first immigration control legislation in the twentieth century was followed by a little debated and much more severe law passed in the months preceding the outbreak of World War I. The Act of 1914, envisaged largely as a security measure, gave the Home Secretary powers to prohibit immigrants from landing and to deport immigrants landed. The Act also imposed a requirement that all aliens register with the police. The Act did not apply to British subjects, and hence was not applicable to the overseas dominions and colonies of the British Empire. Although introduced for temporary security reasons, the Act was renewed after the War by means of the Aliens Restriction Act of 1919. The main provisions of this Act together with amendments contained in a number of subsequent parliamentary orders, continued in force until the Immigration Act of 1971.

The main features of the 1914 and 1919 Aliens Restriction Acts and subsequent Orders in Council were that aliens could be refused entry into the United Kingdom at the discretion of an immigration officer; that for aliens without a visible means of support, only a short stay in the United Kingdom was permissible unless the immigrant secured a work permit issued by the Ministry of Labor; and that aliens could be deported by the courts or by the Home Secretary if such an act was deemed, "conducive to the public goods". The right of political asylum to those likely to be persecuted on return to their country of origin was also affirmed in this law.

From this point, immigration of aliens into Britain declined sharply, although this was for principally economic reasons rather than immigration restrictions. Unemployment in Britain between the wars was at a continuously high level, and the international nature of the economic depression resulted in some return migration to Britain of former emigrants to the colonies and dominions.[12] Because of the break, caused by World War II, in the statistical series it is difficult to calculate the number of migrants for this period. The best estimate is that between 1931 and 1939, the net movement of population to the United Kingdom was about 60,000 annually. This

---

[11] John A. Garrard. *The English and Immigration.* London: Oxford University Press (for the Institute of Race Relations). 1971. P. 57.

[12] Paul Foot. *Immigrants and Race in British Politics.* London: Penguin. 1965.

inflow, composed mostly of Jews and other refugees, and immigrants from Ireland, accounted for about 30 percent of the total population growth during that period.[13]

World War II

World War II produced two main substantial additions of immigrant blocks to the population. The first was the substantial group of Polish immigrants. This group was composed partly of the members of the Polish Second Corps, known as General Anders' Army and numbering around 70,000. This corps had distinguished itself in Italy in 1943 and 1944. Most of its members were inclined to the right in politics, were anti-Russian and unwilling to return to Poland. There were an additional 50,000 or so Poles who had fought in France and had found their way to the United Kingdom. To assist this group, the Polish Resettlement Act of 1947 was passed. The Act was one of the few constructive legislative initiatives in the field of immigration, since it established a Polish Resettlement Corps with the express purpose of resettling Polish excombatants in British society. The resettlement scheme was "remarkably successful". It was designed to cope with the housing, education and employment needs of Poles eligible under the plan.[14] Although some elements of the scheme were employed in later immigration cases, such as the European Voluntary Workers in 1946 to 1948, the Hungarian refugees in 1956 and the Uganda Asians in 1972, it remains the most substantial coordinated attempt at integrating a large immigrant group into British society.

The Polish Resettlement Act of 1947

The distinctive feature of the resettlement effort was the recognition that resettlement had dimensions other than the economic and that it embraced not only housing, but health, welfare and education as well. The National Assistance Board ran a number of hostels and camps which, in 1949, housed a populatioin of 16,400, the main housing burden falling on local government and the private sector. However, Polish settlers were widely dispersed, so that only 25 percent of them were in London in 1952, others settling in Lancashire, the West Riding and throughout the Midlands.[15]

[13] Royal Commission on Population. 1949.
[14] Sheila Patterson. "Immigrants and Minority Groups in British Society", *The Prevention of Racial Discrimination in Britain*. S. Abbott, ed. London: Oxford Univeristy Press (for the Institute of Race Relations). 1971.
[15] J. Zubrzycki. *Polish Immigrants in Britain*. The Hague: Nijhoff. 1956.

Difficulty with the English language was rapidly identified as being the most important obstacle to a rapid assimilation of Poles to the prevailing English culture. The Committee for the Education of Poles in Britain was formed by the Minister of Education and the Secretary of State for Scotland with the main object of assuring "that those who do not elect to return to their country are fitted for resettlement in this country and overseas". The policy was thus to provide the Poles with instruction in English as soon as practicable and to reduce, in number and scale, educational institutions maintained by the Committee as soon as Polish students could be safely transferred to British educational institutions. Certainly there appears to have been virtually no evidence that Polish children have faced extensive difficulty in coming to terms with the English language. On the other hand, there still remain those among the older generations whose grasp of English is rudimentary. The extensive social network of Poles in Britain, embracing religious, political, social and intellectual life, may have helped to take the edge off the incentive to learn for a number of those who first arrived in Britain as mature men and women.

Regarding the welfare and health aspects of Polish resettlement, the Polish army had brought with it numbers of highly skilled medical and allied personnel. There were in existence at the time of the resettlement effort three large Polish hospitals, staffed exclusively by Poles and maintained by the Ministry of Pensions. Additionally, the Ministry of Labor and National Insurance established a Central Polish Resettlement Office. The functions of this office were to give advice to the many Poles who wished to emigrate from Britain as well as to give advice on a "very wide range of subjects including legal problems concerning marriage, divorce and property in Poland".[16]

Despite the positive efforts made by the Labor Government to make special provisions for Polish integration, the process was not entirely without friction. Resistance to Polish settlement was strongest among the trade unions. Their campaign against the Poles was based on fears, however unfounded, that "they were now to be thrown in large numbers on the British labor market and that they would jeopardize the maintenance of full employment; bring down the British workers' living standards or wages; destroy the hard earned liberties of trade unionists; accentuate the housing shortage; and eat food that Britain could hardly spare".[17]

In a fair assessment of the effort to resettle Poles in Britain after World War II it must be noted that, even allowing for the relatively short term nature of the program, it was still a well thought through and imaginative plan. It embraced many aspects of the resettlement process which are important to immigrants making a fresh start in a foreign country, and was

[16] *Ibid.*   [17] *Ibid.*

not restricted simply to employment. It gave some recognition to the importance of maintaining Polish language and culture, even if the main goal was to anglicize Polish settlers as much as possible. It was executed by a Labor administration in the face of considerable resistance from some of the most important sections of Labor Party support which, in the light of prewar unemployment experience, might have been only too easy to understand and actively sympathize with. Furthermore, the program made scarce resources available to Poles at a time when the most powerful period of national austerity and reconstruction was imposing great hardships on the indigenous British. If one is to explain it, one must surely look to the strong ties of emotion, perhaps tinged with guilt, which British people felt for wartime allies (the invasion of whose country by Germany had been the occasion for Britain's entry into the War); as well as to the combination of flexibility in approaching social problems in Britain which the war encouraged, on the one hand, and the powerful and effective system of administrative controls, which had yet to be dismantled, on the other.

Work Permit Holders and Commonwealth Immigrants

The treatment of the Poles contrasts favorably with the treatment of other European in-migrants to Britain in the years immediately following the War. At a time of great manpower shortage for certain kinds of work, notably hospital work, agriculture, coal mining, textiles and building, considerable numbers of Europeans were recruited to work in Britain under a number of different schemes. Many of the in-migrants were displaced persons or prisoners of war when they volunteered for jobs covered by short term (12 months) work permits. The total number of European Voluntary Workers recruited by all schemes has been placed at 100,875,[18] and the most frequently represented national groups were Lithuanian, Ukrainians, Latvians, and Yugoslavs. For these, however, conditions were much harder than for Polish immigrants who were covered by the Polish Resettlement Corps. Work permits were issued for twelve months and transfers between jobs were not permitted, although extensions within specific jobs were allowed. After 1947 European Voluntary Workers were not allowed to bring in their dependents, for fear of strain on housing and other social services. Some initial accommodation costs were paid by the British Government, and a limited amount of hostel provision was made, but equality in the workplace was limited to pay and hours worked. A number of national agreements between employers and unions specifically gave priority to indigenous British workers in such matters as redundancy and promotion.

[18] Juliet Cheetham. "Immigration", *Trends in British Society Since 1900*. A.H. Halsey, ed. London: Macmillan. 1972.

TABLE 5:2

Net Migrant Flows, United Kingdom, Since 1964, by Citizenship of Migrants

Citizenship[a]	Mid-Year to Mid-Year, in 000s						
	1964-65	1966-67	1968-69	1970-71	1971-72	1972-73	1973-74[d]
Aliens	22	30	21	21	15	27	23
Canada, Australia, New Zealand	1	5	−2	−5	6	3	6
Other Commonwealth[b]	55	45	57	42	37	43	21
United Kingdom	−136	−175	−144	−98	−97	−77	−122
All migrants beyond the British Isles[c]	−58	−95	−68	−39	−39	−5	−72
of which: inflow	223	231	228	227	201	225	183
outflow	281	326	296	266	240	230	225

Notes: [a] Pakistani citizens are included in "Other Commonwealth" up to and including 1971-1972, but in "Aliens" thereafter.
[b] Including United Kingdom passport holders from East Africa from mid-1967.
[c] Excluding net immigration due to direct traffic with the Irish Republic which may have averaged some 10,000 persons per annum during the 1961-1971 intercensal period.
[d] Provisional figures.

Sources: *Social Trends*. London: HMSO 1975, Table 1.17.

The European Voluntary Workers benefited less rapidly from an easing of the restrictive conditions under which they were admitted than some of the later arrivals from Europe. Thus, many of them left Britain for other countries. Estimates of those who had left by 1956 for the United States or Commonwealth countries stated that 48 percent of Lithuanians, 44 percent of Estonians, 26 percent of Ukrainians and 23 percent of Latvians and Poles had left Britain.[19]

Those, mainly Germans, Italians, Austrians and Spaniards, who immigrated later, under the same regime of work permits, faced lesser delays in winning the right to bring in their families and, notably in the case of Italians settled in the areas north of London, established successful permanent settlements. Their civil rights were, however, more restricted than those of the largest group of postwar economic immigrants, those who came from 1948 onwards from the poorer Commonwealth territories of the Caribbean, the Indian subcontinent, the Mediterranean and the Far East.

The work permit scheme did not originally apply to citizens of the British Commonwealth who, under the British Nationality Act of 1948, were allowed to enter Britain freely, to find work, to settle and to bring their families. Partly encouraged by employers and the Government, increasing numbers of Commonwealth citizens from former British colonies and dependencies did precisely that. First, from the Caribbean territories and Guyana, then from India and Pakistan, and finally with smaller but quite substantial flows from some African countries, Malaysia and Hong Kong. Substantial numbers flowed in during the fifteen years from 1948 onwards. Between the census years of 1951 and 1961 the enumerated population of West Indian origin rose from 15,300 to 171,800; that of Indian origin from 30,800 to 81,400; that of Pakistan from 5,000 to 24,900; and that from the Far East from 12,000 to 29,600.

The rising tide of "colored" immigration led to an increasing social unease about immigration and to political agitation for its control. The preferential status of immigrants from colored Commonwealth countries was steadily whittled away in a succession of legislative and administrative measures: the Commonwealth Immigrants Act of 1962; the Immigration White Paper of 1965; the Commonwealth Immigrants Act of 1968; and the Immigration Act of 1971. Britain retreated from the principles of the 1948 British Nationality Act which was increasingly criticized as idealistic but unrealistic. Under the 1962 Commonwealth Immigrants Act, a system of employment vouchers for Commonwealth immigrants was introduced, and employment vouchers for unskilled and semiskilled work were progressively phased out. Even vouchers for those with specific skills or qualifications, or with specific jobs, were cut back from a level of 30,130 in 1963, to 4,980 in 1967 and to 2,290

---

[19] *Ibid.*

by 1972, when the system of employment vouchers was finally abolished. Because those Commonwealth citizens who entered the United Kingdom before January 1, 1973 and settled were entitled to bring in their wives, and their children under 18 (and in exceptional cases other close dependent relatives), the numbers of migrants from these Commonwealth countries continued to grow. By the 1971 Census the enumerated population of West Indian origin had grown to 299,580; that of Indian origin to 274,545, more than three times the total ten years previously; that of Pakistani origin to 131,885, more than five times the total ten years previously. The total population of these ethnic origins in the United Kingdom was substantially greater. By 1971 more than half the population of West Indian ethnic origin, and about four in ten of those of Indian or Pakistani ethnic origin had been born in the United Kingdom.

Conditions of the Work Permit Scheme

Under the Immigration Act of 1971 it has been necessary, since 1973, for most immigrants seeking work in the United Kingdom to be in possession of a work permit. There are exceptions for certain kinds of work and for immigrants who are patrials[20] or European Economic Community nationals. The work permit has to be applied for to the Department of Employment by the prospective employer, who is obliged to satisfy the Department that the worker in question is qualified and required for a specific job, that the employment is necessary, and that there is no suitable British or long term resident foreign labor available. There is also a need to satisfy the Department that the wages and conditions offered are not inferior to those offered to indigenous workers. Work permits are issued initially for twelve months and although they have in practice normally been automatically renewable on application by the employer to the Home Office, there is no right of renewal.[21] Department of Employment permission is necessary for a work permit holder to transfer to another employer, and such permission is

[20] Patrials are, a) citizens of the United Kingdom and colonies who have that citizenship by birth, adoption, naturalization or registration in the United Kingdom, or who were born of parents one of whom had United Kingdom citizenship by birth, etc. in the United Kingdom, or one of whose grandparents had such citizenship at the time of the birth of the relevant parent; b) citizens of the United Kingdom and its colonies who have at any time been settled in the United Kingdom and who have been ordinarily resident in the United Kingdom for five years or more; c) Commonwealth citizens (i.e. not necessarily citizens of the United Kingdom and its colonies) born or adopted by a citizen of the United Kingdom and its colonies by birth in the United Kingdom; d) the spouse of a patrial (provided that she/he is a Commonwealth citizen); and e) the former wife of a patrial and citizen of the United Kingdom and its colonies provided that she is a Commonwealth citizen.

[21] Ian A. MacDonald. *The New Immigration Law*. London: Butterworths. 1972.

TABLE 5:3

"Colored" Population of Great Britain: Mid-Year Estimates of the
Population of New Commonwealth and Pakistani Ethnic Origin, 1966-1974

	Mid-Year to Mid-Year, in 000s							
	1966-67	1967-68	1968-69	1969-70	1970-71	1971-72	1972-73	1973-74
Population at the beginning of period	1,016	1,103	1,217	1,320	1,411	1,501	1,583	1,673
Births	45	47	50	52	52	49	47	45
Deaths[a]	−3	−3	−4	−4	−4	−4	−5	−5
Natural increase	42	44	46	48	48	45	42	40
Migration	45	70	57	43	42	37	48	31[b]
Population at end of period	1,103	1,217	1,320	1,411	1,501	1,583	1,673	1,744
Percent of Home Population at end of period	2.1	2.3	2.5	2.6	2.8	2.9	3.1	3.2

Notes: [a] Including deaths of children of New Commonwealth ethnic origin born in the United Kingdom. [b] Provisional figures.

Sources: Population Trends No. 2. HMSO, Winter, 1975.

by no means automatic. Work permit holders, except those from the Commonwealth, are required to register with the police until such time as the restrictions attached to the work permit are removed. A work permit holder may apply to have the time limit and other restrictions attached to his employment removed after four years. Applications are normally granted automatically, although there are grounds for refusal if the worker in question has not observed the time limit or conditions of the permit, or is undesirable because of his character, conduct or associations, or is a risk to national security.

Numbers of Work Permit Holders

The object of the work permit scheme is principally to promote a supply of labor from overseas where the domestic supply is inadequate. Special quotas for the hotel and catering industry, and for resident domestic workers and nursing auxiliaries are fixed annually by the Department of Employment in consultation with the trade unions and employers. With the growth of unemployment in the British economy the numbers issued have declined steadily and by the middle of the decade from 1970-1980, were at an historically low level. The composition of the total also changed. In the latter part of the 1960s and the early part of the 1970s the majority of permits were issued to workers in the hotel and catering industry and in hospital employment. By 1975 the largest single group of work permit holders was from the United States and the number issued to workers from other countries with highly developed economies, such as Japan, South Africa and Switzerland had also risen to a relatively high level, indicating the increasingly nonmanual character of those entering the country on work permits.

Civil and Social Rights of Work Permit Holders

Male work permit holders (not including seasonal workers in the hotel and catering industry or resident domestics) are entitled to bring in their wives, and their dependents under 18 years of age, for the period of their authorized stay. The dependents themselves may also work. A similar concession is not available for female work permit holders. There have been cases where schools and hospitals, acting on the advice of local educational authorities or hospital boards have refused to accept the dependents of permit holders because of the allegedly temporary nature of their presence, although these cases have been the exception.

The ratio of dependents to work permit holders is low. In 1975, for example, the proportion of dependents among the total number of work permit holders and their families entering the United Kingdom from Commonwealth and foreign countries was only around 20 percent, with Americans alone accounting for more than one-third the total, comprising 1,807 out of 4,514. In 1975, 21,843 work permits were issued to non-European Community nationals and 8,235 to persons from Commonwealth countries.[22] Of the foreign permit holders, Americans numbered 5,241, Spaniards 2,728 and Filipinos 1,986. Of the Commonwealth permit holders, Malaysia, as a country of origin, was represented by 1,350, Hong Kong by 1,025 and Mauritius by 849 permit holders. Holders are required to register with the National Insurance Scheme, and they and their dependents in Britain are eligible in return for the full range of social security benefits. Public housing is the responsibility of local housing authorities. Under the Race Relations Act of 1976 it is no longer lawfully possible to discriminate in the provision of goods or services including housing on the grounds of nationality. Lengthy residence qualifications may, however, in a number of areas effectively prevent access by work permit holders to public housing. Similar residence criteria may also affect the ability of a work permit holder or his family to obtain installment or other credits.

Immigrant Workers Free of Work Permit Control

Certain categories of workers may enter without work permits, even though they are neither patrials nor European Community nationals. The main groups in question are doctors and dentists and Commonwealth citizens coming on a "working holiday". The latter are normally admitted for 12 months, extensible for an additional two years. Other groups include the employees of overseas organizations and firms, the self-employed (providing that they can show that they have the necessary funds to conduct their business), *au pair* girls who are notionally in Britain to learn English and a small number of seasonal workers living in agricultural camps who stay for the harvest season and then leave (in recent years around 2,000 on the average). There are other minor categories. Until recently, medical and nursing students could normally expect to be allowed to take up employment in the United Kingdom after completion of their studies there. In 1976 and 1977, however, there were reports of student nurses from overseas being warned that their earlier expectations of a job on completion of training probably would not be fulfilled, owing to the greater supply of United Kingdom nurses.

Records of workers entering free of work permit control are not

---

[22] *Department of Employment Gazette*, May, 1976.

maintained. However, overseas doctors were said, in an official estimate, to have numbered 20,000 in 1973, or 26.9 percent of all active doctors.[23] Many hospitals, particularly geriatric and mental hospitals in Britain's older cities, are staffed nearly completely by overseas nursing staff.

Patrials

Under the 1971 Immigration Act those who qualify as patrials do not need work permits to take up employment or to settle permanently in the United Kingdom. No official statistics of patrials entering and leaving the country exist. The net balance of migration traffic in recent years shows Australia, New Zealand and Canada as those countries in which the majority of overseas patrials is likely to be found. The net balance of migration has clearly not been in favor of Britain. Patrials are in an even more privileged position in regard to entry and settlement than European Community nationals, since they neither require residence permits for periods of stay in excess of six months, nor have to register with the police.

Commenting on the notion of patriality Ann Dummett noted, "The United Kingdom has no written, single constitutional document, readily available and generally regarded as a fundamental source of law. Nor does it have any law which clearly defines its own citizens, or nationals, separately from those of countries outside it."[24] Because of the large number of citizens of Commonwealth countries who, prior to independence, were entitled to citizenship of the United Kingdom and its colonies under the British Nationality Act of 1948, pressure built up to distinguish, in law, between those United Kingdom citizens who in some sense "belonged" to the United Kingdom itself, and those United Kingdom citizens whose closest ties were in some other territory within the Commonwealth. The first step in making these distinctions had been made in the Commonwealth Immigrants Act of 1962 which, in the face of fierce opposition from the Opposition Labor Party, had removed from Commonwealth citizens, and from most colonial citizens not of recent United Kingdom descent and holding United Kingdom passports issued in the colonies, the right to enter the United Kingdom freely and to settle. The next step was brought about as a result of the claims made by another group of United Kingdom passport holders: those who at the time when the African countries in which they lived became independent had been offered United Kingdom passports which were not colonial passports but were issued by the United Kingdom High Commission on behalf of the United Kingdom government. These people, largely of Indian

[23] House of Commons *Hansard*, Feb. 5, 1975.
[24] Ann Dummett. *Citizenship and Nationality*. London: The Runnymede Trust. 1976. P. 9.

TABLE 5:4

Residence Permits Issued to European Community Nationals
in Great Britain, by Country of Origin, for the Years 1973-1975

Country of Origin	Years			
	1973	1974	1975	1976
Belgium	138	101	71	72
Denmark	339	305	292	271
France	1,613	1,568	1,267	1,045
Germany	1,344	1,084	883	725
Italy	2,239	2,144	1,764	1,440
Luxembourg	8	6	6	5
the Netherlands	721	561	397	382
TOTAL	6,402	5,769	4,680	3,940

Sources: Department of Employment *Gazette*, May, 1974, April, 1975, May, 1976, May, 1977.

origin, were ethnic minorities and often rather unpopular, in the countries in which they lived. They found themselves there largely because a succession of British administrators found their presence convenient, whether as indentured laborers to build the railways, or as traders and clerks in the local bureaucracy. It seems clear that there was a deliberate British Government intention to offer the members of this group the safety net of full United Kingdom citizenship at the time of independence, first in Kenya, then in other African countries.

The pressure to exclude these United Kingdom citizens became acute when some tens of thousands of United Kingdom citizens in Kenya, ethnically Indian by descent, found their livelihoods threatened or removed by the Africanization policies of the Kenyan government in 1968. The possibility that these out-migrants from Kenya might come to England had been foreseen by the then British government when these citizens had been issued United Kingdom passports. To prevent the arrival of these "colored" and, therefore, politically embarassing United Kingdom citizens and to break the pledge which had been given at the time of independence, the British government of the day passed the Commonwealth Immigrants Act of 1968, which specified, under Section 1 of the Act, that holders of United Kingdom passports issued outside the British Isles would be subject to immigration controls unless the holders, or one of their parents or grandparents, had been born, naturalized or adopted in the United Kingdom or in a Commonwealth country already self-governing by 1948. In other words, the notion of patriality was invoked.

The result of this Act was to create a new class of citizens who were "stateless in substance though not in name".[25] In practice, the British government has been steadily admitting this new class of nonpatrial United Kingdom passport holders from East Africa under a quota system, with the intention of regulating the flow. Between March, 1968 when controls were instituted and June, 1975, 83,272 such people were admitted, and it was estimated that a further 45,000 at that point still remained in East Africa, not all of whom were expected to come to the United Kingdom.[26] Furthermore, when a rapid evacuation of United Kingdom passport holders of Asian extraction from Uganda became imperative in 1972, as a result of measures taken by President Amin, some 28,000 were admitted to Britain in two months; and a major temporary relief operation was undertaken in an effort to house the evacuees and help those of working age to find jobs.

European Economic Community and Immigration

The category of patrial is important not simply in relation to immigration into the United Kingdom, but also because patrials constitute the class of citizens entitled, under the 1971 Treaty of Accession between the United Kingdom and the European Economic Community, to the benefits of European Communities membership as United Kingdom "nationals". The adoption of a narrow definition of nationality for the purpose of the Treaty of Accession arose partly from the reluctance of other European Communities member states to expose themselves to the risk of large scale in-migration of overseas United Kingdom and its colonies' citizens following Britain's entry into the European Communities. Concern in the United Kingdom, however, was more frequently expressed at the possibility that European Economic Community membership, entailing as it did freedom of movement between member states, might result in large scale in-migration into the United Kingdom from the other European Communities countries. The likelihood of increased migration from other European Communities countries at the time of the signing of the Treaty of Accession seemed small to those aware of the trends in migration over the last decade. In-migration, from the European Economic Community, whether for work or settlement has been declining both relative to other sources and absolutely. Work permits to European Communities nationals had fallen from 31,441 out of a total of 56,426 issued in 1961 to 10,981 out of a total of 48,000 issued in 1972. Given the more rapid development of the German, Belgian, Dutch and French economies it seemed implausible that European Communities nationals would look to the

---

25 *Ibid.*
26 House of Commons *Hansard*, Nov. 2, 1975.

United Kingdom as a place to which they would migrate. Irish in-migrants are an exception in this case, but on their freedom to visit or to work in the United Kingdom there are no restrictions.

Civil and Social Rights of Workers Free of Work Permit Control

Access to full citizenship rights within the United Kingdom is not identical for all immigrants who enter the United Kingdom free of work permit control. The most favored groups of all are patrials, whether of United Kingdom or of Commonwealth origin. They are entitled to settle and they may apply for United Kingdom passports. They are not liable to deportation, are entitled to vote, to perform jury service, to stand for public office, to work in the public services, including the nationalized industries, and to enlist in the armed forces. Next in status are the Irish who, although not Commonwealth citizens, share all these rights, but who may normally not apply for United Kingdom passports and who may be deported for certain offenses where they have not been resident in the United Kingdom for five years or more.[27] Next come nonpatrial Commonwealth citizens and other British subjects who, are subject to entry controls and, unless they have United Kingdom issued passports to work permit control. They are entitled to the full range of voting and other citizenship rights. They are less privileged, however, than European Communities nationals with regard to immigration and deportation. However, for nonpatrial United Kingdom passport holders from East Africa, for instance, there is no other country to which they may be "returned". Next to this group, and because of their favored immigration and working status, more privileged in a number of ways, are European Economic Community nationals. They may not vote or participate in the other citizenship rights to which Commonwealth citizens have access, but they have full access to housing, social security, and education including state vocational employment schemes on terms equal with full United Kingdom citizens. Finally there are other aliens, admitted under work permits, but who have neither citizenship rights nor immunity from deportation who, in common with European Community nationals, may apply for permanent settlement status after they have been resident in the United Kingdom for five years. Alien work permit holders and their families are also entitled to the full range of social security rights and benefits, but dependents may not be admitted if they require treatment for a medical condition of which they were aware before they entered. In addition, educational authorities may decline to accept children whose period of

---

[27] These rights have been in some degree modified by the temporary legislation introduced to counter terrorist activity originating in the Ulster conflict.

residence is six months or fewer. Children admitted during the final six months of a work permit holder's period may not be accepted by a school even though the permit holder himself intends to apply for renewal of his permit, renewal normally being automatic.

Protective Legislation

Legislation to protect the civil rights of minorities in Britain was conceived primarily in response to the needs of colored people in Britain. At the date of the 1971 Census, the proportion of immigrants with brown skin and from Commonwealth countries was smaller than that of immigrants from other sources. The Race Relations Act of 1965 made it unlawful to discriminate on the grounds of race, color, or ethnic or national origin in certain places of public resort, such as hotels, restaurants, theaters, swimming pools and the like. The Act set up a Race Relations Board to receive complaints of discrimination, and to seek a voluntary settlement of differences where the Board found, on investigation, that a *prima facie* case of discrimination existed.

Research in the period following 1965, notably by Political and Economic Planning and Research Services and by academics operating under the aegis of the Institute of Race Relations established that substantial discrimination in employment, housing and the provision of goods and services was practiced against minorities in Britain; and that the incidence of discrimination was greater against the colored minorities than other European settlers. A Race Relations Act of 1968 attempted to redress these problems by enlargening the scope of anti-discrimination legislation to include employment, housing and the provision of goods and services, and by giving to the Race Relations Board the powers to bring to court cases where it had found prima facie evidence of discrimination but had been unable to secure a voluntary settlement between the complainant and the offender. The Act also established a statutory Community Relations Commission with the task of promoting "harmonious community relations" and supporting the many voluntary organizations addressing themselves to the relations among the British majority and the minority groups.

It appears clear in retrospect that, faced with widespread discrimination rooted in widely shared cultural values and social attitudes, a system which must rely on complaints from individuals is inadequate to encompass the problem. Individuals often will not know that they have been discriminated against, and even where they do suspect it, they may lack the courage or resources to pursue the matter. Nowhere was this more clearly brought out than in the findings of research conducted by Political and Economic

Planning and Research Services at the beginning of the 1970s.[28] Even at the manual worker level there was a substantial level of discrimination. An Asian or West Indian would, when applying for an unskilled job, face discrimination in at least one-third, and perhaps as many as one-half of all cases. This implied tens of thousands of cases annually, compared with the 150 employment complaints received by the Race Relations Board in 1973. There was a decline in discrimination against ethnic minority purchasers of housing, but an unequal treatment of minorities in the public housing sector, where apparently neutral allocation practices were resulting in concentrations of colored tenants in certain less favored, inner city, public housing projects.

The Race Relations Act of 1976

The main provisions of the Race Relations Act of 1976, which replaced the Act of 1968, include the prohibition of discrimination on the grounds of color, race, nationality, ethnic or national origin in employment, housing, education, the provision of goods and services, advertisements and in access to private clubs other than certain bona fide membership clubs which are specifically designed to cater for a particular ethnic group, such as the London Scottish Rugby Club or the Indian Workers Association. The law has been extended to cover indirect discrimination, by making unlawful practices which, whatever their intentions, may be shown to have a disproportionately adverse effect on members of ethnic minorities. This is a radical departure from the previous conceptions of discrimination and recognizes, in the light of American experience, that racial minorities may be denied equal opportunities by selection tests which are not directly related to performance and penalize those with below average educational backgrounds.

The main instrument of change envisioned by the Act is a new Commission for Racial Equality, which combines the functions of the preceding Race Relations Board and Community Relations Commission and succeeds them. In carrying out its investigative and law enforcement work the Commission is given certain powers by the Act to subpoena evidence and to issue nondiscrimination notices requiring cessation of the practices in question. Unless appealed, these notices have the force of law.

[28] David J. Smith. "Racial Disadvantage in Employment", *PEP, Broadsheet Series and Major Reports,* 40:544, 1974; 42:560, 1976. *See also,* N. McIntosh and David J. Smith, "The Extent of Racial Discrimination", *PEP, Broadsheet Series and Major Reports,* 40:547, 1974; and David J. Smith and Ann Whalley. "Racial Minorities and Public Housing". *PEP, Broadsheet Series and Major Reports,* 41:556, 1975.

Other Measures to Promote Integration

It has, in fact, been a feature of recent British history that no coordinated attempt has been made to help new minorities to integrate, with the exception of the Poles and, to a lesser extent, evacuees from Uganda. Nonetheless, a small number of specific initiatives have been taken, of which the most substantial have been measures taken to help local authorities.

Local Government Act of 1966. Under this Act some fairly substantial expenditures have been incurred over the years, virtually all of it on educational staff to teach English to immigrant children. The great virtue of this scheme was and is that it was theoretically related to need and not to a cost ceiling. However, local educational authority effort has been uneven; some local authorities with substantial concentrations of immigrants have spent little or nothing and there has been little guidance or encouragement from central government to develop a common policy or to share the positive lessons which individual local authorities have learned. The optional character of the provisions under Section 11 of the Local Government Act of 1966 derives partly from the earnest desire of central government to be seen acting constitutionally, that is, not to be interfering with those areas of responsibility which are notionally the preserve of local government. The nonintervention has to be seen in the context of the traditionally laissez-faire attitude of government toward immigration and its consequences. The basis for assessing eligibility under the 1966 legislation has, in recent years, become unsatisfactory, since records of immigrant children at school are no longer kept, while the economic recession has discouraged local authorities from incurring any extra expenditure, however small.

The Urban Program. The Urban Program was launched in 1968 in a context of concern over the effects of Commonwealth immigration. It was designed, like the Local Government Act of 1966, to be an optional program of financial assistance to local authorities, but it had a fixed initial budget. The kinds of projects seen as acceptable for funding were numerous and have included holiday schemes, day-care facilities for families and young children, schemes to meet the special needs of ethnic minorities, advice centers and legal services, to name just a few of the major categories. Some funds have gone directly to immigrant organizations, or to projects run by black people. The Urban Program was optional in character. Thus, some local authorities which should have made use of its provisions have failed to do so. In retrospect, the explanation of these deficiencies seems clearly political. The Urban Program was originally viewed as an initiative to tackle the problems of integration and the adjustment to immigration. However, the criteria were drawn so wide, and the problems to the solution of which the Urban Program was said to be directed became so various that its impact on the needs of immigrant communities or on the wider needs of the areas in which they lived may have been devoid of any significance.

Educational Policy and Immigrants. The official diagnosis of the educational problems posed by immigration was couched principally in terms of problems for the host community rather than for immigrants themselves. A circular providing official guidance to local education authorities issued by the Minister of Education in 1965 (Circular No. 7) recommended, on educational grounds, that no school should have more than about 30 percent of its enrollment as immigrant children. In other words, dispersal of immigrant children was seen as the appropriate educational response to the presence of immigrants. However, by the early 1970s it had come to be increasingly doubted by educationists whether dispersal served any educational function, either for the children of immigrants or for indigenous children. Research within the Inner London Education Authority strongly suggested that, at any rate, so far as West Indian children were concerned, the density of immigrants was only of slight importance in determining academic attainment of either indigenous children, or of the West Indians themselves. Social class composition was of substantially greater importance.[29] Other evidence pointing in the same direction appeared to suggest the same lack of relationship in respect to other immigrant groups.

More positive steps to deal with the educational problems of immigrant minorities and their children were taken with the establishment, following the Government White Paper, of an Educational Disadvantage Unit and Center for Information and Advice on Educational Disadvantage.[30] These two bodies had a wide brief to tackle the needs of those suffering from educational disadvantage, but the needs of children from minority groups were a specific part of that brief. The political and social pressures which resulted in a diversion of the Urban Program away from what might have been a set of measures to deal with the consequences of immigration towards a generalized program had already shown themselves at the outset of the new educational initiative. To some extent, the omens were not auspicious. A draft directive emanating from the European Economic Commission in Brussels in 1976 calling for, among other things, the provision of mother tongue teaching within school hours for the children of in-migrant workers was modified under strong British and German pressure to make this provision optional and to restrict its application to the children of European Communities nationals. The British demand stemmed from the fact that the Department of Education and Science had no power to require local

---

[29] Christine Mabey. *Social and Ethnic Mix in Schools and the Relationship with Attainment of Children Aged 8 and 11.* London: Center for Environmental Studies. Research Paper No. 9. 1974.

[30] Department of Education and Science. *Educational Disadvantage and the Needs of Immigrants.* London: Her Majesty Stationary Office, Cmnd 5720. March, 1974.

education authorities to make the necessary curricular provisions. However, the educational and social merits of the proposal appear not to have been seriously entertained by the Department of Education and Science which displays signs of traditional departmental thinking about the rapid assimilation of immigrants into English culture, a position apparently more rigidly held in 1976 than the policy adopted under the Polish Resettlement Act of 1947.

The Voluntary Community Relations Movement

Finally, there are many voluntary committees, normally known as community relations councils. The local councils, controlled by voluntary executive committee on which elected local government representatives of the major political parties have usually been heavily represented, have attempted to run a number of community schemes of an educational and welfare kind involving members of ethnic minorities. The more active local community relations organizations have attempted, through publicity and pressure, to alert their local communities to the realities of racial inequality and to the need for a sensitive local government. The less active have been content with organizing multiracial soirees, ethnic evenings, or perhaps short summer schools aimed specifically at children from immigrant backgrounds. It is hard, except in a small number of cases, to point to any concrete success for the local community relations movement. Where success exists it appears to have been the result more of the exceptional personality of the full time community relations officer in charge of the local effort, and less of the application of a successful formula. The greatest achievement of the local community relations councils has probably been to educate some of the local socially and politically elite, both from the majority and from the minorities. With rare exceptions, their impact on local public opinion or on the real disadvantages of ethnic minorities appears to have been trivial, and even their successes may well, like the Urban Program, have provided the alibi for the absence of any serious effort at local level to change local government policies and practices.

Conclusions

Postwar immigration in Britain has been a phenomenon which was willed in the early stages of European migration, and tolerated for its economic benefits in the later, initial stages of migration from colored Commonwealth countries, but later rejected. Now it has fallen to an insignificant level, except for the remaining dependents of those who arrived to settle and work some years ago. Its effect has been to add an approximate 6 to 7 percent to the population of the United Kingdom directly, and more, if children born to immigrants in Britain are taken into account. The traditional laissez-faire stance of public policy has been only occasionally modified, and then mainly in times of (in humanitarian terms) crisis, as with the Polish excombatants, Hungarian refugees and Ugandan evacuees. Only in recent years, and largely because of fears of racial tension, have any substantial signs emerged of positive central government responses to the presence of immigrants. So far, the most thorough response has been in the sphere of protective legislation, though there have been some attempts in the educational field to provide extra financial resources. Britain is still far from asking itself whether the newer immigrant minorities in its midst should receive the kind of public affirmation of their individuality that older minorities with a clear geographical base, such as the Scots and the Welsh, have secured. The relatively small size of the new immigrant minorities and their fragmentation seem unlikely to disturb this neglect in the near future, although low educational attainment and high unemployment among young British born blacks are fueling racial tensions in the major cities.

On the immigration front too, it seems likely that a continuing policy of low immigration will be adopted by governments who will have every reason to expect popular support. Britain's unfavorable economic performance relative to other European Community states is unlikely to render it attractive to European Community nationals. The growth of the tourist industry may impose certain strains on the labor market, but the inclination appears to be to resolve these by drawing on the pool of domestic unemployed or at most on short term work permit holders. An apparently declining birth rate has failed so far to arouse any enthusiasm for increased immigration but, rather, has inspired relief at the population implications.[31]

Insofar as Britain can be said to have an immigration policy, it is a policy designed to contain the social problems of past immigration by eliminating virtually all future inward flows. Its geographical situation as an island would make this policy easier to enforce than in other European Economic Community states with land frontiers, even were it not for its lesser economic attractions. Whether it does contain and resolve the social problems consequent on past immigration will depend partly on the growth of articulacy and self-consciousness among the newer immigrant minorities. It must, at any rate, be said that the legal framework for the attainment of full equality of opportunity for minorities is a benevolent one, so that to a limited extent at least, the wind is set fair.

---

[31] Population Panel. *Report of the Population Panel*. London: HMSO, Cmnd 5258. March, 1973.

III

Countries of In-Migration:
Northwestern Europe

6

Austria*

ERNST GEHMACHER
Institute for Empirical Social Research, Vienna

Recent In-Migration

BETWEEN World War II and the beginning of the 1960s, in-migrants to Austria stayed only to migrate later to another country. Until the dissolution of the Empire in 1918, in-migration to Austria, and in particular to Vienna, was a rural-urban migration from hinterland to the metropolis. The migrants were citizens of the Empire and their migration presented no legal definitional problems.

At the end of World War II, there were returning Germans and refugees from the Eastern Communist countries whom Austria received, quite often under pressure from the occupying Allied powers. On the other hand, Austria concurrently lost quite a few of her nationals who migrated primarily to Germany, or to Switzerland, or who emigrated overseas.

During the 1960s, Austria continued to lose her nationals to her Northwest European neighbors, but began to receive foreign workers, at first from a variety of countries, but later on primarily from Yugoslavia and Turkey. These workers treated Austria as a way station on their trek to the industrial complexes in Germany.

Starting with the European economic recession in 1967 and 1968, Austria began to lose her role as a way station of migrants north and, by 1970, she

---

* Translated from German by Daniel Kubat.

joined the other countries in Europe, relying on foreign workers to perform the indispensable, but unpleasant jobs. In August, 1973, the number of valid work permits in Austria reached 244,000 and estimates of all foreign workers in Austria including the illegals reached about 280,000.

In 1966, foreign workers represented two percent of all employed persons, but in 1973 their percent rose to 8.7. Such a rapid development in the number of foreign workers brought with it a need for a governmental in-migration policy which, until then, rested on some old legislation. Namely, until the end of 1975, regulations for foreigners working in Austria dated to 1945 and were based on regulations valid for Germany and imported to Austria in 1937. Naturally, the regulations, unsuited to Austrian conditions as they were, were amended over the years by various edicts tailored to meet the cooperation principle (*Sozial-Partnerschaft*) governing the relations between the organizations of employers and labor.

The Austrian government was able, at last, to produce a new Act on employment of foreigners in Austria (*Ausländerbeschäftigungsgesetz*), ratified by the Parliament (*Nationalrat*) on March 20 and by the Cabinet (*Bundesrat*) on April 4, 1975. The new law became effective on January 1, 1976.

The new Act came about not only because of the steadily increasing number of foreign workers in Austria, but also because of indications that the economic boom was a temporary phenomenon and that the act of importing labor ultimately means immigration. The new Act remains flexible enough either to encourage or to discourage in-migration and it secures wide powers for the government to encourage out-migration of foreigners if need be.

Austria does not consider itself an immigration country. On the other hand, being a small country, and a labor exporting one, it proffers empathy for the sending countries. There are about 100,000 Austrian nationals working elsewhere in Europe. The close cooperation between industry and labor in Austria produces a constantly shifting equilibrium of interests and compromises making it difficult to articulate its in-migration policy.

Regulations on In-Migration

The employment of foreign workers in Austria was subject to an old German regulation of 1933. Paragraph 2 of the Continuity in Legal System Act (*Rechtsüberleitungsgesetz*) of 1945 reinstituted the 1933 German Act on employment of foreigners. According to this law, an employer needed an employment permit (*Beschäftigungsgenehmigung*) to employ a foreigner who needed a work permit. Both permits were issued by the local branch of the Labor Office (*Arbeitsamt*) subject to local conditions. The permits were issued for a period not to exceed 12 months at a time. The permit expired

TABLE 6:1

Foreign Workers in Austria, by Proportion of
All Employed Persons, 1961-1977[a]

Year[b]	N	Foreign Workers % of Labor Force
1961	11,600	0.5
1962	13,500	0.6
1963	16,900	0.7
1964	21,500	0.9
1965	32,500	1.4
1966	46,900	2.0
1967	60,900	2.6
1968	62,500	2.7
1969	82,400	3.5
1970	109,200	4.6
1971	148,500	6.0
1972	186,465	7.4
1973	226,384	8.7
1974	218,340	8.2
1975	185,200	7.0
1976	173,900	6.5
1977[c]	181,100	6.7

Notes: [a] Estimated population in Austria in 1976: 7,512,000.

[b] 1961 through 1971 estimates based on annual mean values.

[c] Estimate on the first six months basis.

Sources: *Bundesministerium für soziale Verwaltung;* Hauptverband der österreichischen Sozialversicherungsträger (Vienna).

automatically with a change of employment. The state was able to retain a full control over the labor market by this double permit system.

Until 1962, all permits were handled individually irrespective of the built-in bureaucratic delays as large scale in-migration was not taking place. After 1962, the expansion of the labor market was creating more vacancies than the cumbersome bureaucratic system was able to fill. This time, the cooperation between the employers and the unions exerted a sufficient pressure on the government to begin issuing the permits liberally. Annual quotas were set for individual industrial sectors, again after consultation with the respective industries and unions. The quotas were interpreted leniently, meaning they could be raised during any given year. In addition to the quota system, the previous system of individual admission remained in force.

TABLE 6:2

Percent Distribution of Foreign Workers
Subject to Quota Arrangement[a] in Austria,
by Country of Origin, Annual Average Between 1962 and 1972

| | Country of Origin | | | | | | | | |
| | | | | Yugo- | | | | | |
Year	Germany	Greece	Italy	slavia	Spain	Turkey	Other	N	%
1962	24	8	27	16	4	2	19	6,450	100
1963	23	7	16	26	4	2	17	10,351	100
1964	17	4	9	38	5	14	13	14,525	100
1965	10	2	7	53	3	16	9	25,180	100
1966	7	1	4	67	2	13	6	38,112	100
1967	5	1	2	75	1	12	5	50,255	100
1968	5	1	2	76	1	11	5	47,092	100
1969	4	1	1	74	b	13	7	54,053	100
1970	3	b	1	75	b	15	6	75,105	100
1971	2	b	1	77	b	15	5	98,140	100
1972	2	b	1	79	b	13	4	122,702	100

Notes: [a] Produces considerably lower figures than the estimates from all sources, see Table 6:1.
[b] less than 0.5 percent.

Sources: H. Werner. *Freizügigkeit der Arbeitskräfte: Mitteilungen aus dem Arbeitsmarkt und Berufsforschung* (Nürnberg), 1973, No. 4, Table 37; Bundesministerium für Soziale Verwaltung (Vienna).

Thus, a fluidity was built into the admission of foreign workers. It consisted in the fact that individual workers were being admitted by branches of the Labor Office which were acting independently of each other; also, the quota admissions varied depending on the pressure exerted by individual industries.

The new legislation now in force revises the previous admission regulations to allow for a greater control of the influx of foreigners. The quota system remains, but only the Minister for Social Affairs *(Sozialminister)* has the right to undertake any changes. Thus, the quota system is now centralized and, only in special cases, may the stipulated number of workers be exceeded: a sudden need for specialized personnel; newly founded enterprises in danger of not getting off the ground without additional labor; replacement of foreign workers who have just left; or needs in health and welfare fields.

The new legislation allows the government to act "in the national interest" and sets a ceiling on importation of foreign workers for reasons either of the national economy, or of public concern. Such a ceiling can be stipulated by the Minister for Social Administration either for the whole country or for the individual states *(Länder)*, after consultations either with the Federal or State ministry for commerce, trade and industry. This provision also entails a limitation on free movement of foreign workers in Austria.

Technically, regulation of internal migration rests on the requirement of a work permit which is valid only within the administrative area of the issuing authority and which is also restricted to a given job vacancy. To be able to change jobs freely, the alien must have lived continuously in Austria for eight years. The work permit to which he becomes eligible, then, *(Befreiungsschein)* is issued for two years at a time. In case of marriage to an Austrian national resident in Austria, the residence requirement is waived.

The new legislation offers no articulated policy on in-migration, it offers only mechanisms to pursue any policy advantageous at the moment. For instance, the quota system may be set high or low, a refusal of a work permit leading necessarily to a forced out-rotation. The legislation provides for a numerical control of foreign workers, but has nothing to say about selection criteria. That is, it allows in-migration of primarily unskilled workers. In 1965, the proportion of skilled workers among the foreigners in Austria was 17 percent but it dropped to 12 percent in 1969.

The language barrier does not allow the foreign workers, now primarily Yugoslavs and Turks, to move up the occupational ladder. However, there is a shortage of skilled workers in Austria which the foreigners could fill. The chronic shortage of skilled workers and tradesmen, brought about by the out-migration of Austrians, was felt even during the recession of 1975.

Since it is the unskilled workers who have the most difficulties in adjusting to life in Austria, a selection criterion favoring skilled in-migrants would go a long way toward solving Austria's worries about integrating her foreign workers. Austrians do not like, however, the thought of competing with foreign workers, and the Austrian government is careful, especially in the Yugoslav case, not to contribute toward that country's loss of skilled labor.

Demographic and Economic Backdrop

During the last decade of the 1960s, the demographic structure of Austria has improved so that now it is able to anticipate an enlarged influx of its own young persons into the labor market. The strong birth cohorts have come of age and will be supplying the country with labor well into the decade of the 1980s. In addition, out-migration of Austrians has all but ceased during the last few years due to the labor market readjustments in Germany and in Switzerland.

The ability of Austria to continue accepting new in-migrants is likely to decrease even though its current job situation appears much better than that in the rest of Europe. There are, of course, regional needs to be met in Austria. In particular, Austria's primary city, Vienna, has not been able to replace its own population since 1918 and its own supply of young labor force entrants has been diminishing by about 20,000 annually since 1970. Vienna will remain attractive to the Yugoslavs, for instance, as the Austrians from the westernmost parts of the country do not migrate east.

It is true that wages and standard of living are not at a par with other western European countries. On the other hand, both cultural and geographic proximity and economic stability make Austria an attractive land for Yugoslavs and Turks.

In the short run, importing labor has proved a bonus for Austria. It has allowed the country to remain expansionist and to attract investments.[1] Also, the large number of single foreign workers to Austria represents only a minor taxing of the social infrastructure. In a way, Austria has "saved" the normal costs attendant to a bringing up and training of labor recruits,[2] even though it has exported its savings again through Austrian nationals abroad.

Only marginally can the foreign workers depress the wages and retard the improvement of the working conditions for the Austrians, as they are often concentrated in certain enterprises and certain industries and, thus, not directly in competition with Austrian workers. No doubt, exploitation occurs, since the more inarticulate the foreign workers are, the less they are able to defend themselves. Those attempting to offer their services on a black labor market are, of course, those most likely to suffer abuse.

In the long run, the effects of importing labor were not always positive.[3] Rather, they frequently resulted in an upward pressure on wages and prices; discouraging of a rationalization of production; maintaining of unproductive plants and branches of industry; postponing of social costs becoming due when the workers age or when they bring in dependents; overpopulation in areas where quaintness and picturesqueness are selling points of the tourist industry; and delinquency of foreigners' children.

The proportion of foreign workers varies by regions. In 1975, western Austria, especially Vorarlberg, showed the proportion of foreign workers in the labor force as 18.2, Salzburg as 9.8 and Vienna as 10.5 percent of all employed persons. Southern Austria has few foreign workers, but has a high unemployment rate.

[1] F. Butschek and E. Walterkirchen. *Aspekte der Ausländerbeschäftigung. Monatsberichte des Österreichischen Instituts für Wirtschaftsforschung.* Vienna: 1974.

[2] IFES. *Ökonomische und Soziale Kosten-Nutzen-Rechnung der Gastarbeiterbeschäftigung in Wien.* Report to the City of Vienna. Vienna: Institut für empirische Sozialforschung. 1972.

[3] F. Butschek. "Wanderungen und ihre Folgen", *Europäische Rundschau,* 3:69-78, 1975; Salzburger Institut für Raumforschung. *Grenzen und Probleme der Beschäftigung von Gastarbeitern im Lande Salzburg.* Salzburg: 1974.

TABLE 6:3

Distribution of Employed Persons in Austria,
by Selected Economic Branches with Above Average
Proportion of Foreign Workers, 1977

Economic Sectors with a High Proportion of Foreigners[a]	N All Employed	Percent Foreigners
Agriculture and Related	43,876	11.8
Textile Manufacturing	72,841	20.8
Manufacture of Musical Instruments, Sportsgoods and Toys	6,834	25.1
Manufacture of Products from Rubber and Synthetic Materials	19,777	23.0
Manufacture of Earthenware and Related	37,105	11.2
Manufacture of Metal Products	7,210	13.9
Heavy Construction	144,527	14.0
Hostelries and Restaurants	72,861	16.6
All Employed	2,404,028	6.9

Note: [a] All economic branches with at least 10 percent of foreign workers.

Source: Bundesministerium für soziale Versicherung.

Research Backdrop

The new legislation must be viewed against a background of research in the area of foreign workers. A Consortium for Economic and Social Research was founded in Vienna in the summer of 1971. One of its tasks was to address the issues surrounding the adaptation of foreign workers to life in Austria. Representatives to the Consortium, in addition to interested social scientists, came mainly from the unions and from industry. A study undertaken by the Consortium yielded useful data and some recommendations.[4]

A report drawing heavily on the study was produced by the Council of Economic and Social Advisors to the government[5] to serve as a basis for the new legislation.[6]

[4] Gastarbeiter-Kreis. *Gastarbeiter-Wirtschaftliche und Soziale Herausforderung.* Vienna: Europa Verlag and Österreichischer Wirtschaftsverlag. 1973.

[5] Beirat für Wirtschaft-und Sozialfragen. *Möglichkeiten und Grenzen des Einsatzes ausländischer Arbeitskräfte.* Report to the Austrian Government. Vienna. 1976.

[6] *Ibid.*

Four questions were highlighted in the report: 1) admission of foreign workers; 2) selection of foreign workers by occupational criteria; 3) strategies for worker rotation; and 4) strategies for foreigners integration. Clear recommendations, however, cannot be gleaned from the report which suggests "an optimal mix" of answers to the four issues without specifying what the optimal mix would be. "The process of integration at a first level is accommodation at work. That represents a basis which is the purpose of taking the employment in the first place or of offering it in the case of an employer. This first level of integration is viewed positively both by the foreign worker and the host country, that is her economy and her population. . . However, at the second level of integration, the issue emerges of whether or not workers' rotation should be encouraged due to the difficulties posed by the two cultures."[7] Social integration presupposes finding a sufficiently large network of friends among the Austrian population, thus representing a third level of social integration. Finally, retaining a bicultural orientation without feeling inferior in either culture would represent the fourth level of integration, a model for which are, for instance, the Slavic minorities in southern Austria. To achieve a biculturalism, however, without solving the question of naturalization must be considered either wishful thinking or a political smoke screen.[8]

Pressure Groups

Austria has difficulties coming to grips with long term policies in matters of in-migration. Its short term policies have always been influenced by an interaction of various pressure groups. There are, essentially, four distinct political bodies which have vested interests in the issue of foreign workers: industry, unions; churches, and government.

Industry and Unions: Because of the relationship of cooperation between industry and labor in Austria, it is difficult to separate their policies. The institution of cooperation *(Sozialpartnerschaft)* is a form of planning economic policy where the workers participate in the process of decision making. In its Austrian variant, it is mainly a matter of ironing things out between two bureaucracies: that of the Austrian Labor Union *(Österreichischer Gewerkschaftsbund)* and the Federation of Workers and Employees *(Kammern für Arbeiter und Angestellte)* on one hand and the Chamber of Commerce *(Bundeskammer der Gewerblichen Wirtschaft)* and the Austrian Manufacturers Association *(Vereinigung Österreichischer Industrieller)* on the other.

---

[7] Gastarbeiter-Kreis. *Gastarbeiter-Wirtschaftliche und Soziale Herausforderung.* Vienna: Europa Verland and Österreichischer Wirtschaftsverlag. 1973.

[8] Naturalization may, but need not, be granted upon request after a ten year continuous residence in the country.

TABLE 6:4

Estimated Proportion Distribution[a] of Foreign
Workers in Occupational Skill Categories, in
Austria, 1973 and 1976

Skill Levels	June, 1973 %	June, 1976 %
Manuals	96.4	92.9
Highly skilled	4.8	
Skilled	10.4	
Semi-skilled	32.0	
Unskilled	49.2	
Non-manuals	3.6	7.1
Total %	100.0	100.0

Note: [a] Based on probability sample of enterprises employing at least 15 persons.

Sources: Bundeministerium für soziale Verwaltung, Arbeitsmarktvorschau, 1974/1976 (Vienna).

Naturally, the industry pressures for larger quotas of foreign workers and the unions prefer to protect their own workers from an undue competition. On the whole, however, controversies are contained and only acceptable compromises are presented to the public.

Churches: The dominance of the Catholic Church in Austria is indisputable. One of its arms, Supradiocesal Group to the Questions of Foreign Workers, ÜDAG *(Überdiözesane Arbeitsgemeinschaft für Gastarbeiterfragen)* functions as an organ of public conscience in matters of social welfare of foreign workers. Officially, the pressure ÜDAG can exert is limited to the field of public opinion. Unofficially, however, its pressures can be channeled through the opposition party, Austrian Popular Party *(Österreichische Volkspartei).* In a reaction to the new Act on employment of foreigners, ÜDAG took a position that "it became clear that the foreign worker is being considered only in his role as worker...In addition, his legal position has become narrowed to the extent that the work permit allows him only one employer, one enterprise and one place to live. He can be shipped out should his health deteriorate such that his eligibility for a work permit becomes voided... Furthermore, the new Act does not differentiate between those who worked in Austria a short time and those who have lived there for years with their families and are well integrated into the society."[9]

[9] ÜDAG. *Das Österreichische Ausländerbeschäftigungsgesetz vom 20. Marz 1975: Geist und Ungeist einer Leistungsgesellschaft.* Vienna: Überdiözesane Arbeitsgemeinschaft für Gastarbeiter Fragen. 1975.

Government: The official role of the government is to set and to monitor admission quota for foreign workers. Until now, there was, basically, no conflict in this regard between the governing Socialist Party and the opposition party; they are, after all, indirectly represented in the cooperation system between industry and labor.

The only independent role the Austrian government plays in the matter of foreign workers' in-migration is in the diplomatic relations with the sending countries; primarily, then, with Yugoslavia. Paradoxically, the minor disagreements the two may have center on the Slavic minorities in southern Austria. Only in connection with that issue does the Yugoslav press mention the fate of its workers in Austria. Yugoslavia's position on its own nationals abroad is ambivalent, although the country clearly sees itself as a protectress of "her nationalities" abroad who are, actually, Austrian citizens.

Governmental initiative in improving services for foreign workers consists, for example, in broadcasting news four times a week for five minutes in Serbo-Croatian languages and, once a week, in Turkish. A concession to Yugoslavia is that children of Yugoslav workers in Austria are receiving additional school classes in German and three to five school classes weekly in Yugoslav languages and civics, based on a Yugoslav suggested curriculum outline. This is a direct result of a conference on such issues held in Belgrade in May, 1975.

Outlook

There is no clear cut policy on in-migration into Austria; only mechanisms are spelled out to regulate the inflow of aliens into the country. In this respect, foreign workers in Austria enjoy fewer rights than elsewhere as their dependents may move in, but remain ineligible for work permits. Austria does have a residence permit system but does not allow aliens to stay in the country without a work permit. Foreigners expecting to stay in Austria longer than three months must demonstrate either that they have employment, or some other source of income for the duration of their stay.

Austria's in-migration policies are developed in an ad hoc fashion and as a response to economic pressures. The latter are, however, mediated by the peculiarly Austrian system of cooperation between the unions and industry, the unions having the upper hand as their party is in power. The new Act dealing with the presence of foreign workers in Austria provides wide discretionary powers to the government in that it can set quotas on the number of persons to be employed and can issue regulations limiting the number of foreign workers either by region or nationwide.

Thus far, industry was interested in having a pool of foreign workers from which to draw and select, the latter function foregone by the government. The unions considered that their nationals should be assured some occupational mobility and protection from unpleasant and hard jobs to be offered to the foreign workers.

The social conditions of foreign workers in Austria have generated some concern on the part of the Catholic Church, which tends to see itself as the spokesman for the public conscience, its political power having been curtailed. It seems, however, that the voices of humanitarian concern are not being listened to so attentively as are the political protestations from the governments of the sending countries. The Austrian government pretends to think that, as a small country and as an employer of relatively few foreigners — mostly from nearby countries — it can afford to take a somewhat opportunistic view and get away with it. On the other hand, when pressed, it is quick to respond, especially to the claims of Yugoslavia.

On the whole, however, Austria's position on matters of in-migration remains unchanged. Austria is not an immigration country. Nonetheless, Austria indulges in importation of labor to feed its short run economic upswings. It remains to be seen whether the country will be able to discourage, during the economic downswing, a large part of its foreign workers from staying without incurring too much of an adverse international publicity. More likely than not, Austria will have to toe the line informally prescribed by the larger European labor importing countries, which would mean, integrating the country's foreign workers.

7

The Benelux Countries:
Belgium, the Netherlands, Luxemburg

GUNTHER BEYER
European Center for Population Studies

Introduction

BELGIUM, the Netherlands and Luxemburg were the first countries in Europe after World War II to sign a treaty in 1948 for a closer cooperation in matters of joint political, economic and social administration. This was the first treaty towards the unification of Europe, preceding the creation of the Council of Europe (1951), the Coal and Steel Community (1952), the West European Union, and the European Economic Community (1957) now referred to as the European Communities.

The Benelux countries were highly industrially developed before the War and the last three decades after the War have a considerable economic growth in common, although varying demographic pictures characterize the individual countries. It is the latter which directly influenced the in-migration policies in the individual Benelux countries.

The economic expansion of these countries demanded a growth of the labor force which could not be met domestically. By 1974, there were approximately 450,000 foreign workers in the three countries, the population total for which is about 23 million. The proportion of foreign workers in the three countries varies from about 2 percent in the Netherlands to 24 percent in Luxemburg, Belgium registering now about 8 percent of its population as alien nationals.

The in-migration policies in the Benelux countries have been dependent thus far on the two complementary trends of economic expansion and

The Politics of Migration Policies

TABLE 7:1

Estimated Number of Workers from Selected
(Association Treaty and Recruitment) Countries
in the Three Benelux Countries, in 1974

Countries of Origin	Countries of Arrival			
	Belgium[a]	The Netherlands[b] (000s)	Luxemburg[c]	Total
Algeria	3	—	—	3
Greece	8	2	—	10
Italy	85	10	11	106
Morocco	30	23	—	53
Portugal	3	4	3	10
Spain	30	20	2	52
Tunisia	—	1	—	1
Turkey	10	33	—	43
Yugoslavia	3	9	1	13
All Others	76	80[d]	19	175
Total	248	182	36	472

Notes: [a] Estimated population in Belgium in 1974, 9,788,000.
[b] Estimated population in The Netherlands in 1974, 13,491,000.
[c] Estimated population in Luxemburg in 1974, 357,000.
[d] Includes 25,000 persons from Surinam and the Netherland Antilles.

Sources: *Servizio Migranti* (Rome), 1975, No. 8.

demographic contraction with the consequence of importing labor from abroad. The new in-migrants from other than the neighboring countries brought with them new problems of adaptation attracting the attention of politicians and social planners. The economic recession of 1974 and 1975 required that the individual countries come to terms with the importation of labor and the issue of in-migration and immigration respectively. Until this time, all in-migration measures were ad hoc and not always consistent with the existing recommendations issuing from the supranational bodies like the Council of Europe, the International Labor Office or the various policy branches of the European Communities.

BELGIUM

The coal and steel industry of Belgium has been relying on foreign workers as far back as the nineteenth century. By 1890, there were as many as

170,000 foreign workers in Belgium. The economic expansion and the declining birthrate after World War I combined to favor in-migration. There were about 340,000 in-migrants in 1938, primarily from Italy and Poland. After World War II, in-migration from Poland all but ceased; the neighboring countries developed their own labor shortages and Belgium turned to workers from the Mediterranean countries. The number of aliens in Belgium rose from 368,000 in 1947 to 805,000 in 1974 when they constituted somewhat over 8 percent of the total population.[1] The majority of foreign workers are now from countries with whom Belgium has a labor recruitment agreement. The inflow of aliens with divergent cultural backgrounds had already begun in the late 1950s. In 1964, 85 percent of all in-migrants were arriving from the Mediterranean basin and only 8.5 percent that year came from the neighboring countries.[2]

Demographic Trends

The recent growth in the Belgian population is due mostly to the aliens in the country. Representing 8.2 percent of the total population in 1974, they accounted for 16.8 percent of all births. Not only have the in-migrants a higher fertility while in Belgium, but also their in-migrating families tend to be larger than Belgian families. The net in-migration accounted for most of the population increase during the last few years. Between 1970 and 1974 the number of registered aliens in Belgium increased by 119,426,[3] while the number of Belgian nationals remained the same despite the 5,000 persons added through naturalizations during that period.

The census of 1970 indicated that the average age of aliens is younger than that of Belgians. The birth rate of aliens was 23 and 21 and the death rate 5.5 and 4.8 per 1,000 nationals in 1970 and 1974 respectively. In the city of Brussels the modal age of foreign workers in 1970 was between 20 and 24 years; men aged between 20 and 29 years represented 38 percent of the number of alien men, while women in the same age category represented 35 percent of alien women.[4]

---

[1] G. Dooghe. *De Bevolking in Belgie. Demografisch Overzicht.* Brussels: Centrum voor Bevolkings-en Gezinstudien. Technical Report No. 10. 1976.

[2] Fr. Denis. "Toekomstbeeld der Immigratie in Belgie", *Maandblad Arbeid*, 6:465-478. 1965; N. Fineau. "Free Movement of Migrant Workers in Belgium", *Migration News*, 23(3):21-24. 1974.

[3] G. Dooghe. *De Bevolking in Belgie. Demografisch Overzicht.* Brussels: Centrum voor Bevolkings-en Gezinstudien. Technical Report No. 10. 1976.

[4] *Bulletin de Statistique*, 62:438. 1976.

TABLE 7:2
Migratory Flows of Aliens Into and Out of Belgium,
by Selected Countries of Out-Migration, by Proportion Males, Between 1971-1975

Countries of Origin and Percent of Male Migrants		Years						1971-1975
		1971		1973		1975		
		In	Out	In	Out	In	Out	Net Migration
EEC (except Italy)	N	26,154	21,729	29,895	24,439	29,352	26,026	21,996
Percent	M	51	46	50	49	49	50	61
Italy	N	10,931	7,132	9,340	7,653	7,003	6,808	9,146
Percent	M	60	57	59	57	59	58	66
Greece	N	727	480	643	821	809	758	36
Percent	M	48	42	49	49	56	49	88[a]
Spain	N	2,304	2,112	1,542	2,781	1,224	2,720	−4,718
Percent	M	45	44	49	46	54	47	44
Turkey	N	3,197	637	2,951	843	7,323	799	18,139
Percent	M	53	58	54	57	54	54	55
Yugoslavia	N	786	208	854	454	810	404	2,002
Percent	M	56	57	64	67	60	69	60
Other Europe	N	2,786	1,460	3,086	1,914	3,371	2,039	5,904
Percent	M	49	50	49	49	50	51	48
All Others and Total	N	62,708	41,608	64,250	49,431	69,886	50,308	88,417
Percent	M	54	51	53	52	54	53	60

Note: [a] Absolute number; net migration of females was −52.
Sources: Institut National de Démographie. Mouvement de la population étrangère. Statistiques Démographiques (Brussels), 1976, 4:85-98. Figures compiled.

In-migration Regulations

Article 128 of the Kingdom of Belgium guarantees all aliens the same legal protection given to nationals. The legislation of March 23, 1958, stipulates that aliens in Belgium need a valid passport, sufficient means of subsistence, must not be known to the police as criminal, and must abide by regulations protecting public peace and order and safeguarding the national security.[5]

The Royal Edict of November 6, 1967 restricts employment in Belgium to aliens holding a valid work permit. There are three classes of work permits: Class A, is for workers of member states of the European Community, allowing free movement and is issued upon request; Class B, is valid for one worker for one employer, for one industry and for a specified period, which is usually one year; and Class C, is valid for special designated occupations usually of the professional or related nature but not stipulating a specific employer.[6]

Belgium presently maintains bilateral agreements with Algeria, Morocco, Tunisia, Turkey and Yugoslavia which regulate the recruitment of workers.[7] The agreements control the issuing of work permits, usually those of Class B. Whereas, in the past, entry into the country depended on the individual's ability to secure work, these agreements streamline the matter. Until 1967, aliens were eligible for a full equality in employment with the nationals after a ten year stay in the country. Now the waiting period has been reduced to five years for the nationals from preferred countries. Aliens married to Belgian nationals, or who are parents of Belgian children, are in the same legal position as Belgians in matters of work mobility.

The Royal Edict of November 6, 1967 introduced stricter controls on the employment of foreigners. Aliens seeking work in Belgium were, as a result, required to go through the consular offices abroad. The National Employment Office *(Office National de l'Emploi)* checked the application and awarded a work permit only if no resident in Belgium was willing or qualified to fill the vacancy. This procedure slowed down the influx of new aliens into Belgium, particularly beginning with the year 1970.

The restrictive policies on in-migration brought with them illegal in-migration, a new problem for Belgium.[8] Under pressure to act on it, the Minister for Employment and Labor issued a form of amnesty dated April 1, 1974. The order was intended to regularize the illegal stay of those already in the country and working. The ministerial order required that all aliens illegally in Belgium prior to April 1, 1974 must register with the National

[5] *Revue Trimestrielle de Droit Belge*, 30:291f. 1970.

[6] *Moniteur Belge*, 11:11. 1967; *Revue Trimestrielle de Droit Belge*, 31:28, 1971, 32:463. 1972.

[7] G. Campioli. "Les Étrangers en Belgique. Notes sur la Littérature Sociologique et Quelques autres Travaux", *Studi Emigrazione*, 13:219-234. 1976.

[8] C. Braeckman. *Étrangers en Belgique*. Bruxelles: Edition Vie Oeuvrière. 1973.

Employment Office by October 31, 1974 or apply for a work permit through their employer. The number of illegal aliens in the country was estimated at that time to be about 20,000.

In another effort to solve the difficult problem of monitoring aliens and to regularize their stay, a new legislation was put into effect in October, 1976. It reduced, to six years from ten, the number of years an alien must stay in the country and work to be eligible for a free work permit. Foreign workers, covered by a special agreement with Greece, Malta, Morocco, Switzerland and Turkey need now only four years of stay and political refugees need only three years of continuous stay and work to qualify for this permanent work permit. The last two groups can obtain a permanent work permit after only one year if their families accompany them and they appear well settled.

On the other hand, the new legislation all but bars in-migrants to Belgium unless specifically recruited. Those from the member states of the European Communities are, of course, exempt from any restrictions. The new measures were enacted to yield to the pressure from labor unions to stabilize the labor force and to limit the inflow of unskilled workers. The unions expected the new measure to push up wage levels in those branches of industry and the service sector which have been employing large numbers of foreign workers at relatively low wages. It should be kept in mind that Belgium has the highest unemployment of the Benelux countries and that Belgium unemployment is considered to be linked with the relatively large foreign labor force.

Integration of Aliens

With recent legislation to restrict in-migration of workers, Belgium has joined most of the other labor importing countries in Europe. The present strategy is to integrate those aliens already in the country and to discourage others from coming. Of course, Belgium had a well developed system of alien integration. In the case of recruited labor, preparatory steps to a potential integration was taken before the arrival of foreign workers. The incoming workers were informed about their legal and social welfare rights, housing, language and vocational training programs, and about the conditions for naturalization. The information was offered in languages of the major in-migrant groups. One specific point made was to stress the legal status of the wife.

Useful information to in-migrants is being disseminated by the mass media in the respective languages. There are, for example, regional and local "welcome stations" offering interpreter service during the first few weeks of stay. In addition, there are now about 25 local and provincial advisory councils to deal with foreign workers' adjustment problems.[9] The in-migrant workers have the right to join trade unions and to interest themselves in local politics. They may vote for candidates to community consultative councils and can be elected to the councils. In 1975, 25 workers held seats on these councils.

A ministerial decree of October, 1969 provides for language training in French for aliens working in Belgium. The wording of the decree is such, however, that it requires an initiative on the part of the potential users. Consequently, it remains unexploited. Children under 16 years of age are subject to compulsory school attendance. The mother tongue of the in-migrants is not normally taught at school; the consular services of the sending countries offer language courses, but their effectiveness is difficult to evaluate. Many large firms offer language courses in French since it saves the cost of interpreters in the long run. Without the knowledge of French, however, chances for an occupational improvement remain slim. The national employment office sponsors vocational training courses for all. At first these were not well taken advantage of by the foreign workers but, since 1973, the courses have been in demand. Unfortunately, at about the same time, budgetary restrictions forestalled any expansion, or improved staffing of such courses.

The in-migrant workers to Belgium are eligible for all social welfare provisions as are the nationals. In addition, they receive a reimbursement of up to 50 percent of the costs of travel for their dependents joining them in Belgium. The newly arrived dependents receive assistance when looking for employment. Furthermore, the government subsidizes pastoral services for most denominations the in-migrants may belong to.

Naturalization

The Act of March 17, 1964 on naturalization of aliens, stipulates a continuous residence in the country for ten years to be eligible for Belgian citizenship. However, after six years of stay, an alien may apply for ordinary naturalization and be considered a Belgian subject. The difference rests in the type of passport one carries, only fully naturalized persons carry Belgian passports. Naturalizations do not seem to take place very fast. Between 1963 and 1972, for instance, there were approximately 12,000 naturalizations in toto. The annual number of naturalizations varies considerably.[10]

[9] P. Baton. *Coéducation d'Enfants Belges et Étrangers*. Brussels: Institut de Sociologie de l'Université Libre de Bruxelles. 1968.

[10] *Migration News*, 1:38. 1974.

THE NETHERLANDS

An exception among the industrial countries of Europe, population growth in the Netherlands has always been fairly rapid. With a population of 13.5 million, the Netherlands are today the largest of the Benelux countries and the only one with an active out-migration policy pursued since World War II. This policy strived to ease the population pressure at home by actively encouraging emigration. Around 1960, however, the need for labor at home discouraged emigration. Until that time the annual goal of the emigration policy was to send between 40,000 to 50,000 persons overseas.[11] Thus, during the fifteen years since the War about one-half million Dutch emigrated. The Netherlands government assisted emigrants financially at a cost of 2,000 guilders (about 500 U.S. dollars in 1950) per person.[12]

While actively pursuing a policy of emigration, the country was, nonetheless, receiving in-migrants. They were World War II displaced persons and refugees, political refugees (12,000 Moluccans, 3,000 Hungarians, 1,500 Czechoslovaks; and recently, a few hundred Ugandans and Chileans), and about 300,000 repatriates from Indonesia, the former Dutch East Indies. Added up, the number of in-migrants coincided with the number of emigrants.[13]

The need for additional and low cost labor which began to be felt around the end of the 1950s was initially met by Italians and Spaniards. The economic boom in Europe kept the nationals of the neighboring countries employed at home despite the agreement of 1964 whereby the nationals of the European Economic Community could move freely between the member states. The Netherlands were able to fill the gaps in their labor force by employing workers from their former dependencies, Surinam and the Netherlands Antilles. These workers were nationals of the Kingdom of the Netherlands. An estimated 150,000 Surinams were living in the Netherlands in 1975. In 1976, however, about 10,000 of them returned home after Surinam gained independence in November, 1975.

Despite the relatively heavy in-migrations, the proportion of aliens in the country has remained low for largely three reasons: 1) the former Dutch subjects are not being registered as aliens; 2) the Netherlands did maintain a

[11] W. Steigenga. *Industrialization — Emigration. The Consequences of the Demographic Developments in the Netherlands.* The Hague: Martinus Nijhoff. 1955; T. van den Brink. "Some Quantitative Aspects of Future Population Development in the Netherlands", *Some Aspects of Migration Problems in the Netherlands.* G. Beyer and J.J. Oudesgeest, eds. The Hague: Martinus Nijhoff. 1952. Pp. 40-58.

[12] J. Tinbergen. "Investment, Balance of Payment and Welfare". Lecture. Utrecht, October 17, 1951.

[13] C. Bagley. "Immigration and Social Policy in the Netherlands", *New Community*, 1:25-28. 1971; H. Verwey-Jonker, ed. *Allochtonen in Nederland.* The Hague: Government Printers (second edition). 1973.

TABLE 7:3

Aliens in the Netherlands by Countries of Origin[a]
Since 1956 (as of January 1)

Year	European Community Except Italy	Italy	United Kingdom	Yugo-slavia	Spain	Morocco	Turkey	Others	Total
1956	50,063	3,993	4,531	953	233	10	47	46,650	106,480
1957	50,181	5,372	4,968	892	290	10	51	46,013	107,777
1958	49,497	6,518	5,182	889	300	8	59	48,140	110,593
1959	48,235	5,972	5,368	910	298	10	66	47,441	108,299
1960	47,608	5,232	5,668	858	329	10	72	47,241	107,018
1961	47,126	5,930	5,936	809	416	10	87	47,437	107,751
1962	47,627	8,509	6,022	788	1,487	17	163	48,265	112,869
1963	49,030	10,501	7,137	1,009	5,056	32	305	54,407	127,477
1964	49,798	11,441	7,838	1,266	8,470	257	1,172	54,550	134,792
1966	49,223	12,663	8,445	1,592	19,521	5,484	8,744	59,237	164,909
1967	50,593	14,172	9,919	2,985	23,412	1,427	14,464	75,450	192,422
1968	51,723	14,236	9,469	1,726	18,433	12,587	12,324	60,878	181,376

TABLE 7:3 (continued)

Aliens in the Netherlands by Countries of Origin
Since 1956 (as of January 1)

Year	European Community except Italy	Italy	United Kingdom	Yugo-slavia	Spain	Morocco	Turkey	Others	Total
1973	62,272	19,269	13,464	11,618	31,362	27,901	46,018	70,457	282,361
1974				12,900	31,300	33,205	62,600		316,300
1975				13,800	29,100	42,200	76,500		350,500

Note: [a] Nationals from nonmember states of the European Community (except Italy and United Kingdom — the latter only since 1974) who showed more than 10,000 persons in 1973 (in that year, Germans numbered 36,808 and Belgians 20,477). Returnees from Surinam, Antilles, and Moluccan Islands not included.

Sources: Ministerie van Justitie; H. Werner. "Migration and Free Movement of Workers in Western Europe", *International Migration* (Geneva, The Hague), 12(4):311-327. 1974; *Dutch Statistical Yearbook*, 1977. P. 28.

policy of worker rotation; and 3) the population of the Netherlands had been increasing by about 216,000 persons annually while the inflow of foreign workers at first was about 10,000 annually until the mid-1960s. In 1975, however, foreign workers numbered about 150,000. They were being supplemented by some 20,000 border commuters from Belgium and by about the same number from Germany. The total alien population was estimated to be 370,000 persons. Some 110,000 Dutch were estimated to be working in Germany and other neighboring countries.

In-migration Policy

The in-migration policy of the Dutch government was neither restrictive nor encouraging during the last 15 years or so. The government was anxious to assure that not too large an influx of foreigners would take place. This concern stemmed not only from economic considerations which at times looked quite promising, but rather from social considerations for the population density and the adaptation of in-migrants to the Dutch society. The government favored in-migration of single workers for a stay not to exceed three years. In this matter, the government found support from industry, unions, the churches and various private welfare organizations dealing with foreign workers.

Stricter admission standards for foreign workers went into effect in 1970. The recruitment of workers began to be channeled either through the recruitment offices abroad or through the Dutch consular offices and the number of provisional work permits became restricted.[14] A check at home also had to be made to verify that there was an employment vacancy and no indigenous workers available to fill it. The government attempted to check the inflow of unrecruited in-migrants entering illegally. An estimate for 1972 indicated about 20,000 illegal in-migrants in the country, representing about 12 to 15 percent of all foreign workers.

Starting with 1974, the policy of short term in-migration was being revised. An amnesty was declared for all workers illegally in the country. From this, about 12,000 illegal aliens became legalized. However, several hundred of the illegal in-migrants had to leave the country. The amnesty allowed the government to start insisting on an almost total restriction on new in-migration. Now, the work permit is being keyed to the job and to housing and is issued centrally by the Ministries of Economic and Social Affairs. To obtain any employment without a permit is now virtually impossible. The ceiling on work permits reflects the rising unemployment in the Netherlands.

[14] H. ter Heide. "Labor Migration from the Mediterranean Area to the Benelux Countries", *Population and Family in the Low Countries*. H.G. Moors et al., eds. Leiden: Martinus Nijhoff. 1976. Pp. 132-148.

Of course, workers from the member states of the European Communities remain unaffected by the new situation, as do the workers from countries who have an Association Treaty with the Netherlands, or where the Netherlands still entertain recruitment offices, such as in Morocco and Tunisia.

The Netherlands government tried to solve the problem of foreign workers by suggesting various policies of worker rotation. A much discussed plan envisaging a lump sum payment and a repayment of the old age pension contributions (12% of one's wages) was never realized.[15] Another plan to relate return migration to a development program in the country of origin proved difficult to operate. It consisted of offering returnees a training in technical and industrial skills over and above those acquired during their employment in the Netherlands. The plan was opposed by the unions and by the public which saw in it a discrimination in reverse and an unnecessary strain on the public purse.

Another alternative to solve the problem of in-migrants has been before the Parliament since 1975. This proposal entails rather harsh measures: in-migration should be restricted as much as possible and illegal in-migrants sent home; work permits should be issued to employers, but not to individual workers; and work permits should carry a mandatory maximum of two years, be tied to a specific job description, limit geographical mobility of foreign workers and there should be a fixed ceiling on the number of permits issued.[16] Thus far, there has been considerable public sentiment against the proposed measures. The proposed Act did pass the Second Chamber of Parliament recently and it needs to pass now the First Chamber to become a law. There is a strong opposition to this legislation by organizations of foreign workers who are being supported by several Dutch civic action groups. Their main argument is that the law will allow action to be brought against only the illegal in-migrant and not against his employer who profits by employing him.

The In-Migration Policy in Force

In principle, in-migration is open to all persons in possession of a valid identification document and falling under the various intergovernmental agreements between the Netherlands and the labor supplying countries, which include: Greece, Morocco, Tunisia, Portugal, Spain, Turkey, Yugoslavia and the member states of the European Communities. The in-migrant must have some means of subsistence, or a guaranteed job and acceptable housing.

---

[15] *Ibid.*

[16] F. Lüscher. "Justice and Migration", *Migration Today*, 20:107-109. 1976.

TABLE 7:4

Annual Arrivals and Ratios of Arrivals to Departures for Aliens
in the Netherlands, by Major Sending Countries, Between 1965 and 1972

Year	Italy		Spain		Portugal		Morocco		Yugoslavia		Turkey	
	Arr	Ratio[a]	Arr	Ratio	Arr	Ratio	Arr	Ratio	Arr	Ratio	Arr	Ratio
1965	2,645	166	11,407	228	1,061	528	5,287	723	577	217	5,444	518
1966	2,364	142	8,910	138	1,438	328	9,111	557	967	250	6,890	409
1967	1,444	84	2,508	34	546	126	1,234	51	373	48	1,564	47
1968	1,675	111	3,430	98	756	274	2,783	291	1,280	242	4,580	294
1969	2,064	153	5,738	205	820	497	3,395	756	2,964	325	7,725	652
1970	1,921	140	7,632	236	1,212	635	5,938	1425	4,991	427	7,009	585
1971	1,835	123	7,683	182	1,170	696	3,827	544	5,159	302	10,167	551
1972	1,287	107	4,072	83	773	405	2,304	120	2,396	357	6,822	171

Note: [a] A value of 100 represents a perfect balance between arrivals and departures; higher values represent percent multiples of arrivals over departures and vice versa.

Sources: Central Bureau voor de Statistick; H. Werner, "Migration and Free Movement of Workers in Western Europe", International Migration (Geneva, The Hague), 12(4):311-327. 1974.

A medical examination is also required to receive a work permit which is issued by the local magistrate. Residence permits are issued by the Aliens Registration Office and are either for a limited or an unlimited period of time. The in-migrant may appeal his case by writing to the Minister of Justice should he feel discriminated against in the matter of the residence or work permit. The in-migrant must not be a known criminal, nor may he represent a threat to public order. He must obey and respect the laws of the country. Naturalization of foreigners is possible after five years of uninterrupted stay; the number of naturalizations taking place annually remains small and is not more than a few thousand.

Once the in-migrant has been admitted, he enjoys the same rights as the Dutch: employment is obtained or changed through the Employment Office and the in-migrant is guaranteed the same minimal wages as the Dutch workers. The newcomer is also required to pay taxes and must contribute to the social security plan, including old age pension and the health insurance program as well as unemployment insurance. Union membership is not compulsory, but it has been increasing rapidly after the Dutch unions created sections specifically to answer the needs of foreigners. After one year in the country, the alien may bring his family, provided he has suitable accommodations. There are several social aid organizations which assist foreigners searching for housing and there are social services developed to meet the needs of in-migrants. The major problem remaining is that of language, and this is being overcome by radio and television language broadcasts, which offer information on topics of interest covering the Netherlands and the respective home countries. Attention is also paid by the information media to inform the in-migrants about the rights of their family members, especially of their wives. Additional information, also in the respective languages, is printed and distributed by the unions.

Children of in-migrants are subject to the same schooling provisions as are the Dutch. There are approximately 12,000 foreign children enrolled in school, not including children of parents from the former dependencies of Surinam, the Dutch Antilles and the Moluccan Islands. The sending countries provide additional schooling for children of their nationals. In 1976, there were 686 such schools. Furthermore, in schools with a large proportion of in-migrant children, teachers from the principal sending countries are often employed on the teaching staff.

The Dutch government subsidizes language programs at work and offers adult education programs evenings. It is also running various adult retraining programs so that the foreign workers can improve their employment qualifications. There are, presently, about 25 such vocational schools. The efforts of the government are being supplemented by the efforts of the Foundation for Socio-Cultural Cooperation, created to meet the issues of social and cultural adaptation of in-migrants.

With the exception of taking part in the local elections (local and municipal councils), the foreign workers are not eligible to vote even though they may interest themselves in politics. On the whole, the provisions the Netherlands have for the foreign in-migrants are those of an immigration country official disclaimers notwithstanding. The foreign workers in the Netherlands consider that they have as many rights and as many freedoms as they may wish.[17] Their numbers are not likely to decrease in the foreseeable future, as the government economic forecasts call for a reduced, but continuing, in-migration to guarantee the smooth development of the economy.[18]

LUXEMBURG

The wealth of Luxemburg is based on the country's iron ore deposits and the national wellbeing reflects the fluctuations in the price of steel. Given Luxemburg's small size and its geo-political location, it is not surprising that international economics are an essential element in the prosperity of this "gift of iron", as Luxemburg is often called.[19] The correlation of Luxemburg's Gross National Product and the production of steel is undeniable. Luxemburg's high standard of living is due chiefly to two causes: the economic make-up of the country and the proportionately large labor force, which is mostly a result of the contribution of aliens to the working age population. The proportion of foreign workers in Luxemburg is perhaps the highest in Europe. Some foreign workers commute daily across the border from Belgium, Germany and France, but most of the workers are in-migrants.[20]

In the decade of the 1950s, net in-migration averaged about 1,000 persons annually and this number increased to about 2,000 net in-migrants annually during the decade of the 1960s. Since about 1970, the net annual intake of foreigners is about 2,500 persons, including children of aliens born in Luxemburg.[21] In 1975, about 25 percent of Luxemburg's population was foreign born.

[17] E. Bovenkerk. "Dutch Immigration Policy and the Myth of Return", *International Migration*, 13:147-150. 1975.

[18] K. van der Windt. "Bevolking en welzijn in Nederland. Eindrapport Commissie Muntendam", *Nederlandse Staatscourant*, 30:6-17. 1977.

[19] G. Als. *Luxemburg: Historic, Geographic and Economic Profile*. Luxemburg: Service Central de la Statistique. 1976.

[20] H. Heyden. "Diskussion über die Ausländerbeschäftigung im Europa", *Bundesarbeitsblatt*, 24(1):33-36. 1973.

[21] Service Central de la Statistique et des Etudes Economiques (Luxemburg). *Projections Démographiques 1974-2000*. Luxemburg: Ministère de l'économie national. Débats parlementaires sur le projet de budget 1975. Pp. 10. Mimeo. 1975.

TABLE 7:5

Foreign Workers in Luxemburg,
by Selected Countries of Origin, Between 1961 and 1972

Countries	Years								
	1961	1962	1964	1966	1968	1969	1970	1971	1972
Germany	3,700	3,700	3,700	3,900	3,900	4,000	3,900	3,900	3,800
Belgium	2,900	3,100	3,900	4,600	4,800	5,100	5,600	6,200	6,700
France	1,400	1,600	2,700	4,000	4,300	4,600	5,000	5,500	6,200
Italy	10,500	11,300	11,300	12,400	11,300	11,100	11,000	11,000	10,900
Spain	100	300	900	1,200	900	1,100	1,200	1,700	1,700
Portugal	—	100	400	900	1,100	1,800	3,700	6,300	8,500
Total including All Others	20,900	22,400	25,200	29,400	28,600	30,100	33,100	37,500	40,900

Sources: Office National du Travail (Luxemburg); H. Werner. *Freizügigkeit der Arbeitskräfte und die Wanderungsbewegungen in den Ländern der Europäischen Gemeinschaft. Mitteilungen aus der Arbeitsmarkt-und Berufsforschung* (Nürnberg), 1973, No. 4. Adapted.

Demographic Trends

Demographically, the native population is not replacing itself. Foreigners represented about 10 percent of the total population in 1947; 13 percent in 1960; 18 percent in 1970; and 23 percent in 1974. Demographic projections up to the year 2000 estimate the proportion of foreign population to reach about 34 percent.[22] In absolute numbers that would mean 130,000 aliens to 252,000 native born. In 1976, foreigners numbered 84,000 in Luxemburg. On the whole, however, the age and sex composition of the alien population in Luxemburg does not promise much of a natural growth. In 1972, females represented 20.8 percent of the Portuguese, 4.2 percent of the Spanish and one percent of the Yugoslav in-migrants. In the same year, 9,700 of 40,900 foreign workers were females. Births to foreigners numbered 1,303 in 1967, and 1,591 in 1974, representing 12.2 percent of all births, which was less than the proportion of aliens in the population of the country.[23]

In-Migration Policy in Force

The National Labor Office controls all recruitment of labor, and prospective employers direct their requests to that office. Recruitment officers abroad arrange for medical examinations and the selection of workers to whom they issue work permits. Upon arrival, the work permit holders are rechecked at the local police precinct, a feature of alien control distinctive to Luxemburg. The Ministry of Labor is the final instance in the work permits. Belgian citizens have been exempted from work permits since 1926, Dutch workers since the inception of the Benelux Treaty and nationals of the European Communities receive work permits upon request.

In-migrant workers have been on an equal footing with Luxemburg nationals since March, 1954. In 1957, a bilateral agreement with Italy was the first bilateral agreement on the recruitment of labor. It was followed, since then, by similar agreements with other countries of the Mediterranean basin. Foreign workers' rights extend to the working conditions, wages, dismissal procedures, assistance by the employment office in changing jobs, occupational training (although they have no special programs only for foreign workers) and union membership. In contrast to Belgium and the Netherlands, aliens have not as yet the right to be represented on the community consultative councils, nor are there plans to give them the right to take part in the local elections.

A Social Service Program was instituted in 1964 to foster the social integration of foreigners. The program encompasses such diverse activities

[22] *Ibid.*

[23] G. Als. *La population du Luxembourg.* Luxemburg: Service Central de la Statistique. 1975.

as helping to search for suitable housing, orientation of foreigners as to health care, and financial assistance for the cases of repatriation. New housing for foreign workers totals now four homes with 260 beds each for single workers. Of the new construction of 2,600 dwelling units annually, some 40 percent go to foreign workers. In addition, the employers of foreign workers receive a governmental subsidy for housing construction for their workers.

The children of foreigners are required to attend school as are children of nationals. The government of Luxemburg, however, subsidizes the instruction of these children in their native tongue. Exact statistics on the utilization of such a language program are, unfortunately, not available. In many instances it is the schooling of their children which discourages foreigners in Luxemburg to return home. Those few who do return, report the difficulties their children face in schools back home. Essential information on legal matters and changes of governmental migration policy are broadcast or distributed in printed form in the major languages of in-migrants. There are also radio and television language courses for foreigners.

Naturalization in Luxemburg is difficult. It can take place only after a continuous residence of 10 years or, in exceptional cases, after 5 years of continuous residence.[24] The naturalization figures have doubled since 1950 even though they remain relatively low. Naturalizations represent only 0.75 percent of the number of foreign workers in the country in any given year.

A Comparative Overview

Short term measures of population policies dealing with in-migration cannot be an end in themselves. They must be integrated with a wide range of policies of social welfare. It is true that population policies are hardly mentioned in the discussions of social policies. If they are referred to, they deal strictly with the demography of the foreign workers and their families.[25]

The economic circumstances surrounding foreign workers in the Benelux countries have evolved as follows: 1) all three countries have witnessed in-migration of labor at first from the neighboring and then from more distant countries; 2) large in-migration of labor adversely affected wages especially in those sectors of industry and services already characterized by low wages; 3) in-migrant labor had beneficial effects on the national economies during the period of growth. The link, however, between in-migrant labor and national economic growth is quite complex, involving relationships between

[24] *Ibid.*

[25] D.J. van de Kaa. "Demographic Change and Social Policy: A European Perspective", *Demographic Change and Social Policy*. M. Buxton and E. Craven, eds. London: Centre for Studies in Social Policies. 1976. Pp. 62-71.

a greater labor mobility, lower wages and higher investments. On the other hand, limiting the number of foreign workers during periods of economic recession does not necessarily bring a corresponding drop in the national unemployment; 4) should the number of foreign workers in the country diminish, the average wages are expected to rise because there would be, a) fewer wage earners in the low paying jobs while, b) investment in labor saving devices would depress the level of employment. It seems that at a certain stage of economic development foreign labor is indispensable given an interdependent and/or complementary production structure.[26]

The social circumstances of foreign workers seem to be: 1) they do receive equal pay for equal work as the native born but they do not receive equal work. That is, foreign workers are overrepresented in jobs paying low wages and having unpleasant working conditions. During recessions, e.g. in 1967-1968 and 1974-1975, particularly in Belgium and the Netherlands, foreign workers showed a higher level of unemployment than the nationals, but even in 1977 they did not show any sign of wanting to return home; 2) in theory, foreign workers enjoy all the civil rights except the right to an elected national office. In practice, there are a number of pressures which tend to place the foreign workers at a disadvantage. In any case, even the disadvantaged situation appears to the foreign workers as a preferable option to returning home. The effort to facilitate worker rotation or out-migration was not successful, as shown in the case of the Netherlands. For humanitarian reasons, it is even difficult to repatriate the illegal in-migrants; and 3) the demographic impact of in-migration can be quite significant as in the case of Luxemburg. However, labor recruitment did proceed mostly unaware of the demographic requirements of the country. If in-migrants are accepted for the purpose to fill the gap in the domestic demographic structure, they should be given a just chance to settle permanently and to enjoy all the privileges bestowed on the nationals. In particular, the children of in-migrants born or educated in their new countries should not be denied naturalization should they desire it. Such an enlightened policy must, by necessity, be very selective[27] and it would have been at odds with a policy to import cheap labor.

The question presents itself whether the economic growth and welfare of labor importing countries will continue to require additional in-migration with the naturalization of aliens, or whether the labor importing countries will not have to realize rather soon that they must come to terms and live without such an irresponsible intake of foreign labor.

[26] M.H. Bussery. "Incidence sur l'Économie Française d'une Réduction Durable de la Main-d'Oeuvre Immigrée", *Économie et Statistique*, 3:37-45. 1976.

[27] H. Wander. *Demographic Aspects of the Active Population.* Paper before the Seminar on the Implications of a Stationary or Declining Population in Europe. Strasbourg, Council of Europe. September, 1976. Pp. 12.

8

France*

YANN MOULIER
National Foundation for Political Sciences

GEORGES TAPINOS
*National Institute for Demographic Studies and
Institute for Political Studies*

Immigration History

RARELY a country of emigration, France became a country of immigration during the peak of the overseas European emigration movement. Records in France list 100,000 foreigners in 1800, 38,000 in 1851, 800,000 in 1876 and 1,150,000 in 1911. Just before World War I, immigrant population in France was 2.8 percent of the total population and 3.2 percent of the labor force.

Migration to France followed the general migration patterns in Europe before World War I, that is, they were primarily individual and economically motivated. Even though the pace of industrialization in France was uneven and restricted essentially to large scale enterprises and heavy industry, the country was still able to attract a fair number of foreign workers from neighboring countries.

In the two single attempts in France to regulate the inflow of foreign labor from abroad by bilateral treaties, in 1908 and in 1911, France entered into agreements with Italy and Poland to assure a supply of manpower for agriculture, coal and metal working industries respectively. The treaties

---

* Adapted from the French by Daniel Kubat.

covered administrative matters in France, but did not express the logistics of recruiting and transporting the workers and the yield of the treaties proved disappointing.

World War I and After

World War I exacerbated the chronic labor shortage in France and the government saw itself compelled to look for additional labor in the colonies. During the War, France accepted 500,000 workers. The entry of the French government into labor recruitment required an expansion of the governmental administrative apparatus dealing with foreigners. By 1917, the administrative controls included the issuing of ID cards, and of work and residence permits.[1] After World War I, France experienced a heavy immigration. Between 1921 and 1930, close to two million persons were admitted into France as immigrants and France ranked second, after the United States, in volume of immigration. In 1931, the 2.7 million foreigners represented 6.5 percent of the population in France.

The immigration to France after World War I was of a different character than the immigration prior to the War. In the first place, the source countries changed from Northwest Europe to Southern and Central Europe, in particular Italy, Spain, Portugal and Poland. There was also a fair number of Russian *emigrés* settling in France. Secondly, the skill levels of the new immigrants were, on the whole, lower than the skill levels of the earlier immigrants. The new immigrants found their employment in the new chemical industries and in the newer branches of the metal working industries, although the traditional placement of immigrants in construction, mines and textile factories continued. The third distinguishing characteristic of the post World War I immigration was the system of recruitment. The potential migrants were actively recruited abroad and often transported into France collectively. This was done primarily through the recruitment offices of the *Societé Générale d'Immigration*, de facto an arm of the Association of Mines and Metallurgy Industries. The administrative aspects of immigration in France as well as the medical selection and screening of immigrants were still left to the French government. Starting with 1926, the French government took a greater role in the selection and recruitment process of foreign workers abroad and began to control the regional distribution of immigrant labor at home as well, in an attempt to channel the foreign workers to agriculture and to avoid intrasectorial mobility toward

[1] J.C. Bonnet. *Les Pouvoirs Publics Francais et l'Immigration dans l'Entre Deux Guerres.* Lyon: Université du Lyon II, Centre d'Histoire économique et sociale de la région lyonnaise. 1976.

industry.[2]

Immigration to France was never completely interrupted during the depression of the 1930s, although the Act of 1932 gave explicit priority to the indigenous labor and to migrants already settled in France, thus proving an effective curb on the continued influx of new migrants. There were also various financial incentives being offered to foreigners to leave France. The effects of such measures, however, are difficult to evaluate; although some of the immigrants undoubtedly left as a result of these measures, new immigrants, mostly refugees from Spain, Germany and Central Europe, added to the number of foreigners in the country. In 1936 there were 2.2 million foreigners in France, one-half million fewer than five years earlier. Naturalizations, however, may have accounted for some of the nominal loss of foreigners. World War II eased the problem of unemployment at home and the French labor force was diminished by 300,000 workers transferred to Germany under the Vichy regime in the German occupied portion of France.

World War II and After

The number of foreigners working in France in 1946 has been estimated at 935,000. At that time, the French economy was well below its prewar capacity. The French government took a keen interest in matters of population in the interest of a rapid rebuilding of the country. Abandoning the essentially laissez-faire attitude to immigration, the French government adopted a population expansion policy.

At this time the French government was being informed by two essentially disparate counsels: The French National Demographic Institute *(Institut National des Etudes Démographiques)* which counseled for the immigration of families;[3] the economically oriented State Planning Office *(Commissariat Général au Plan)* which counseled for the short term labor infusions according to demand. The First Plan of economic recovery and development (1946-1951) projected immigration needs ranging between one and one-half million persons.[4] Such a large number of immigrants needed to be administratively encompassed. For that reason, the French government created a National Immigration Office *(Office National d'Immigration)* in 1946 to handle all foreign migration into the country. The Ministerial Order of October, 1945, provided a *code des nationalités* (naturalization) and

---

[2] *Ibid.*

[3] L. Chevalier. *Problèmes Francais de l'Immigration.* Paris: Cours de Droit. 1947.

[4] G. Tapinos. *L'Immigration Étrangère en France (1946-1973).* Paris: Presses Universitaires Françaises. 1975.

introduced a distinction between a labor permit and a resident card, the two of which had previously been linked together.

France was not successful in its immigration plans. By 1954, the proportion of foreigners in the country was 3.6 percent of the entire population; only slightly less than eight years earlier. Italy was expected to become the main sending country for in-migrants and a bilateral agreement in 1947 which projected the in-migration of about 200,000 Italians proved inadequate, as only 49,000 Italians in-migrated to France in the years following the agreement. The Office tried to direct migrants to specific regions in France and to specific occupations suffering from labor shortages. These same regions and jobs were, of course, not always attractive. Over the years, an adaptive response was developed by would-be immigrants: illegal immigration. It was illegal only in terms that it was not channeled through the Office.[5] The major source of manpower immigration was Algeria. Between 1946 and 1949, 265,000 Algerians entered France, well above the 85,000 figure planned for by the Office. Of course, residents of Algeria were citizens of France starting in the year 1947 and thus were exempt from the controls imposed on other immigrants by the Office. In 1948, there were about 100,000 Algerians in France and the estimate for 1954 was 240,000. The National Immigration Office was reorganized and its administrative priorities were placed on immigration of whole families instead of on the specific priorities of industries or manpower short geographic areas. In this respect, the immigration *per se* gained ascendance over the philosophy of immigration as a stop-gap measure for manpower shortages.

The First Expansion: 1956-1966

Between 1956 and 1966, the Office registered a threefold increase in immigrant registrations as compared to the previous ten year period. The total of the officially processed immigrants for this period was 966,000, 38 percent of whom were Spanish immigrants. During this period there were 305,000 naturalizations and in 1965, the entire number of aliens registered in France reached 2,323,000. Including Algerians into the total, aliens in France increased by about one million during this period.[6]

Initially, the reasons for the increase in immigration to France lay in the fact that all the countries of Northwest Europe began to enter their own "economic miracles" in the middle of the 1950s, thus starting large scale migrations originating in the countries of the Mediterranean basin. France, due to its military involvement in Algeria and demographic insufficiency,

---

[5] L. Gani. *Syndicate et Travailleurs Immigrés*. Paris: Editions Sociales. 1972.

[6] G. Tapinos. *L'Immigration Étrangère en France (1946-1973)*. Paris: Presses Universitaires Françaises. 1975.

began to experience an acute scarcity of labor. Economically, France remained attractive to immigrants, an attractiveness which was later ceded to Switzerland and Germany in particular. Until the French conflict with Algeria was finally settled in 1962, France had lost some manpower to military draft. Prior to that, however, Italy eventually did become one of the important labor producing countries for France. In 1957, France attracted about 90,000 Italian workers who enjoyed numerical dominance among the immigrants to France until 1960, when they still represented 53 percent of all migrants in that year. Soon after, however, Spanish immigration gained an ascendancy which lasted until 1966, when their numerical majority in the immigrant inflow was taken over by the Portuguese. In the mid-1960s the economic attractiveness of the European Communities countries surpassed that of France and migrants followed the promise of better jobs and higher wages, despite the ease with which France allowed the in-migrants to bring their families. All in all, the attractiveness of increased wages and, perhaps, of better working conditions, seem to have had a greater persuasiveness than family unity.

A prominent feature of the in-migration movement to France during this period is the liberality of control over entry into the country. The liberal controls were not only a function of the emerging freedom of movement among the member states of the European Economic Community, but were also a product of the fact that the residents of the French colonies or territories, with allegiance to France, had, de facto, free movement privileges: by finding a job upon arrival, they were issued residence and work permits. The practice of entering France and then, of "immigration from within", persisted as it was simpler than to try to register with the Office. The National Immigration Office presented bureaucratic obstacles to a population unaccustomed to such even after a restructuring and streamlining of the immigration procedures. As a matter of fact, the French government issued regulations in 1964 to streamline the immigration "from within". The regulations were issued primarily in response to the needs of the Portuguese who, at that time, still needed permits from their own government to emigrate. These were illegal emigrants from Portugal and thus ineligible to avail themselves of the services of the Office. The restrictions in Portugal were directed toward the categories of persons deemed illiterate, those subject to be called into the military, and those coming from areas plagued by high unemployment, all three categories, no doubt, overlapping.

Immigration from Within: Numerically, how significant were the "regularizations" of the illegal immigrants? In 1956, 28 percent of foreign labor entrants were those who became "regularized" in that year. The corresponding figures for 1961 and 1969 were 46 percent and 80 percent respectively.

Even though immigration by "regularization" helped France to meet the numerical goal of its immigration plan, it has essentially weakened the administrative grip of France on the allocation of immigrants to areas and occupations most in need of manpower. The system of work permits was devised to regulate the distribution of foreign workers. Work permits issued to first time applicants were valid for one year, for one job, and for one *departement*, an administrative region the size of a large county. The second time around, permits were issued for three years, but for one job and in one region. After that, the permits were issued with a ten year validity, without geographical restrictions. Political refugees and aliens who had had a work permit for at least ten years, did receive a permanent work permit without any restrictions when working for an employer.

To avoid being locked into unattractive jobs or areas, the illegal immigrants sought suitable jobs first before applying for a work permit. This resulted in a high rate of job turnover, as the types of jobs available to illegal immigrants were seldom those preferred for long term employment. In 1975 the French government simplified the work permit system to cut down on the initial employment turnover.

Algeria and Immigration: Immigration to France, although responsive to the economic fluctuations, remained immune to the changes in the French native born labor force. The demustering French at the end of the Algerian War in 1963 did not affect the inflow of foreigners into France. At the same time, the inflow of Algerians to France increased considerably. The French labor force increased by a total of 430,000 workers in 1962; the foreign labor force by about 100,000. Between 1962 and 1965, net immigration to France was 717,000 workers of which 324,000 were repatriates, 100,000 were Algerians and 283,000 were "true" foreigners. The return of the "French" required in particular new housing and resettlement services, inducing a boom in the construction industry which, in turn, attracted additional foreign labor. Furthermore, the general resurgence of the French economy brought about transformations in the French occupational structure, making it possible for foreigners to be accepted into branches of industry previously not open to them. The increase of alien employees in industry between 1962 and 1968 was high compared to the French nationals: 29 percent versus 5 percent. The share of industrial jobs held by aliens increased from 9.5 percent in 1962 to 11.4 percent in 1968. That meant that alien workers increased numerically by a factor between 2 to 6, depending on the branch of the industry.[7]

[7] Commission Emploi. *Rapport (Préparation du VIe Plan)*. Paris: Documentation Française. Vols. I and II. 1972.

TABLE 8:1

Recent Immigration of Persons and Families to France,a
by Country of Origin, Annually, Since 1970

Country	1970		1971		1972		1973		1974		1975		1976c	
	Fams	Pers	Fams	Pers	Fams	Pers	Fams	Pers	Fams	Pers	Fams	Pers	Fams	Pers
Algeria	1,212	3,123	1,590	4,502	1,685	4,094	2,239	5,421	2,317	5,663	1,744	4,249	2,345	5,328
Italy	2,384	4,073	2,064	3,360	1,879	3,221	1,766	2,788	1,732	2,798	b	b	b	b
Morocco	2,239	5,925	2,790	5,939	3,758	9,041	5,301	12,075	6,095	13,798	5,159	10,801	7,164	16,140
Portugal	20,082	47,033	21,963	46,492	18,951	38,217	16,672	31,861	12,563	23,398	10,922	18,490	7,593	12,411
Spain	5,623	10,644	5,109	9,636	4,535	8,385	3,569	6,255	2,898	4,709	1,927	2,842	975	1,500
Tunisia	1,739	3,731	1,897	3,962	2,201	4,223	2,569	4,763	2,457	4,347	2,434	3,871	2,325	3,782
Turkey	182	359	346	763	534	1,169	1,171	2,732	2,261	5,551	2,729	6,991	2,961	8,124
Yugoslavia	1,924	2,703	2,057	2,517	1,884	2,374	2,006	2,523	1,833	2,395	1,199	1,571	824	1,113
Others	1,750	3,361	1,984	3,675	2,233	4,271	2,455	4,229	3,128	5,379	1,795	3,007	2,010	3,400
Total N	37,135	80,952	39,800	81,496	37,660	74,995	37,748	72,647	35,284	68,038	27,909	51,822	26,197	51,798

Notes: a Estimated population of France in 1975, 52 million.
b Data for families on nationals from the European Community not provided starting 1975.
c Eleven months only.

Source: Office National d'Immigration.

The Second Expansion: 1969-1973

The economic recession in 1966 and 1967 depressed immigration to France, but not so heavily as it depressed in-migrations to the other countries of the European Communities. An explanation may be sought in the nature of immigration to France, immigration being usually less responsive to economic conditions than worker in-migration. Between 1966 and 1973, net immigration to France reached 901,000 persons of which 210,000 were Algerians. This represents a faster immigration than that which took place during the preceding period. The peak period of immigration took place between the years 1969 and 1972. In 1970, the annual record high of 174,000 foreigners entered France to work. The economic expansion was rapid: in 1969, 90,000 new industrial jobs were created, more than the entire number of new jobs created during the preceding five years.[8]

Immigration from Algeria: In 1969 France and Algeria entered into an agreement to regulate the inflow of Algerian nationals (not French citizens anymore) to be about 35,000 annually. In 1971, construction and public works suffered a mild slowdown, reducing the inflow of new, primarily unskilled immigrants. The decline in immigrants averaged about 20 percent per year as compared to the base year of 1969. In 1972, there was a general decline in immigration from Algeria and in the number of immigrants from elsewhere.

The First Restrictions: Standardization of Admissions

Admission of immigrants to France has been based on distinguishing among the various countries of origin of immigrants. France distinguished between bona fide foreign countries whose emigrants were subject to the standard immigrant selection criteria, and between countries enjoying the status of favored nation. The latter status was extended essentially to countries which had been French colonies or administrative territories, for instance Algeria or the countries of Subsaharan Africa. Countries or territories still under French administration, such as some islands in the Caribbean, fall under the statute of free circulation of persons.

For all other foreign countries' citizens, immigration to France is subject to regulations as to the volume of immigration desired and other conditions and selection criteria as they may be imposed from time to time. Immigrants must be in possession of a valid work permit usually restricted as to duration, type of employment and geographic location where the job may be held.

[8] *Ibid.*

Immigration is subject to the administration by the National Immigration Office.

In actuality, control of immigration and keeping track of immigrants already in the country is rather difficult, for several reasons. Initially, the entrants from the French Caribbean may migrate freely and they were estimated to number between 150,000 and 180,000 in 1976 and to have had an immigration volume of about 10,000 persons annually. Secondly, nationals from the European Communities, previously allowed free movement only to jobs in which they were working for an employer, as of 1977 are allowed to enter France and practice professions independently. In the third place, until 1972, nationals from the favored nation status countries were able to enter the country de facto illegally as tourists and apply for "regularization" later. Many workers entering France from Algeria return home again after a year's stay or so and may be remigrating several times in succession. An agreement, initiated in 1964 between Algeria and France, to regulate migration between the two countries has not been successful. A subsequent agreement from December, 1968, attempted to lock Algerian immigrants into a controlled migration by use of residence permits.

The annual quota fixed by this agreement was reduced to 25,000 annually, as compared to the 35,000 annually stipulated earlier. Furthermore, the Algerian "tourists" were given nine months to find a permanent job and acquire a work permit in France or, they had to return home. All in all, too many categories of immigrants exempt from the "normal" immigration procedures made it difficult for the Office to keep track of immigration and to control it in any meaningful way. In 1973, the Arab community in France became subject to a racist campaign and terrorist activities directed against her members. A general nonunion strike of protest was organized and the Algerian government suspended out-migration completely in December, 1973.[9]

The major culprit for the inefficiency of the Office was the immigration from within, the practice of "regularizing" the de facto illegal in-migrants. In 1968, only one out of four vacancies going to foreign workers was filled through the Office. The only employment sector in which the Office had any modicum of success was in coal mining.

To deal with the problem of the immigration from within, the French government issued regulations in July, 1968, based on the regulations of 1964 which set the employment priority by immigration status. The 1968 regulations limited the practice of "regularization". However, three exceptions to the restrictions were allowed, effectively weakening an implementation of the restrictions: 1) Portuguese were exempt from having to immigrate

[9] S. Adler. *People in the Pipe-Line. The Political Economy of Algerian Migration to France 1962-1974.* Boston: Massachusetts Institute of Technology. September, 1975. Mimeo.

from abroad through the Office (in 1968 and 1969 about 90 percent of Portuguese immigrating to France have immigrated from within); and 2) household employees were exempt from the regularization restrictions (these were mostly Spanish or Portuguese women); and 3) skilled workers in designated occupations were also exempt.

The restrictions largely covered new immigrant workers. On the other hand, the reuniting of families was encouraged and was facilitated by the Office. A lesson learned earlier had been that once male immigrants have entered the country, their dependents were bound to follow. In discouraging new immigrants from Morocco, Tunisia, Turkey and Yugoslavia from gaining an immigration stream momentum, the Office was able to preclude a mass rejoining of families at a later date. In this respect, the new restrictions had some effect and "regularizations" did decline. As a consequence, an increasing number of employers had to turn to the Office to get their manpower. The French government set up a new National Employment Bureau to centralize information on job vacancies and placements.

The three categories of immigrants exempted from the restrictive policies began, soon enough, to gain in importance in proportion to the decline of other immigrants. All illegal immigrants were required to register with the National Immigration Office; if they belonged to one of the exempted categories, they would receive a favorable treatment. The Portuguese represented about one-half the number of all immigrants processed through the Office, not counting Algerians. Employers, particularly those in the construction industry began to reclassify their vacancies upward to make them fall into the designated categories and to have their employees "regularized".

By 1972, France had redefined the categories of immigration source countries into one category subject to the screening by the Office. At first, this was directed only at the illegal immigrants. The redefinition brought with it, at least for a time, new categories of exemptions, but those too were meant to be of a temporary nature, dictated as they were by political considerations, as were those in the case of Portugal.

Regulations of 1972: The measures credited with the largest effect on the control of immigration were those based on the Ministerial Orders *(Circulairs)* signed Marcellin, Fontanet, and Gorse, and issued January 24, February 23, and September 26, 1972 respectively. In substance, the Orders referred back to the labor force regulations of 1945 which gave an absolute priority in allocating jobs to the indigenous labor force and to the bona fide immigrants already in the country. The residence permit became the new control mechanism and it was to be issued only in connection with a work permit. New immigrants could obtain a work permit only by signing a work contract for a job channeled and specified by the Office. The Office had to make sure there was no person already in the country qualified to fill the job and willing to take it. Furthermore, the employer was now liable to provide housing for workers recruited for him from abroad.

Such measures were decided upon mostly because of the development of immigration which renders the "impression that migratory flows have a certain autonomy from the very indicators of economic growth which should be guiding them".[10] The autonomy of migratory flows came about in four ways. In the first place, it was a result of the total volume of immigration required to meet the objective of the Plans. The Fifth Plan (1966-1970) foresaw about 100,000 immigrants annually, but 138,000 were effectively registered not counting in-migrants from Algeria. Secondly, migration inflows seemed to follow their own rhythm. Thus, net in-migration remained about 20,000 to 30,000 persons below the annual expectations during the years 1966 to 1968. Between 1969 and 1970, however, the number of immigrants substantially overshot the projected needs. In toto, the Office registered 1,194,000 workers and their families between the years 1966 and 1972. This represented an annual intake of about 170,000 persons. Net immigration during that period was 128,000 annually, coming essentially short of the projected worker immigration. Thirdly, the ethnic composition of immigrants had changed. That is, the Spanish were succeeded by the Portuguese, their numbers subsided in turn and immigrants from North African countries took their place. In each case new cultural needs came to the fore. In the fourth place, the disparities between the official forecasts and needs and the actual migration patterns were best seen at the level of specific industries. Construction and metal working industries had not suffered any great shortage of manpower, but agriculture had. Domestic employment and some specific industries also failed to attract the desired manpower. In other words, a reshuffling of workers among the various branches of industry took place, but not in correspondence with the distribution of the initial work permits.

Even though exact data are lacking, the autonomy of immigrant redistribution in the French economy can be summarized as to the direction of the drift: from nonemployed to worker status, as in the case of wives and children of immigrants and in the case of student immigrants; from the primary sector to the secondary sector of industries and within that from construction to metal working, and from large enterprises to smaller ones; from industry to service jobs; and from working for an employer to self-employment. An improvement in income and social status seemed to accompany these shifts and some social mobility of immigrants did take place.

[10] Commission Emploi. *Rapport (Préparation du VIe Plan)*. Paris: Documentation Française. Vols. I and II. 1972.

The Second Restriction: Suspension of Immigration

The highest immigration registration to France was in the years 1969 through 1971. After that a sharp decline of legally immigrating workers took place. This was due partly to the restrictions on the immigration from within, first enforced in 1972, and it was due also to the suspension of the out-migration from Algeria starting with September, 1973. The French government declared full immigration stoppage in July, 1974, in response to the rapidly worsening economic situation. The decline in immigration was substantial. While there were 213,000 immigrants to France in 1970, their number dropped every year thereafter so that in 1974 there were only 64,000, in 1975, 26,000 and in 1976 there were no immigrant workers registered by the Office. On the other hand, immigration of dependents of workers already in France continued, averaging between 30,000 to 35,000 persons annually. It was temporarily stopped in 1974, but was allowed to resume in 1975. This type of immigration became supplemented by admission of refugees from Chile, Cambodia, South Vietnam, Laos and Lebanon. These new immigrants brought with them high occupational skills, until then found only infrequently among immigrants to France. As a matter of fact, about 70 percent of the number of workers who previously immigrated to France had been unskilled.

A corresponding decline in seasonal workers took place, even though the decline was not too rapid. Between 1973 and 1975, the seasonal workers coming to France declined in numbers from 142,000 to 124,000. On the other hand, the number of workers who were nationals of member states of the European Communities, remained stable at around 10,000. All in all, the new French policy became centered on stabilizing the number of foreigners in France and, thus, effectively closing France to new immigration.

Distribution of Foreigners in France

By the end of 1975, 4,196,000 foreigners were living in France. Paris and environs housed about 35 percent of all aliens, while the other major concentrations of aliens were in south France. In Paris and the surrounding metropolitan area, 14 percent of the population were foreigners, other regions had a lower proportion of foreign nationals, except Corsica, where close to 23 percent of the population were aliens. In toto, 7.7 percent of the entire population in France in 1975 were aliens. Due to the unbalanced sex structure of the foreign population, who were primarily young males, the birth rate of aliens did not add substantively to the overall population increase.[11]

[11] R. Nadot. "Les Effets de l'Immigration sur la Natalité en France depuis 1953", *Population*, 18. 1963.

TABLE 8:2

Percent Distribution of "Earned" Naturalizations of Aliens in France,
by Selected Countries of Origin Since 1962,
and the Total of "Acquired" Naturalizations Since 1968[a]

Countries of Origin	Naturalizations in Percent									
	1962-1966	1967	1968	1969	1970	1971	1972	1973	1974	1975
Total N	108,744	45,663	29,935	30,116	27,986	32,554	27,851	26,651	24,028	26,674
Algeria	—	—	1	2	2	3	2	2	2	3
Italy	35	32	31	32	26	25	24	22	22	22
Morocco	3	5	3	3	3	4	4	5	4	5
Poland	13	8	8	8	6	6	6	5	5	4
Portugal	2	2	3	4	5	7	10	12	15	14
Spain	24	26	30	30	27	30	32	29	28	24
Tunisia	5	9	5	5	6	7	6	7	7	6
Other[b]	18	18	19	16	25	18	16	18	17	22
Total Percent	100	100	100	100	100	100	100	100	100	100
Acquired Naturalizations N	—	—	8,352	8,281	7,014	7,435	7,403	6,965	12,058	14,726

Notes: [a] Earned naturalization (*per décret*) is awarded after the alien has met the eligibility criteria including the stipulated residence in France. Acquired naturalization (*par déclaration*) is awarded to aliens marrying a French national. Prior to January, 1973, only alien women marrying Frenchmen were eligible for the citizenship.
[b] None of the other countries supplied enough aliens to exceed the lowest numbers listed in the Table.

Sources: Ministère du Travail: Direction de la Population et des Migrations; Ministère de l'Interieur.

In 1974, Algerians claimed the largest share of all aliens, with 21 percent of the total; second were Portuguese, with 20 percent, then Spaniards with 14 percent and Italians with 13 percent of the total. Moroccans represented 7 percent and Tunisians about 4 percent of the total, while other nationalities lagged behind.[12]

Aliens in the Labor Force: As of the end of 1973, 1.9 million aliens were employed in France, of whom 430,000 were Portuguese and about as many were Algerians; Spaniards numbered 250,000 and Italians 210,000, Moroccans 165,000 and there were 90,000 workers from Tunisia. About 70,000 workers were from the European Community countries other than Italy; there were also 60,000 Yugoslavs, 50,000 workers from other African countries and 35,000 Turks. Workers from the European Communities were most likely to have white collar jobs. Construction alone employed about one-half million foreigners. Aliens represented 8.5 percent of the total labor force, but in construction and in the health auxiliary service occupations their proportion ran close to 30 percent. Compared to the French nationals, nine out of ten foreigners held blue collar employment while six out of ten Frenchmen did manual labor.

The Role of Immigration in France

The French experience with immigration is unique. France has not been an immigration country like the traditionally immigration countries overseas, nor has it been an emigration country, as most of the other countries in Europe. The experiences of France vis-à-vis immigration rests on two historical circumstances: the demographic development and the bimodal industrialization.

Demographic Development: France is perhaps the only country in Europe where the decline in fertility preceded the decline in mortality, starting toward the end of the 18th century.[13] France did not experience demographic pressures characteristic of its neighbors such as Great Britain or Germany. Since the end of the 19th century, immigration had played a key role in the growth of the French population even though the growth remained quite modest.

---

[12] INED. *VIe Rapport du la Situation Demographique de la France.* Paris: Institut National d'Etudes Demographiques. March, 1977.

[13] *Démographie Historique. Population* (Paris). Special issue. 30:1-265. 1975; J.J. Markowitch. "L'Industrie Francaise de 1789 à 1964", *Cahiers de l'ISEA* (Paris), Series A.F. No. 6. 1966.

TABLE 8:3

Percent Distribution of Foreign Immigrant Workers in France by Major
Occupational Divisions, for the Year of Immigration, Since 1969

Occupational Divisions	Years						
	1969	1970	1971	1972	1973	1974	1975
Agriculture, fishing, forestry	9.9	11.2	13.9	12.8	11.7	12.7	5.3
Heavy industry including mining	3.8	3.3	2.3	1.2	1.4	3.6	7.8
Manufacturing and mechanical	17.9	20.2	15.9	19.1	19.2	15.8	7.4
Construction and Public Works	40.8	34.4	29.9	27.2	31.8	29.0	14.3
Food processing	1.3	1.5	1.7	1.6	1.3	1.5	1.3
Textile, Leather, Wood processing	6.9	6.1	7.2	7.4	6.9	5.3	4.2
Other Industries	2.7	2.6	2.0	3.0	2.9	3.0	3.7
Business and Commerce	5.4	6.7	8.8	10.4	10.8	12.9	24.0
Health and Personal Services	8.5	10.8	13.4	12.9	9.6	9.0	13.8
Other Services	2.7	3.2	3.9	4.4	4.4	7.2	18.0
Total N[a]	167,802	174,243	136,004	98,074	132,055	64,461	25,591

Note: [a] Excludes Algerians.

Source: Office National d'Immigration.

Industrialization: The development of the French economy does not fit the industrialization model predicated on the "take off" principle.[14] The frequent upsets in the French political history did not encourage, paradoxically, any major transformation of French economic structure which tended to evolve slowly and gradually. There are two factors which have underlined this slowness of French economic development: 1) agriculture remained a significant sector of French economy. An exodus of the rural population did not occur to any great extent until around 1950; and 2) the growth of the industrial sector was limited to large enterprises and the heavy industry and did not spill over into the rest of the economy so that its fairly high rate of growth remained isolated. Whereas the heavy industry and the large industrial enterprises had a growth rate of about 3 percent annually between 1915 and 1938, small industries, crafts and trades showed a rate of growth of only 0.7 percent annually during the same period.[15]

Immigration: Immigration provided the connecting component necessary for the development of the French industry. The immigrating workers allowed the French population to switch directly into tertiary occupations without the evolutionary stop over in the secondary industries. Service occupations and lower level civil service jobs were being entered by in-migrants from the French countryside. The chronic need for seasonal workers in agriculture was also being met by immigration, especially in south France where large scale plantings of vines and sugar beets had developed during the last century. Furthermore, the low birth rate of the French indigenous population left some small enterprises in want of additional workers thus creating vacancies for immigrants.

The economic depression in the 1930s affected the immigrant labor force in particular in the heavy industry and encouraged a diffusion into small scale shops and agriculture.[16] Spanish and Italian farmers were sprinkled among the French farming population; a parallel situation has developed in the 1970s with the Portuguese.[17]

---

[14] J. Marczewski. "Y-a-t-il Eu un 'Take Off' en France?", *Cahiers de l'ISEA* (Paris), Series A.D., No. 1:69-94. 1961; J.J. Markowitch. "L'Industrie Francaise de 1789 à 1964", *Cahiers de l'ISEA* (Paris), Series A.F. No. 6. 1966.

[15] J.J. Markowitch. "L'Industrie Francaise de 1789 à 1964", *Cahiers de l'ISEA* (Paris), Series A.F. No. 6. 1966.

[16] J.C. Bonnet. *Les Pouvoirs Publics Francais et l'Immigration dans l'Entre Deux Guerres.* Lyon: Université du Lyon II, Centre d'Histoire économique et sociale de la région lyonnaise. 1976.

[17] M. Poinard. *L'Émigration Portugaise et les Retours.* Paris: OECD. Rapport du groupe de travail sur l'émigration. 1971.

Prospects

Immigration remained of crucial importance in the demographic and economic development of France after World War II. The new politics of . French immigration now, thirty years of sustained immigration later, are intent, in the first place, on "freezing" the foreign population at its present level.[18] In the past, social and economic dislocations brought on by the heavy immigration of the 1920s were followed by stabilization policies in the 1930s.[19] In the present, the stabilization policies of the 1970s have to deal, on one hand, with the problems posed by out-migrating aliens and, on the other, with the problems of integration of the second generation of migrants into France. To facilitate the latter, naturalizations have become quite liberal in 1973.

The problem of unemployment is persistent, especially among the youth. In this respect France resembles Germany and takes similar measures towards stabilization of the employment market. For instance, usual subsidies and investment. write-offs are not available in regions and to enterprises employing a disproportionate number of aliens. The attempt to introduce a stoppage of immigration of dependents of aliens already in France has faltered due to political opposition. The pressure of migration is threatening to bring about a migration policy essentially alien to the country's immigration tradition.

---

[18] A. Michel. *La Nouvelle Politique de l'Immigration*. Paris: Secretariat d'Etat. 1977.

[19] J.C. Bonnet. *Les Pouvoirs Publics Francais et l'Immigration dans l'Entre Deux Guerres.* Lyon: Université du Lyon II, Centre d'Histoire économique et sociale de la région lyonnaise. 1976.

9

Federal Republic
of Germany *

URSULA MEHRLÄNDER
Friedrich Ebert Foundation

Introduction

THE historical German economic miracle has always been very much dependent on the increasing supply of labor. The building of the Berlin Wall in 1961 effectively shut off a major source of labor from eastern Germany and economic expansion dictated that Germany's own labor supply had to be augmented by the importation of labor from abroad.

The German Federal Government was responsive to the needs of German industry for a large pool of labor. Foreign labor began to be systematically recruited abroad, primarily in the countries in the Mediterranean basin, and the government set up a network of labor recruiting German commissions whose activities were specified in bilateral agreements with the sending countries.

The economic primacy of labor needs was not questioned. Soon, however, the conditions of foreign workers in Germany brought out questions regarding the social integration of the "guest workers". These questions acquired a new salience for the German government when a further supply of workers was effectively throttled by the Federal regulations in 1973. Despite the out-migration of some workers, there has continued to be an influx of family members. In 1975, foreign workers and their families numbered over four million, representing over 6 percent of the total

---

* Translated from German by Daniel Kubat.

population in the Federal Republic of Germany.

After World War II, Germany experienced the heaviest migrations in Europe. The millions of refugees, displaced persons and its own repatriated nationals and emigrants, turned Germany into a country of migrants. Despite the enormous experience of settlement and resettlement to the present, Germany does not acknowledge its status as an immigration country. Its aliens are considered strictly temporary residents.

Employment Regulations for Aliens

Most of Germany's labor needs were met through recruitment abroad. By December 20, 1955, the Federal Republic of Germany had entered into a bilateral agreement with Italy. This agreement may still be seen as a prototype agreement. It was preceded by extensive consultations between the Federal Government, the Federal Employment Agency, the German employers and the labor unions, on the one hand, and the interested parties in Italy, on the other. Italy, at this time, had a surplus of manpower. German enterprises needed an expanding labor supply. The unions felt that their own interests could be served only if the foreign workers were guaranteed employment equality to safeguard the competitiveness of German nationals.[1]

The treaty establishing the European Community in 1964 made the original agreement with Italy obsolete: freedom of movement for nationals of all member states assured the Italians all the rights stipulated in the original agreement. The recruitment of labor agreement was then updated and supplemented on February 23, 1965.[2]

In the middle of the 1960s, Germany was employing about 280,000 foreign workers, somewhat less than half of whom were Italians. The rest consisted mainly of Spaniards, Yugoslavs, Greeks and Turks. Their stay, too, became a basis for a number of bilateral agreements on the recruitment of labor with Spain (1960), Greece (1960), Turkey (1961) and Portugal (1964). Employment of Tunisians became regulated contractually in 1965; a second agreement with Morocco was concluded in 1966, three years after the first. With Yugoslavia, Germany entered into an agreement in 1968, regularizing the stay of a substantial number of Yugoslavs, who were already in Germany.

Implementation of all recruitment agreements was suspended in November, 1973. The workers' protection clauses contained within the agreements,

---

[1] R. Lohrmann. "Politische Auswirkungen der Arbeitskräftewanderungen auf die Bundesrepublik Deutschland", *Ausländerbeschäftigung und Internationale Politik*. R. Lohrmann and K. Manfrass, eds. Munich, Vienna: Oldenburg. 1974. Pp. 103-140.

[2] U. Mehrländer. *Soziale Aspekte der Ausländerbeschäftigung*. Bonn-Bad Godesberg: Neue Gesellschaft. 1974.

TABLE 9:1

Foreign Workers in Germany by Proportion of Males to Proportion of All Workers,
by Proportion from Major Sending Countries, Since 1959a

Year[b]	Total Foreign Workers	% Males	% All Workers	E.C. Except Italy	Italy	Greece	Yugo-slavia	Spain	Other Europe	Turkey	Non-European and Other	Total %
1959	166,829	81.1	0.8	24	29	2	4	1	28	—	12	100.0
1960	279,390	84.5	1.3	17	44	5	3	3	18	1	9	100.0
1961	475,722	—	2.3	14	44	9	3	10	13	1	6	100.0
1962	655,463	82.1	3.0	12	41	11	4	13	11	2	6	100.0
1963	811,213	79.3	3.6	11	37	13	5	14	11	3	6	100.0
1964	932,932	77.8	4.1	10	31	15	6	15	10	7	6	100.0
1965	1,164,364	76.9	5.5	8	31	16	6	16	8	10	5	100.0
1966	1,314,031	74.7	6.1	7	30	15	7	14	10	12	5	100.0
1967	1,023,747	71.1	4.9	7	27	14	10	13	11	13	5	100.0
1968	1,014,774	70.5	4.9	7	28	13	10	11	11	14	6	100.0
1969	1,372,059	70.6	6.4	6	25	13	16	10	10	16	4	100.0
1970	1,838,859	71.0	8.5	6	20	12	21	9	11	18	3	100.0
1971	2,168,766	71.6	10.0	5	19	12	22	8	11	20	3	100.0

TABLE 9:1 (continued)

Foreign Workers in Germany by Proportion of Males to Proportion of All-Workers, by Proportion from Major Sending Countries, Since 1959a

Year[b]	Total Foreign Workers	% Males	% All Workers	E.C. Except Italy	Italy	Greece	Yugo-slavia	Spain	Other Europe	Turkey	Non-European and Other	Total %
1972	2,316,980	70.8	10.6	6	18	12	20	8	9	21	4	100.0
1973	2,520,100	65.1[c]	11.6	6[c]	17	10	20	7	10[c]	24	6[c]	100.0
1974	2,150,580	68.3	10.5	6	14	10	20	7	10	27	6	100.0
1975	1,932,604	68.5	9.7	6	14	10	20	6	10	27	7	100.0
1976	1,873,835	68.8	9.4	7	15	9	20	6	10	27	7	100.0

Notes: [a] Estimated population for the Federal Republic of Germany in 1976 was 61,542,000.
[b] Through 1972, midyear count; 1973 to 1976, December estimates.
[c] Estimated.

Sources: Heinz Werner. "Freizügigheit der Arbeitskräfte und die Wanderungsbewegungen in den Ländern der Europäischen Gemeinschaft." *Mitteilungen aus der Arbeitsmarkt- und Berufsforschung,* 1973, No. 4, pp. 326-371, Table 1; Bundesanstalt für Arbeit. *Ausländische Arbeitnehmer: Beschäftigung, Anwerbung, Vermittlung, Erfahrungsbericht 1972/73.* Nürnberg, 1974; Die Beschäftigungslage Ende Dezember 1974 und Ende März 1975 im *Bundesgebiet* und in den *Landesarbeitsamtsbezirken.* Nürnberg 1975; *Amtliche Nachrichten der Bundesanstalt für Arbeit* (ANBA), 1976, No. 3, pp. 301, 321; No. 10, p. 1100; *DIW-Wochenbericht,* 1976, No. 46, p. 423; ANBA, 1977, No. 6, p. 776.

however, remained in force.

Naturally, nationals of the member states of the now nine European Communities countries remained unaffected. The freedom of movement and employment of these states was guaranteed by the original Treaty (Regulation No. 38/64 EEC, Directives No. 240/64 EEC; and No. 22164 EEC).

Residence and Work Permits

In principle, no foreigner has the right to enter and to live in the Federal Republic of Germany. In actuality, only those foreign nationals entering the country with an intent to pursue gainful employment are subject to the application of the Aliens Act of April 28, 1965 and its Implementation Regulations of September 10, 1965.[3]

The Aliens Act does not apply to persons under 16 years of age. Furthermore, nationals of the European Communities are entitled to a residence permit upon application.[4] Residence permits may stipulate geographic areas and time limits. At first, a residence permit is granted for one year only and is tied to a designated employment. Before extending the residence permit, the issuing authority, the Aliens Registration Bureau *(Ausländerbehörde)*, may reconsider if the conditions which were prevailing at the time of first issuance still hold. Thus, the Aliens Registration Bureau has wide discretionary powers. After an uninterrupted stay of at least three years, the residence permit may be granted for two or more years.

A foreigner, who has been in Germany, legally, for at least five years and is considered to have integrated himself into the economic and social life, is eligible to receive a domicile permit *(Aufenthaltsberechtigung)*. Once granted, the permit allows its holder to move within the country without restriction. Legally, the domicile permit may be revoked should "national interest" so dictate, or should the permit holder be declared an undesirable (The Aliens Act, Art. I, Sections 8 and 10).

Work permits are issued by the Federal Labor Office *(Bundesanstalt für Arbeit)*. All aliens intending to work in Germany need a work permit. There are two classes of work permits: a general permit, issued normally for one year and geared to the labor conditions prevailing, or to special needs of certain industries; and, there is a special work permit *(besondere Arbeitserlaubnis)*, issued to aliens who have a steady employment record for the preceding five years, or who have been living in Germany legally for the last eight years or more, or who are married to a German citizen. This permit may carry a geographical limitation and is normally issued for five years.

---

[3] *Bundesgestzblatt*, I:353, 1341.
[4] *Amstblatt der EWG*, 57:1073. 1961; 62:965ff. 1964.

After a ten year stay in Germany, aliens may be issued work permits without time limitations. General work permits are tied to residence permits. They expire when the residence permit expires, or if the alien remains outside Germany for more than three months.

Recruitment of Labor Abroad

The majority of foreign workers in Germany come from countries in the Mediterranean basin. Generally following the same steps in the recruitment procedures a German employer first notifies his nearest Employment Office *(Arbeitsamt)* about his manpower needs, indicating the number of workers desired, the required skill levels and, then frequently indicates a specific desired nationality to cut down his interpreter costs. The Employment Office checks first whether the needs can be filled locally, or whether there are any Germans available. When no Germans are available, the request is routed to the Federal Labor Office in Nuremberg. From there, the appropriate German commission in a sending country is notified. In 1971, the Federal Labor Office entertained commissions in Athens, Belgrade, Istanbul, Lisbon and Madrid. The German commission contacts the appropriate employment agency of the sending country which prepares a list of suitable candidates. The staff of the German commission selects from among the candidates and gives them a medical examination. Each recruited worker is provided with a one year work contract, a general work permit and a residence permit (until 1973 the worker was provided with an ID card entitling him to same). Workers recruited as a group are then provided transportation paid for by the employer.

Workers recruited by individual contracts followed the same procedures. Also, until 1971, workers were able to secure a visa, which served as a general work permit, and which was obtainable directly from German consulates abroad.[5]

Until November, 1973, when Germany suspended all labor recruiting abroad, the elasticity of its economy allowed the employers to have some say in matters of labor recruitment. By tying the new recruits to their jobs for one year, they were able to assure themselves an ample labor supply and were able to continue to provide for their workers' wages and working conditions at such levels which might not have been competitive in a tight labor market.

The short history of foreign worker in-migration into Germany shows a rapid increase until about 1965, when their number reached 1.2 million, that is, 5.5 percent of the labor force. At that time, unemployment was only 0.7

---

[5] Bundesanstalt für Arbeit. *Ausländische Arbeitnehmer-Beschäftigung, Anwerbung, Vermittlung, Erfahrungsbericht 1970.* Nürnberg: Bundesanstalt für Arbeit. 1971. P. 89.

percent and the number of job vacancies 650,000.[6]

The recession of 1966 and 1967 slowed the influx of foreign workers considerably; some returned home and the influx through new recruitment practically ceased. The number of foreign workers from nonmember countries of the European Economic Community (their nationals retained the freedom of movement) declined to 900,000. The number of all unemployed was 460,000 in 1967 and the number of job vacancies dropped to 300,000 during the same year.

The recession did not last long and the new economic upswing brought in foreign workers in unprecedented numbers. By September, 1973, they numbered 2.6 million and their proportion to the native labor force rose to 12 percent. The peak year of 1970 registered only 150,000 unemployed, and 800,000 job vacancies. The situation worsened toward the end of 1973 with 270,000 unemployed and 570,000 vacancies, which was still an enviable situation compared to most other industrial countries. In September, 1977, there were 0.9 million unemployed and only 237,000 vacancies.[7]

The energy crisis, coupled with a pronounced recession, made itself felt by 1973 and curtailed the free play of market forces with respect to German labor conditions. This time, the foreign workers did not respond to the worsened economy by returning home, as they did once before. The decline between September, 1973 through March, 1975 in the number of foreign workers in Germany was 18 percent despite the unemployment among them of 6.3 percent in December, 1975. During a previous recession, between June, 1966 through January, 1968, the number of foreign workers in Germany decreased by 31 percent. What happened was that the foreign workers in 1975 had a longer tenure in Germany than previously, they had their families with them and they were able to collect unemployment benefits which, in most instances, were higher than the wages they could earn at home. In September, 1977, there were about 80,000 unemployed foreign workers.[8]

In-Migration Curbs

Not until it became clear that costly energy would remain a permanent fixture of modern industrial nations did the Federal Government decide to interfere in the market play of labor supply. Starting in 1971, entry of workers from the recruitment agreement countries became restricted to those duly processed by the German commissions abroad. In June, 1973, the

---

[6] U. Mehrländer. *Beschäftigung Ausländischer Arbeitnehmer in der Bundesrepublik Deutschland unter Spezieller Berücksichtigung von Nordrhein-Westfalen.* 2nd ed. Köln and Opladen: Westdeutscher Verlag. 1972. P. 90.

[7] ANBA, 25(11):1389. 1977; *Statistisches Jahrbuch*, respective years.

[8] ANBA, 25(11):1390. 1977.

Federal Government published its new Action Program on Employment of Foreigners.[9] The main thrust of the new directives was the reordering of priorities away from employment to integration of foreign workers into the social structure of the country.

Not wanting to abrogate the various agreements with the sending countries, the Federal Government resorted to enforcing the provisions at home: a stricter supervision of housing supplied by the employer; raising of fees per recruited worker from about 150 dollars to about 500 dollars (1,000 DM); and enforcing penalties for the illegal employment of aliens. On the other hand, integration of those foreigners who have been in Germany for quite some time is expected to be speeded up. For instance, the raised recruitment fees were to be used for language courses and the like. However, the Federal Government is leaning no doubt as to the firmness of its conviction in matters of immigration: Germany is not an immigration country, but it shall do its utmost to assure that those foreign workers and their families already in the country should feel at home; also, they must enjoy all the rights and privileges of Germans, save suffrage, of course. Mandatory rotation, for instance, is unacceptable.

Shortly after issuing the new policy, the Federal Government saw itself forced to declare a complete stoppage of all recruitment activities as of November, 1973. This, of course, did not stop the inflow of aliens into the country even though the arriving dependents were usually eligible only for residence, but not for work permits.

The continuing inflow of dependents caused the social facilities to be strained, especially in the heavily industrial areas of Germany. Regulations suggesting a limit of 12 percent of aliens in any *Kreis*, or administrative district, were being proposed, even though enforcing such regulations proved difficult. The guidelines of "absorptive capacity" for a city or area was more likely an intuitive guess than a thorough assessment of the carrying capacity of housing, schools, recreational facilities and the like. Areas with a high proportion of single foreign workers for instance, living in "barracks" had to be viewed differently than areas where families were making their homes. The residence permits were not to be granted even to the dependents of workers already in the area should these areas be declared overburdened. In any case, the one year residence permits issued were stamped "off limits" for designated areas.[10] As of April 1, 1977, this practice was discontinued, in deference to the anticipated extension of free movement of workers to

---

[9] H. Ernst. "Wende in der Ausländerpolitik?", *Arbeit und Sozialpolitik* (Bonn), 6/7:181-186. 1973; "Bonn: Aktionsprogram für Ausländerbeschäftigung", *Arbeit und Sozialpolitik* (Bonn), 6/7:183. 1973. Editorial feature.

[10] J. Langkau and U. Mehrländer. *Raumordnungspolitische Steuerung der Ausländerbeschäftigung.* Bonn-Bad Godesberg: Bundesministerium für Raumordnung, Bauwesen and Städtebau. 1976. Pp. 43-44.

TABLE 9:2

Percent Distribution of Border Commuters
in Germany by Countries, Between 1959 and 1972

Year[b]	All Commuters	France	Belgium	Holland	Countries Luxem-burg	Denmark	Switzer-land	Austria
1959	7,286	10[c]	4	52	a	a	3	30
1960	12,241	14	3	49	a	1	2	31
1961	28,608	19	6	53	a	a	1	20
1962	41,428	20	7	54	a	1	1	18
1963	46,476	20	6	55	a	1	1	17
1964	47,839	22	5	53	a	1	1	18
1965	51,953	27	6	47	a	1	1	18
1966	52,387	31	7	43	a	1	1	18
1967	35,735	32	8	37	a	1	1	21
1968	34,989	32	8	36	a	1	1	22
1969	42,308	31	7	37	a	1	1	23
1970	53,005	32	7	36	a	a	1	23
1971	62,611	33	7	38	a	a	1	21
1972	72,372	34	6	40	a	a	1	18

Notes: [a] Fewer than 0.5 percent.
[b] Annual average based on March and September figures.
[c] September.

Source: *Amtliche Nachrichten der Bundesanstalt für Arbeit*, corresponding years.

nationals of countries wishing to join the European Communities. In particular, the Ankara Agreement of 1964 provided for a stepwise introduction of a free worker mobility for Turkish nationals.

A New Policy

In August, 1976, an Intergovernmental Commission was established to deal with the policy aspects of integration of foreign workers remaining in Germany. The Commission, consisting of representatives of the Federal and State governments answered directly to the Federal Minister for Labor and Social Affairs *(Arbeit und Sozialordnung)*. Its mandate was to inquire into the legal status of aliens in the country, especially those who have been in the country for some time. "The guiding principle," said the initial document, "remains the balancing of the social and humanitarian claims of foreigners living in the Federal Republic, the interests of their countries of origin and the social and economic interests of the Federal Republic of Germany."[11]

Specifically, the Commission was charged to propose means to improve housing for foreign workers, to suggest ways and means for a suitable language training for foreign dependents and to look into programs encouraging occupational training of foreign youth. Furthermore, social welfare coverage of foreigners on the one hand and the question of naturalization on the other were to be evaluated and local political rights considered. The Commission was thus "in a position to propose a policy on foreign workers integrating both the alien legislation and the employment of foreigners...so that in the future there will be a responsible policy to go by."[12] The Commission completed its task in the spring of 1977. Its main recommendation was that the suspension of recruitment of foreign workers abroad, in effect since the summer of 1973, should remain in force, and that foreign workers already in the country be subject to the following residence permit regulations: after five years stay, residence permit is to be renewed without a time limitation; and after eight years of stay, the worker gains a right of domicile. On the other hand, the spouse of the foreign worker loses her or his automatic right to a work permit previously issued without a reference to the employment situation. The "second generation" of foreigners should benefit through a new program of German for Foreign Workers, starting in 1977. Should the workers express an interest in returning home, all assistance is to be provided. However, the notion of worker rotation or

[11] "Entwurf von Thesen zur Ausländerpolitik eines Ausschusses der Bundesregierung vom 23, Oktober 1975", *epd-Dokumentation* (Frankfurt), 5:4-10. 1976.

[12] W. Dodenberder. "Zwischenbilanz der Ausländerpolitik". Paper read before the Südosteuropa Gesellschaft, Tutzing, Nov. 16, 1976.

lump sum payments as an incentive to leave the country were rejected by the Commission.

Integration of Aliens into the German Society

Regarding economic protection, all workers in Germany are subject to a compulsory social and unemployment insurance. The time spent working within the territory of the Federal Republic of Germany is credited to individual persons. In addition to this territorial limitation, Germany is party to a multinational agreement worked out by the International Labor Office in Geneva and the Council of Europe. This agreement stipulates transferability of credits accumulated in any country covered by the agreement. In addition, for Germany's foreign workers not covered by the European Communities agreements, there are individual agreements with the sending countries assuring the portability of accumulated social insurance (old age pensions) and unemployment insurance credits as well as health insurance and various payments attendant upon employment in Germany. The foreign workers must observe the conditions stipulated for them in the ruling on work and residence permits. In other words, their claims have been exhausted once their residence permit lapses. In general, contributory funds claims are transferable, but claims on social provisions paid out of general tax funds are not unless the claimant remains a legal resident of Germany. Furthermore, there are some restrictions on claims from the contributory funds if the claimant has no valid work permit.

Regarding the social integration of foreign workers in Germany, the issue remains complex. There are four major problem areas: language skill; housing; dependents; and schooling for children.

Language: Data from a large survey of foreign workers in Germany in 1971[13] indicate that only about 10 percent of the recruited workers spoke any German at entry. Eventually, most of them acquired some basic German, but on the whole they remained functionally illiterate in the language. The interest in attending language courses is only minimal, and the availability of courses is uneven.

The failure of the language program has several causes. Initially, the traditional teaching methods proved inappropriate as the emphasis on grammar and sentence structure was not understandable to the foreign workers most of whom have had minimal formal education. Attending a language course after hours proved to be an added burden to workers who would rather use their time for overtime work. The often collective form of

[13] U. Mehrländer. *Soziale Aspekte der Ausländerbeschäftigung.* Bonn-Bad Godesberg: Neue Gesellschaft. 1974.

housing also militated against the necessity of learning German which was equally rarely needed on the job; the system whereby enterprises prefer workers of one ethnic group permits a consequent creation of language enclaves. Furthermore, a natural ghettoization of foreign workers made it unnecessary for those with families to venture outside the circle of kin and friends. Finally, the cultural and political activities of their own government emphasized national identity and dissuaded them from assimilation in the host country.

Parallel to the official, as it were, courses in German, conducted by the various university extension field offices, were the efforts of various voluntary agencies. The most successful of these programs was a televised learn German program under the title of, "Guten Tag" and a new series, "Viel Glück in Deutschland". This latter, a "Sesame Street" type program, was developed by the Goethe Institute for the Ministry of Labor and Social Affairs. Since 1972, most efforts in teaching German to foreigners are being coordinated centrally, on the federal level, and in 1974, a federally supported action, German for Foreign Workers, was initiated.

Housing: Due to acute housing shortages in the industrial areas, the employers were required to provide housing for the labor they imported. The first such arrangement dates to the German-Italian agreement and covers various details such as the number of washrooms, the arrangement of sleeping accommodations, dayrooms, and similar provisions. Principally, such housing was a military barrack. Only recently have the standards been raised which has begun to discourage employers from importing workers.[14]

One survey[15] indicates that in the fall of 1971 about one-fifth of the number of foreign workers lived in housing provided by their employers. Turks and Yugoslavs were more likely to be found in such accommodations than the other groups; from among the Turks who have been in Germany for less than one year, the proportion in collective employer supplied housing was 43 percent. Such housing was minimal: usually more than two persons were placed in a room; and men and women, including married couples, were housed separately. The barracks also suffered from an overdose of house rules against which complaints were most often directed.

Workers who have been in Germany for more than three years usually move into their own apartments and have their families join them. Neighborhoods then develop, giving the area a specific flavor. Attendant to this process is a slackening of standards in services, upkeep and a host of

[14] E. Zieris. *Betriebsunterkünfte für ausländische Mitbürger Nordrhein-Westfalen.* Düsseldorf: Der Minister für Arbeit, Gesundheit und Soziales des Landes NRW. 1972.

[15] U. Mehrländer. *Soziale Aspekte der Ausländerbeschäftigung.* Bonn-Bad Godesberg: Neue Gesellschaft. 1974.

other conditions usually deemed as bad.[16]

Dependents: Both the data from the 1971 survey and the statistics of the sending countries indicate that separation of family members among the recruited workers is quite common. It is higher for Yugoslavs and Turks and lower for Greeks, Italians, and Spaniards.[17] Wives are more likely to follow their husbands then are the children, except the younger children. The older children are left at home with relatives, their schooling often being the decisive issue.

Inasmuch as the reason for coming to Germany was to make and save money, any dependents who join the head of household depress the savings. Residence and work permit regulations in force are such that, apart from the Italians covered by the European Communities freedom of movement agreement, recruited foreign workers have to wait for three years before bringing in their families. In addition, they must demonstrate that there is "adequate" housing for their family. Entry of dependents is restricted to the spouse and unmarried children under 21 years of age. Children under 16 need no residence permit. In the past, the foreigners were usually able to bring their families after one year's stay provided housing was available.

That Germany is not exempt from the general trend in family reunification of migrants is apparent from recent data. In 1974, the number of new arrivals was small and was exceeded by the number of departing workers. However, about 320,000 dependents arrived in Germany in that year.[18] Whether the influx is to be attributed to the "beat the ban" syndrome, namely the expectation that admission policies into the country will be tightened, or whether it is just a natural lag of dependents following the workers, is open to question. In any case, the number of foreigners in Germany at the end of September, 1975 was 4.1 million.

The influx of dependents normalizes the age and sex structure of the German population and provides for a modest growth rate which, without the foreigners, would have been negative during the last few years. Recent figures, however, indicate perhaps a new trend: in 1975 456,000 aliens entered Germany and 655,000 left. For the first time, the leavers included about 40,000 dependents.[19]

---

[16] M. Borris. *Ausländische Arbeiter in einer Grossstadt.* Frankfurt: Europäische Verlagsanstalt. 1973; A. Schildmeier. *Integration und Wohnen.* Hamburg: Hammon. 1975; U. Mehrländer. *Einflussfaktoren auf das Bildungsverhalten Ausländischer Jugendlicher.* Bonn: Verlag Neue Gesellschaft. 1978.

[17] U. Mehrländer. *Soziale Aspekte der Ausländerbeschäftigung.* Bonn-Bad Godesberg: Neue Gesellschaft. 1974.

[18] Presse und Informationsamt der Bundesregierung. "Zuwanderung von Ausländern stark rückläufig", *Sozialpolitische Umschau* (Bonn), 67. April 25, 1975.

[19] *Die Presse* (Vienna), October 12, 1976.

TABLE 9:3

Estimated[a] Percent Age Distribution of
Foreign Workers and Germans Working for an Employer,
by Sex, 1971-1972

Age	Germans[a]		Foreigners[b]	
	M	F	M	F
under 25	17	29	16	32
25-29	10	10	21	22
30-34	15	11	22	17
35-39	12	9	18	12
40-44	12	9	11	8
45 and over	34	32	11	8
Age not indicated	—	—	1	1
Total	100	100	100	100

Notes: [a] Microcensus of April 30, 1971: all working for an employer minus the foreign workers as of March 31, 1972.
[b] March 31, 1972.

Source: Bundesanstalt für Arbeit. Repräsentativ-Untersuchung 1972 über die Beschäftigung ausländischer Arbeitnehmer im Bundesgebiet und ihrer Familien- und Wohnungsverhältnisse. Nürnberg, 1973.

Schooling for Children: In 1972 there were about one million children of foreign workers. About 37 percent of them were between 6 and 16 years of age, and, of compulsory school age.[20] The mandatory schooling for children of aliens was introduced in 1964 after the number of children became substantial.

Normally, schools are administered by the individual German states *(Länder);* there is, however, a Standing Conference of Ministers of Education with powers only to recommend. A recommendation dating to 1971[21] requests an integration of foreign children into their age corresponding grade. A provision for instruction of the mother tongue is also recommended "to maintain the students' links with the language and culture of their home countries".

There are built-in disadvantages in the present way foreigners' children are educated. Their insufficient command of German proves a barrier to a successful progression through grades. At home, children may not find

[20] *Repräsentativ-Untersuchung '72 über die Beschäftigung Ausländischer Arbeitnehmer im Bundesgebiet und ihre Familien-und Wohnungsverhältnisse.* Nürnberg: Bundesanstalt für Arbeit. 1973. P. 23.
[21] Bundesanzeiger, January 8, 1972. P. 5.

TABLE 9:4

Percent Distribution of Foreigners' Children in Germany
by Age and by Activity Status, Major Nationality Groups, 1972

Children	Italian	Greek	Spanish	Portu-guese	Turkish	Yugo-slav	Other	All Children
Age								
under 6	38	43	44	45	46	48	39	42
6-11	221	22	22	20	22	20	21	21
12-16	17	20	17	17	17	13	13	16
older than 16	24	15	17	18	15	19	27	21
Total	100	100	100	100	100	100	100	100
Activity								
in Kinder-garten	7	7	11	—	6	16	13	9
at School	32	36	39	29	28	28	34	32
Appren-ticing	3	3	3	—	3	2	4	3
Working	19	12	14	14	12	14	20	16
At home or unknown	39	42	33	57	51	40	29	40
Total	100	100	100	100	100	100	100	100
N(000s)	257	111	80	18	195	115	177	953

Source: Bundesanstalt für Arbeit, 1973 (see Table 9:3).

much encouragement for their German schooling. One study[22] found that one-fifth of all foreign parents evaded sending their children to school. Alternate instruction is provided in the "para-schools" in the respective mother tongue and during the regular class time. This makes the students miss some of the subjects taught in German. In addition, supplementary training in the mother tongue after school hours and by their own nationals discourages an integration of children into their new society.

Thus, mostly for reasons of indeterminacy as to where one belongs and

[22] U. Mehrländer. *Soziale Aspekte der Ausländerbeschäftigung.* Bonn-Bad Godesberg: Neue Gesellschaft. 1974.

TABLE 9:5

Distribution of Foreign Workers in Germany by
Economic Sectors, September 30, 1976

Sectors[a]	Foreign Workers N (000s)	%	Proportion of all Workers
Agriculture and related (1)	18	1.0	8.6
Mining, electricity, gas, water and related (2,4)	38	2.5	7.7
Manufacturing (3)	1,148	47.5	13.4
Construction (5)	203	8.3	12.1
Trade and Hostelry (6)	110	13.9	3.9
Transport and Communications (7)	71	4.8	7.3
Financing and related (8)	12	3.5	1.7
Public Services (9, without household services)	262	15.3	8.5
Household Services and related	12	1.6	3.6
Social Service Organizations (O)	47	6.5	3.7
No Classification	1	0.1	—
Total	1,971	100.0	9.5

Note: [a] The numerical code in parentheses is the International Industrial Classification of the Economic Activities (SIC), 1968.

Source: Bundestanstalt für Arbeit, ANBA, No. 6, 1977, pp. 732, 733.

what one should learn, children of foreign workers become severally disadvantaged; "illiterate in two languages", they pose a problem for the future in whatever country they will find themselves.[23]

Conclusions

Germany's migration policies have wide ranging effects if for no other reason than that the numbers of its foreign workers are substantial.

Up to the middle of the last decade, the inflow of foreign workers was increasing moderately. The in-migration decreased considerably during the

[23] W. Grossmann. "Sozialisationsbedingungen und Bildungschancen Ausländischer Arbeiterkinder", *Gettos in unseren Schulen?* H. Feidel-Mertz and W. Grossmann, eds. Frankfurt: Gewerkschaft, Erziehung und Wissenschaft, 137:11-25. 1974.

TABLE 9:6

Distribution of Foreign Workers in Germany
by Regions, March 31, 1975 and December 31, 1976

Region[a] Landesarbeits- amtsbezirk(a)	Foreign Workers					
	N (000s)		% by Region		Proportion of all Working for an Employer	
	1975	1976	1975	1976	1975	1976
Schleswig-Holstein/ Hamburg	95	87	4.5	4.7	6.6	6.2
Niedersachsen/ Bremen	148	128	7.0	6.8	6.3	5.4
Nordrhein-Westfalen	613	538	28.9	28.7	10.8	9.7
Hessen	234	211	11.0	11.3	12.5	11.3
Rheinland-Pfalz/ Saarland	103	83	4.7	4.5	7.3	6.2
Baden-Württemberg	515	451	24.3	24.1	15.8	14.0
Nordbayern	107	92	5.0	4.9	7.1	6.0
Südbayern	221	202	10.4	10.8	12.0	10.8
Berlin	86	81	4.1	4.2	11.8	11.3
Unknown	2	1	0.1	—	—	—
Total	2,123	1,873	100.0	100.0	10.6	9.4

Note: [a] District of the State Employment Office corresponds approximately to the political region of the State (Land).

Sources: Bundesanstalt für Arbeit, 1975 (see Table 9:1); ANBA, 1977, No. 9, p. 1235.

first economic slowdown in 1966 and 1967. The resumption of the economic boom and the corresponding rise in the in-migration was not halted until 1973 when the energy crisis and a serious economic recession took place. By then, Germany had acquired over four million foreigners. Whereas the foreigners were at first mostly young males, now they were heads of households with families, effecting a rejuvenation of the country's population.

The German government remains adamant about not wanting any immigrants. However, the country does receive in-migrants and always has. The average stay of the alien population is lengthening. The foreigners' children are calculated into the labor supply projections and there are a host of measures to integrate the foreigners economically and socially.

German industry was interested in the importation of labor and in a policy of worker rotation. In that, it was supported by the conservative political parties, such as the Christian Democratic Union and the Christian Social Union. The labor unions, on the other hand, sided with the foreign workers and were pressing for their full integration as a matter of protecting wages and benefits. They were abetted in that by the Social Democrats, until the fall of 1976 the governing party in Germany in coalition with the Free Democrats, a party of the Liberals.

The official German policy remains that of nonrecognition of the de facto immigration situation. Arguments against immigration are couched in terms of population stability especially in regard to excess concentrations in the traditionally industrial areas like the Ruhr. Furthermore, and perhaps more to the point, the government argues that a total, meaning the political integration of foreign workers in Germany would run counter to the spirit of the various bilateral recruitment agreements with the sending countries. The solution offered is that of a "temporary integration", which is, of course, only political rhetoric.

At the moment, however, governmental policies are being helped by the difficulties in the national economy which discourages industry to ask for additional workers and which mutes the protest of those favoring aliens' integration because their own welfare may be at stake.

10

The Scandinavian Countries:
Denmark, Finland, Norway, Sweden

ALTTI MAJAVA
Finnish Ministry of Labor

The Common Nordic Labor Market

THE governments of Denmark, Finland, Norway and Sweden concluded an agreement on the Common Nordic Labor Market in May, 1954, effective July 1 of that year. The text of the agreement states the intention of the signatory parties to maintain full employment in their own countries; to foster free mobility of workers among the Nordic countries; and to treat the nationals of the other Nordic countries as their own citizens in matters of employment. Thus, no work permit has since been necessary for nationals of the signatory countries and most of the worker recruitment has been channeled through the respective public employment services.

The Nordic countries have also established a regular exchange of information on the local job markets. To monitor the agreement, a permanent commitee was initiated consisting of top civil servants in the national labor market administrations. This Nordic Labor Market Commission meets annually and maintains a set of subcommittees dealing with specific tasks. In 1955, the Commission issued guidelines on employment exchange among the Nordic countries which were revised in 1973.

Since the mid-1960s, the Nordic Ministers of Labor have been meeting regularly to discuss common problems. In November, 1973, the Ministers of Labor meeting as the Nordic Council of Ministers issued a pioneer document entitled *Nordic Cooperation Program in the Field of Labor Market Policy.* An implementation program was adopted by the Nordic Labor Market

Commission. A supplementary document between Finland and Sweden was signed in April, 1973. The chief aim of this document was to strengthen the principle of labor recruitment through the public employment service in the case of labor migrations between Finland and Sweden.

A number of other agreements have a bearing on the workings of the Common Nordic Labor Market. The most important of the agreements is the Nordic Social Security Convention, entered into in 1955. It stipulates equal treatment for all Nordic citizens in regard to welfare and social security including pension benefits. Another agreement to abolish passport requirements for Nordic citizens was signed and put into effect at the same time as the Labor Market Agreement in 1954. In 1958 the Nordic countries established a passport union. In 1969 steps were taken to improve the national statistics on inter-Nordic migrations: thanks to the introduction of the Inter-Nordic Migration Certificate, the population registers of the five Nordic countries, including Iceland, constitute a closed, interrelated system. Although Iceland takes an active part in most areas of Nordic cooperation, it has not joined the Common Nordic Labor Market. However, Icelandic citizens need no work permit in Sweden and Denmark. The work permits are granted liberally to Icelanders in Norway and Finland.

Demographic Data

Vital statistics are accurate and reliable in all the Scandinavian countries, although data on the labor force, especially those on employed aliens, are deficient. In Finland, few data are available on the domiciled aliens. Inter-Nordic migrations are primarily constituted by the migrations of Finns to Sweden, including return migrations, by the recent migrations of Danes to Sweden, and by comparatively lively and balanced migratory movements between Denmark and Norway.

Sweden has received the bulk of inter-Nordic migrants departing from the other Scandinavian countries; Nordic nationals predominate in the alien population in Sweden. In Denmark, the share of other Nordic citizens is comparatively low, fewer than 25 percent of all aliens. On the other hand, there are many nationals in Denmark coming from the European Communities countries. In Norway, 37 percent of all aliens are other Nordic nationals, North Americans being the second largest group of aliens, with 17 percent of the total for aliens. There are great differences in the composition of the alien population in the different Nordic countries. All in all, aliens represent 5.0 percent of the population in Sweden, 1.9 percent in Denmark, 1.7 percent in Norway. In Finland, the estimated number of foreigners is about 12,000 persons, representing 0.2 percent of the total population.

TABLE 10:1

Migration Flows Between the Scandinavian Countries,
by Five Year Periods, Since 1951[a]

Years	From Finland to Sweden	From Sweden to Finland	Net[b]	From Denmark to Sweden	From Sweden to Denmark	Net[b]
1951-55	47,500	15,400	32,100 S	19,700	12,400	7,300 S
1956-60	47,600	14,600	33,000 S	21,000	14,200	6,800 S
1961-65	74,100	20,500	53,600 S	13,700	12,600	1,100 S
1966-70	124,700	36,400	89,300 S	14,000	12,200	1,800 S
1971-75	57,800	71,400	13,600 F	25,600	16,500	9,100 S

Years	From Norway to Sweden	From Sweden to Norway	Net[b]	From Finland to Denmark	From Denmark to Finland	Net[b]
1951-55	11,500	8,400	3,100 S	1,300	1,100	200 D
1956-60	10,400	6,800	3,600 S	1,300	1,000	300 D
1961-65	12,800	7,200	5,600 S	2,800	1,100	1,700 D
1966-70	12,900	11,100	1,800 S	2,500	1,400	1,100 D
1971-75	11,800	13,500	1,700 N	2,700	2,400	300 D

TABLE 10:1 (continued)

Migration Flows Between the Scandinavian Countries,
by Five Year Periods, Since 1951

Years	From Finland to Norway	From Norway to Finland	Net[b]	From Norway to Denmark	From Denmark to Norway	Net[b]
1951-55	...	...	...	16,200	19,600	3,400 N
1956-60	(1,200)	(900)	(400)N	19,600	20,300	700 N
1961-65	1,100	900	200 N	18,600	15,900	2,700 D
1966-70	2,100	1,600	600 N	(12,300)	(10,800)	1,500 D
1971-75	2,300	1,800	600 N	12,400	14,100	1,300 N

Notes: [a] Denmark, estimated population 1975, 5.1 million; Finland, estimated population 1975, 4.7 million; Norway, estimated population 1975, 3.9 million; and Sweden, estimated population 1975, 8.2 million.
[b] The letter after the net figure (D = Denmark, etc.) indicates the country gaining from migration.

Source: A. Majava. *Migrations Between Finland and Sweden from 1946 to 1974: A Demographic Analysis.* Helsinki: Ministry of Labor, Planning Division. 1975.

TABLE 10:2

Percent Distribution of Domiciled Aliens in Denmark,
Norway and Sweden, by Nationality or Area of Origin, in 1975[a]

| | Aliens Domiciled in | | | | | |
| | Sweden | | Denmark | | Norway | |
Country or Area	N	Per-cent	N	Per-cent	N	Per-cent
Nordic Countries	251,511	61.2	22,121	23.5	24,181	38.2
Sweden	—	—	7,462	7.9	7,347	11.3
Denmark	38,352	9.3	—	—	14,147	21.8
Norway	27,476	6.7	10,364	11.0	—	—
Finland	184,102	44.8	2,363	2.5	1.811	2.8
Iceland	1,581	0.4	1,932	2.1	876	1.3
European Community (except Denmark)	35,919	8.7	23,844	25.3	13,500[b]	20.8
Yugoslavia	40,424	9.8	6,896	7.3	1,530	2.4
Greece	17,832	4.3	769	0.8	200[b]	0.3
Turkey	7,003	1.7	8,129	8.6	1,156	1.8
USA	6,310	1.5	5,911	6.3	10,290	15.8
Africa and Asia	12,442	3.0	14,887	15.8	7,519	11.6
Stateless and unknown	4,294	1.0	2,863	3.0	511	0.8
Other[c]	34,951	8.8	6,849	9.4	6,045	9.3
All aliens	410,657	100.0	94,199	100.0	64,932	100.0
Aliens as percent of total population		5.0		1.9		1.7

Notes: [a] Data for Sweden as of November 1, 1975; Denmark, January 1; Norway, December 1.
[b] Estimates.
[c] Mostly other Europe but also Americas and Oceania. Small numbers per country or region.

Sources: The Nordic Council and the Nordic Statistical Secretariat. *Yearbook of Nordic Statistics 1975.* NU 1975:38. Stockholm; B. Puntervold Boe. "Foreigners in Norway". Paper before the Third Nordic Seminar on Migration Research. Mimeo; Sweden: National Central Bureau of Statistics. *Population and Housing Census 1975,* Part 3:3.

Sweden: Immigrants were not received to any noticeable extent in Sweden until the end of World War II. In 1945 there were only 35,100 aliens resident in the country, representing one-half of one percent of the total population. By 1950, the number of aliens increased to 123,700; in 1960 it reached 190,600; and in 1970 there were 407,800 aliens in Sweden, representing about 5 percent of the total population. Immigration had been comparatively small since 1971 and net migration was negative during the years 1972 and 1973. The number of domiciled aliens is now remaining stable. Taking into account the natural increase of the alien population, immigration contributed some 650,000 to the population of Sweden between 1944 and 1970, representing about 40 percent of the population increase.[1]

At the census of November 1, 1975 the total resident population of Sweden was 8.2 million, of which 410,657 were enumerated as alien residents while 231,641 of the Swedish citizens were foreign born.[2] It is estimated that the first and the second generation immigrants in Sweden account for at least 8 percent of its population. The sex ratio of all aliens in Sweden is fairly balanced with 47.8 percent females in 1975. However, the in-migrants from the Mediterranean countries are more likely to be males. Most of the married male immigrants have their wives with them.[3] The immigrants have a young population structure: children under 15 years of age account for 30 percent of all immigrants and persons 50 years of age or older for only 8 percent. This compares with the national figures of 46 and 34 percent respectively.[4] The in-migrants are heavily concentrated in Central and Southern Sweden. Although the largest cities have sizeable numbers of aliens, aliens are "over-represented" in many small municipalities and exceeded 10 percent of the population in 18 municipalities in 1973. There are 278 municipalities in Sweden.[5]

Denmark: Before World War I, Denmark already had a considerable number of foreign workers. After World War II, Denmark's net immigration accelerated, especially during the 1960s. Despite a worker recruitment ban introduced in 1970, the number of foreign workers continues to grow. In 1960 there were 9,300 aliens and in 1970 24,200 aliens holding a work permit. In 1975, the number of alien work permit holders including the nationals of the European Communities countries rose to 41,100.[6]

[1] Rolf Olofsson. *Den utrikes omflyttningen sedan 1944 och des betydelse för Sveriges befolkningsutveckling* (The effect of post-war external migration on population trends in Sweden), National Central Bureau of Statistics, Forecasting Information 1972:14, Stockholm. 1972. P. 61.

[2] Sweden, National Central Bureau of Statistics. Population and Housing Census 1975, Part 3:3. 1977. P. 9.

[3] Jonas Widgren. *The Position of Immigrants in Sweden.* Report for the UN Secretariat, May 26, 1974. Stockholm: Ministry of Labor. 1974. Mimeo. P. 9.

[4] Sweden, National Central Bureau of Statistics. Population and Housing Census 1975, Part 3:3. 1977. Pp. 9, 105.

[5] Nordisk Utredningsserie. *Nordisk Kommunal Rösträtt och Valbarhet* (Voting eligibility in Scandinavia). Report NU 1975:4. Oslo: The Nordic Council of Ministers. 1975. Pp. 50-55.

[6] Denmark: Ministry of Labor. *Betaenkning nr. 589 om Udenlandske Arbejderes Forhold i Danmark* (Conditions of foreign workers in Denmark). Report of a Commission. Copenhagen: Statens Trykningskontor. 1971. P. 18; Nordisk Utredningsserie. *Nordisk Kommunal Rösträtt*

TABLE 10:3

Percent Distribution of Foreign Born Residents in Sweden
by Occupational Categories and by Proportion in Occupational Categories

Occupations (Groups)	Percent Foreign Born per Category	Percent of Foreign Born among All Workers
Code Name		
0 Scientific, technical, etc.	16.7	7.4
1 Administrative and managerial	1.4	5.1
2 Clerical work	7.2	5.6
3 Commerical and sales	4.9	4.7
4 Agriculture,, forestry, etc.	3.0	3.1
5 Mining and quarrying	0.5	10.4
6 Transport and communication	3.1	4.0
7-8 Industrial production	51.3	12.7
90-94 Services	11.5	10.1
Other or unknown	0.5	—
	100.0	

Source: Statens Offentliga Utredningar, 1974:69, Invandrarutredningen 3. Stockholm: Ministry of Labor. Pp. 102-103.

The 94,199 domiciled aliens in 1975 comprised nearly two percent of Denmark's population of 5.1 million. In 1975, 44 percent of the number of aliens were female. Of the domiciled aliens, 24 percent were persons 15 years or younger; those 65 years of age or over represented 2.6 percent. This compares to 23 and 13.5 percent for the respective groups in the total population. About two-thirds of all aliens live in the Greater Copenhagen area.[7]

Norway: The number of foreign workers in Norway remained remarkably stable in the 1950s and 1960s, varying between 13,000 to 16,600 persons between 1952 and 1970.[8] There was some increase in the immigration into Norway in the early 1970s. In August, 1973 (the last official reporting on the stand of aliens employed in Norway) there were 21,200 foreigners working

och Valbarhet (Voting eligibility in Scandinavia). Report NU 1975:4. Oslo: The Nordic Council of Ministers. 1975. P. 33.

[7] Nordisk Utredningsserie. *Nordisk Kommunal Rösträtt och Valbarhet* (Voting eligibility in Scandinavia). Report NU 1975:4. Oslo: The Nordic Council of Ministers. 1975. P. 33.

[8] Norway: Norges Offentlige Utredninger. *Innvandringspolitikk.* Report No. 1973:17 by the Committee of October 16, 1970 on immigration of labor policies. Oslo: Universitetsforlaget. 1973. P. 52.

in Norway,[9] representing about 1.5 percent of the total labor force. In 1974 and 1975 there was a considerable influx of aliens working in the oil industry.[10] Hence, the proportion of aliens in the labor force may have been nearly 2 percent in 1975. Foreign seamen (under 7,000 in June, 1975) sailing on Norwegian merchant ships are not included in these figures. Women represent about one-half the number of immigrants from North, East and Central Europe, but they are underrepresented among in-migrants from Southern Europe and from Asia and Africa.[11] The age composition of the alien population is normal with the exception of the immigrants from North America: 27 percent of these were 67 years of age or over in 1975 and were, no doubt, Norwegian return migrants. Most aliens live in the Greater Oslo area and a few of the other major Norwegian cities.[12]

Finland: Domiciled aliens were, in 24 percent of the cases, 61 years or older in 1973, no doubt being return migrants to their home country.[13] Also, return migration from Sweden between 1973 and 1975 may account for the increase in the number of aliens in Finland from 7,400 to 11,300 persons. In the 1970s the number of valid work permits was stable at about 4,000 permit holders. About 1,100 work permits have been issued to long-time residents while most of the other permits are issued for short periods only.

A considerable part of international migrations in Scandinavia were movements from one Nordic country to another.[14] No significant changes in the flow of migrants occurred after the establishment of the Common Nordic Labor Market. However, out-migration from Finland to Sweden increased sharply during the 1960s and stabilized in the 1970s. Between the years 1956 and 1975 about 815,000 persons moved from one Scandinavian country to another. Finnish emigrants contributed about 37 percent to the total flow and their return from Sweden added another 18 percent. Migration from Denmark to Sweden accounted for 9 percent of the total migration flow and migration from Sweden to Denmark accounted for 7 percent. Migratory movements between Norway and Denmark were in balance and represented 18 percent of the total, while emigration from Norway to Sweden represented

[9] Nordisk Utredningsserie. *Nordisk Kommunal Rösträtt och Valbarhet* (Voting eligibility in Scandinavia). Report NU 1975:4. Oslo: The Nordic Council of Ministers. 1975. P. 66.

[10] Norway: Norges Offentlige Utredninger. Statement No. 107, 1975-1976. The Parliament. 1976. Pp. 16-18.

[11] Bente Puntervold Boe. "Foreigners in Norway". Paper read before the Third Nordic Seminar on Migration Research. Espoo, Finland, May, 1976. Mimeo.

[12] Norway: Norges Offentlige Utredninger. Statement No. 107, 1975-1976. The Parliament. 1976. P. 20.

[13] Nordisk Utredningsserie. *Nordisk Kommunal Rösträtt och Valbarhet* (Voting eligibility in Scandinavia). Report NU 1975:4. Oslo: The Nordic Council of Ministers. 1975. P. 36.

[14] Altti Majava. *Migrations between Finland and Sweden from 1946 to 1974: A Demographic Analysis.* Helsinki: Ministry of Labor, Planning Division. 1975. Mimeo.

6 percent and from Sweden to Norway 5 percent of all migratory movements during the twenty year period.

SWEDEN

Migration Policy: Goals and Administration

The development toward the present-day migration policy in Sweden had its start in the mid-1960s. In 1966, the Swedish government set up a task force to deal with the social and cultural conditions of immigrants. Later, this task force became a part of the National Immigration and Naturalization Board established in 1969. In 1968, the Swedish Parliament adopted new guidelines for the admission of foreigners and the Government appointed a Royal Commission on Immigration to provide a comprehensive picture of the immigrant and ethnic minorities in Sweden. In its final report, published in 1974, the Commission articulated the goals and principles of the Swedish immigration policy. A bill based on the proposals was adopted unanimously by the Parliament in May, 1975.

The new position on immigration holds that if immigrants are to have the same economic and social advantages as the rest of the population, then a restrictive admission practice applying to potential immigrants from non-Nordic areas must be continued. Potential immigrants from outside the Nordic countries must have a work permit and be assured housing prior to entering Sweden. Immigrants will be treated as Swedes regardless of the intended length of stay. A special feature of the new policy is the linking of immigrant and minority affairs. This is not surprising since the most significant minorities, with the exception of Lapps and Tornedal Finns, have resulted from immigration.

The new policy on immigration rests on four premises: 1) international migrations are expected to continue and to give rise to acute social problems which Sweden must be prepared to help solve; 2) a large number of in-migrants to Sweden will settle there permanently and form linguistic and cultural minorities; 3) many in-migrants will eventually return to their own countries and, therefore, they and their children should be afforded opportunities to maintain their own language and cultural heritage as well as an active contact with their own country; and 4) all immigrants are to be treated alike and on an equal basis with Swedes. This means an equality of opportunity, a freedom to retain their own ethnic identity, and a right to partake in the building of the country, politically and culturally.

Administratively, in-migrants and immigrants fall under the same civil administration as Swedes. The Ministry of Labor is responsible for the overall coordination of immigration policy implementation. One of its sections, the Division of Immigration and Citizenship, reports directly to the Minister in Charge of Immigration Affairs. Three bodies, the Commission on Aliens Legislation, the Council on Immigrant Affairs and the Commission on Migration Research are attached to the Ministry of Labor to deal with specific aspects of immigration policy and administration. Other matters relating to immigrants fall under the respective ministerial portfolios. The National Immigration and Naturalization Board has the overall responsibility to implement the policies of the day. The Board is responsible for issuing residence and work permits, awarding Swedish citizenship, coordinating activities of public authorities and voluntary associations, and fostering adjustment of immigrants to Swedish life including taking care of the social welfare of immigrants.[15]

Immigration Regulations

Already before the establishment of the Common Nordic Labor Market in 1954, citizens of Denmark, Finland, Iceland and Norway were entitled to migrate to Sweden without restrictions. The work permit requirement was abolished in 1943 for all Nordic nationals and the visa requirements were abolished after World War II for all except the Finns. For them, visa requirements were abolished in 1949. No passports are required of Nordic citizens for intra-Scandinavian travel. A special Swedish-Finnish agreement attempts to channel migrations of Finns to Sweden through the public employment service of the two countries.

The present Aliens Act was passed in 1954, but has been amended several times since, notably in 1968 and 1975. The current provisions are in force since January 1, 1976.[16] Provisions for residence and work permits reflect the need of Sweden to harmonize immigration with its own resources and economic and political situation. In other words, in granting work permits due regard is to be given to the possibilities to mobilize the domestic resources first, including women, the handicapped and the elderly by means of job retraining, job relocation and similar efforts. In particular, in-migrant labor should not be used to regulate the supply of labor in response to business cycle fluctuations. Furthermore, in-migrant workers are not to be concentrated

[15] Jonas Widgren. *The Position of Immigrants in Sweden.* Report for the UN Secretariat, May 26, 1974. Stockholm: Ministry of Labor. 1974. Mimeo; Jonas Widgren. *Memorandum on Swedish Immigration Policy, January 17, 1977.* Stockholm: Ministry of Labor. 1977.

[16] Jonas Widgren. *The Position of Immigrants in Sweden.* Report for the UN Secretariat, May 26, 1974. Stockholm: Ministry of Labor. 1974. Mimeo; Jonas Widgren. *The SOPEMI Report on Sweden.* Stockholm: Ministry of Labor; OECD Document SME/MI/76:12 (Sweden). Paris. 1976. Mimeo.

in low wage industries only and they must be offered satisfactory working conditions. No ceiling has been set for the number of residence or work permits to be issued.

All non-Nordic citizens wishing to settle in Sweden are required to have employment, housing and work permits arranged in advance, before entering the country. This provision, in force since 1967, requires such aliens to apply for their permits through Swedish embassies and consulates. Applications for work permits are then submitted for approval to the appropriate trade unions and to the National Labor Market Board. Final decision is made by the National Immigration and Naturalization Board. Housing is the responsibility of the employer recruiting the in-migrant.

The first work permit is granted usually for one year, is valid for a specified occupation but is open as to a specific job. Once an in-migrant has been admitted, he cannot be refused a work permit renewal for reasons of job scarcity. After the first year, the work permit is valid for all occupations. After one year's residence in Sweden, an alien may be granted a permanent residence permit in which case neither residence nor work permit need to be renewed for as long as he remains domiciled in Sweden. A spouse and minor children may join a person in Sweden already holding a permit to work, without obtaining their permits in advance. Special regulations apply to political refugees and other persons who have grave reasons for not wanting to return to their home countries because of political conditions there. No specific provisions or arrangements are available nor are incentives provided for in-migrants to return to their home countries. In case of return, social security payments are not refunded. The earned supplementary retirement pension, however, will be paid to all eligible persons 65 years or older regardless of their domicile.

Immigrants and the Job Market

Sweden has concluded agreements on the recruitment of labor with three countries: Italy, in 1947 (suspended in 1976); Yugoslavia, in 1966; and Turkey, in 1967. On the whole, collective recruitment of workers into Sweden has been negligible.[17] Aliens have no unconditional right to employment in Sweden. There are specific regulations for instance of aliens' rights to become entrepreneurs. Generally, however, laws and rules of the labor market apply to immigrants and Swedish nationals alike. Foreign workers are entitled to public employment services, occupational training, unemployment benefits and disability compensation, as are Swedes.

[17] Jonas Widgren. "Immigration in Sweden in 1972", *Migration Research in Scandinavia.* A. Majava, ed. Helsinki: Ministry of Labor, Planning Division. 1973.

Immigrants and Swedes alike take part in collective agreements on work contracts and both have the same rights to participate in trade union activities. Nevertheless, immigrants may be somewhat less protected than Swedish citizens as regards notices of dismissal or layoffs.

Intergovernmental agreements specify job orientation programs for new foreign workers, but orientation courses vary in length and content depending on the employer. Large enterprises may organize effective orientation courses lasting several days and covering all essential aspects of the job and the workplace, safety measures, collective agreements, opportunities for further training, trade unions activities and similar activities. Small enterprises, on the other hand, may offer an ineffective orientation program and usually a short one.

There is close cooperation between employers and trade unions in regard to industrial safety. However, the difference in frequency of accidents to Swedes and in-migrants is still considerable. In addition to warning signs and instructions on how to operate machines in the languages of the in-migrants, interpreters are needed. Thus far, however, immigrant shop-stewards with interpreter skills are rare.

In 1973, a legislative regulation was passed requiring employers to give their immigrant workers a paid leave of up to 240 hours so that the workers can take a course in Swedish. The pay must be the same the worker would have received had he stayed on the job. The bill is retroactive, covering immigrant arrivals before 1973, and it also covers part-time workers. New immigrants must be given information about the language training opportunities, their leave of absence must be granted within sixty days of starting their jobs. The courses in Swedish and in Swedish civics are being offered by voluntary adult education organizations. Thus far, the courses were taken mainly during the off work hours of immigrants, which is not the intention of the bill. Moreover, most of the "old" immigrants, that is those arriving in Sweden before 1973, have not taken advantage of the language and civics program.[18]

Foreign workers are entitled to the same unemployment benefits as are Swedes. Starting in 1975, the Swedish government pays unemployment benefits to immigrants who have not worked in Sweden long enough to be covered or who have not been able to transfer their coverage from their home country. Immigrants have the same entitlements as Swedes falling under the labor market and employment policy. The foremost of such entitlements is vocational training. Each year some 10,000 to 15,000 aliens participate in such programs. Aliens represent about 15 percent of all participants. As a part of occupational training programs, unemployed

---

[18] Jonas Widgren. *The Position of Immigrants in Sweden.* Report for the UN Secretariat, May 26, 1974. Stockholm: Ministry of Labor. 1974. Mimeo.

immigrants may receive up to two or, in certain cases, up to four months of full time instruction in Swedish. Some vocational training courses have been organized experimentally in the language of immigrants, mainly in Finnish.

Housing and Welfare

Immigrants to Sweden are entitled to the same housing benefits as are Swedes. This means that they may receive rent subsidies, loans to newlyweds, and similar.[19] There is little in the way of special housing for immigrants in Sweden. Although many immigrants live in areas scheduled for slum clearance, immigrants in similar socioeconomic situations as Swedes tend to differ but little in the quality of their housing, with the exception of crowding. There is some ethnic "ghettoization" especially in the new housing developments.[20]

Practically all the social benefits available to Swedes are also available to immigrants. Domiciled immigrants are entitled to children allowances, social assistance, and the supplementary pension insurance. In principle, the basic old age pension is available to Swedish citizens only. Nevertheless, as a result of agreements with several countries sending in-migrant workers to Sweden, more than 90 percent of all aliens are entitled to the basic old age pension. However, they must have lived in Sweden for at least 3 to 5 years. The Commission on Immigration is proposing that, after a certain period of residence, all aliens should become entitled to the basic old age pension of the same terms as Swedes.

All residents of Sweden are covered by medical and health insurance. That includes medical expenses, hospital costs, loss of earnings during illness, dental care, and similar. Maternity and child health services are available free of charge to domiciled aliens as well. The overall health of immigrants in Sweden may be considered satisfactory even though they seem to have more than their share of tuberculosis and mental illness.[21] Many immigrants make little use of their equal rights regarding health and social welfare. This may be due to the language barrier but perhaps also to the differing cultural valuation of such services. A Parliamentary resolution in 1973 stipulates that more efforts must be put into creating a network of interpreters to facilitate an integration of immigrants into the Swedish society.[22]

[19] Sweden: Ministry of Labor. *Immigrants in Sweden. A Summary of Swedish Immigration Policy.* Stockholm: Ministry of Labor. 1975.

[20] Jonas Widgren. *The Position of Immigrants in Sweden.* Report for the UN Secretariat, May 26, 1974. Stockholm: Ministry of Labor. 1974. Mimeo.

[21] *Ibid.*

[22] Sweden: Ministry of Labor. *Immigrants in Sweden. A Summary of Swedish Immigration Policy.* Stockholm: Ministry of Labor. 1975.

Education and Related Services

Immigrants and Swedes enjoy an equal access to all educational services, from the kindergarten to the university level. School attendance is mandatory for all children aged 7 to 16. Immigrant children are given special instruction in Swedish and other subjects for a transitional period. A Parliament resolution of 1968 provides for instruction of immigrants in their mother tongue. This auxiliary instruction in the nine year comprehensive school may total six periods a week, two of which may be used for teaching the mother tongue. A bill passed in the spring of 1976 considerably increases the number of hours devoted to the immigrant's mother tongue.[23] The aim of Swedish policy is now to promote an active bilingualism among the immigrant children and, consequently, great attention is being paid to the instruction of and in the mother tongue. A proper command of the native language will not only make it easier for a child to learn another language (that is Swedish), but also will facilitate a healthful emotional development, the new bill argues.[24]

Providing immigrant children with an adequate instruction in their mother tongue is not an easy task in Sweden. At the present time there are about 63,000 immigrant children in the nine year comprehensive schools and about 7,000 students in the upper secondary schools. Among themselves, the immigrant students represent 100 different languages. In areas having too few immigrants, it is difficult to bring together enough students for a class. Recruitment of competent teachers and securing of adequate teaching materials are not easy. Moreover, schooling is a concern of municipalities, affecting the program to teach immigrant children. In about 50 municipalities, there are ordinary classes taught in the immigrant children's mother tongue only in the first few grades. Most of these classes are in Finnish. There are about 850 teachers who are Finns, but the need is twice as great. Other language groups fare much worse.

Many adult immigrants from countries outside of North and Central Europe are in need of a basic education. There are special programs run by voluntary associations or by university extension programs for the functionally illiterate immigrants and for gypsies.[25] A special university extension

---

[23] Jonas Widgren. *The Position of Immigrants in Sweden.* Report for the UN Secretariat, May 26, 1974. Stockholm: Ministry of Labor. 1974. Mimeo; Jonas Widgren. *The SOPEMI Report on Sweden.* Stockholm: Ministry of Labor; OECD Document SME/MI/76:12 (Sweden). Paris. 1976. Mimeo.

[24] Sweden: Ministry of Labor. *Immigrants in Sweden. A Summary of Swedish Immigration Policy.* Stockholm: Ministry of Labor. 1975.

[25] The extension programs are actually independent of universities being offered by a Folkshogskola. It is an institution providing adult education but without university or college credits. It is similar in its function to the North American university extension programs.

program for Finnish immigrants was established in 1973.[26]

Cultural demands of immigrants are now assuming a growing importance and a variety of ethnic voluntary associations have sprung up. Presently, there are nearly 800 immigrant and minority associations in Sweden. The National Federation of Finnish Associations numbers more than 50,000 members and the National Federation of Yugoslavs about 12,000.[27] Immigrants' interests are being promoted by a governmental grant-in-aid system to the existing ethnic voluntary associations. The National Immigration and Naturalization Board started with a subsidy program of immigrant associations in its fiscal year 1975-1976. The grants cover civic activities, theater productions, ethnic press, purchases by local libraries to carry foreign language books, and similar functions.[28]

The main agency taking care of immigrant affairs is the National Immigration and Naturalization Board. Aside from administering work and residence permits and naturalization applications, the Board is also responsible for providing extensive information to the various immigrant voluntary associations and the press, and for running experimental programs on immigrant adjustment. The Board publishes news and information releases in 15 languages and one general publication for the Swedish public. The Swedish government established a Foundation in 1967 to publish an immigrant newsletter in five languages. The newsletter is a weekly and has a circulation of 40,000. There are also special programs broadcast in Finnish, seven hours each week. Finnish television programs total three hours each week. Radio and television broadcasts are now also conducted in Yugoslav, Greek and Turkish. At the local level, about 70 Immigrant Service Bureaus provide information and advice to immigrants. The Bureaus are sponsored by the municipalities. One of their main functions is to provide interpreter services free of charge. The costs of all these services are difficult to estimate, but they are considerable. The state budget for 1976/1977 shows a sum of about 60 million dollars earmarked for education and other special programs for immigrants and refugees.[29]

Civil Rights

An alien has no unconditional right to enter, to reside and to work in Sweden, nor is an immigrant entitled to participate in parliamentary

[26] Jonas Widgren. *The Position of Immigrants in Sweden*. Report for the UN Secretariat, May 26, 1974. Stockholm: Ministry of Labor. 1974. Mimeo.

[27] *Ibid.*

[28] Sweden: Ministry of Labor. *Immigrants in Sweden. A Summary of Swedish Immigration Policy.* Stockholm: Ministry of Labor. 1975.

[29] Jonas Widgren. *Memorandum on Swedish Immigration Policy, January 17, 1977.* Stockholm: Ministry of Labor. 1977.

elections. There are also some limitations regarding eligibility for a civil service appointment, the right to own a business or to acquire real estate. Aliens are exempt from military service. No restrictions are imposed on the alien's right to pursue political activities in Sweden. Immigrants are encouraged to join trade unions and to be active in labor politics. As of 1976, all aliens 18 years of age or more, who have lived in the country for more than three years, have voting rights and are eligible to vote in regional and municipal elections. About 220,000 immigrants became enfranchised in the fall of 1976.[30] The citizenship legislation adopted in 1976 allows non-Nordic citizens to acquire Swedish citizenship after five (seven, prior to 1976) years in the country. Nordic citizens can become Swedish citizens after two years of residence.[31]

DENMARK

Migration Policy: Goals and Administration

In recent years, a considerable number of measures have been proposed and put in operation in Denmark to deal with in-migration. Practical solutions have been found to a wide range of problems, but thus far no explicit goals of Danish in-migration policy have been articulated. There are two governmental documents on in-migration, published in 1971 and 1975 respectively.[32] There are some parallels to the immigration policy of Sweden, but of much more modest proportions.

In formulation in-migration regulations the Danish authorities advert to the domestic employment situation, to the housing and social conditions of in-migrants already in the country, and to the explicit goal of the Danish in-migration policy that all residents of Denmark enjoy the same rights and privileges. There is, however, no central authority to handle in-migration

---

[30] Jonas Widgren. *The SOPEMI Report on Sweden.* Stockholm: Ministry of Labor; OECD Document SME/MI/76:12 (Sweden). Paris. 1976. Mimeo; Dagens Nyheter, Feb. 24, 1977.

In the September, 1976 elections, 59 percent of the eligible aliens voted; 195 out of the 1,200 immigrant candidates were elected to a seat on the municipal and regional councils. In comparison, 92 percent of eligible Swedes cast their ballots.

[31] Jonas Widgren. *The SOPEMI Report on Sweden.* Stockholm: Ministry of Labor; OECD Document SME/MI/76:12 (Sweden). Paris. 1976. Mimeo.

[32] Denmark: Ministry of Labor. *Betaenkning nr. 589 om Udenlandske Arbejderes Forhold i Danmark* (Conditions of foreign workers in Denmark). Report of a Commission. Copenhagen: Statens Trykningskontor. 1971; Denmark: Ministry of Social Affairs. *Betaenkning nr. 761 om Udenlandske Arbejderes Sociale og Samfundsmaessige Tilpasning her i Landet.* (Social and Societal Adjustment of Foreign Workers in Denmark). Copenhagen: Statens Trykningskontor. 1975.

matters in Denmark. Regulations concerning in-migrant workers are issued by the Ministry of Labor; there is a small bureau attached to the Ministry of Social Affairs handling the counseling of in-migrants. Otherwise, in-migrants' affairs are handled by the same offices and branches of the governmental administration as pertain to the affairs of Danes. It is being proposed that the informal cooperation among the various branches of the government in matters of in-migrants be placed on a firmer basis.[33]

In-Migration Regulations

Nordic citizens are entitled to enter, to reside and to work in Denmark without restrictions. Denmark also joined the European Communities in 1973 so that nationals of the member countries do not need work permits to work there. However, they do have to have a special European Communities certificate of residence. Other aliens seeking to work in Denmark must apply from without the country. Regulations concerning work permits were revised several times between the years 1969 and 1973. In practice, a labor recruitment ban has been in force continuously since November, 1970, except for a brief period in 1973. In effect, work permits are now granted only in the case of family reunion, for some designated occupations, and to bona fide political refugees. No work permits are granted to persons who have entered Denmark as tourists.

A work permit is granted for a specified period. At first issuance this period is for one year. During the first two years, the permit is tied to a particular employer. In-migrant workers must undergo a health examination and must register with an unemployment insurance fund. Within the first three months of employment, they are required to register for a 40 hour course in Danish and civics. The employer of foreign workers is required to find them suitable housing, to pay the travel expenses of the workers to Denmark, and in case of a temporary in-migration, the fare back. To change employer, the in-migrant must seek permission through the local Employment Service.[34] An in-migrant worker in possession of his work permit may normally count on receiving a residence permit for his wife and dependent children. Family members of in-migrants are not automatically eligible for work permits.

[33] Denmark: Ministry of Social Affairs. *Betaenkning nr. 761 om Udenlandske Arbejderes Sociale og Samfundsmaessige Tilpasning her i Landet.* (Social and Societal Adjustment of Foreign Workers in Denmark). Copenhagen: Statens Trykningskontor. 1975. P. 31.

[34] Denmark: Ministry of Social Affairs. *Fremmedarbejder i Danmark.* Copenhagen: Ministry of Social Affairs, Information Section. 1974. Pp. 12-15; Denmark: Ministry of Social Affairs. *Betaenkning nr. 761 om Udenlandske Arbejderes Sociale og Samfundsmaessige Tilpasning her i Landet.* (Social and Societal Adjustment of Foreign Workers in Denmark). Copenhagen: Statens Trykningskontor. 1975. P. 42.

Employment

In-migrant workers are accorded equality of treatment with Danes with regard to wages, working conditions, work safety, unemployment insurance, and similar programs. As for work safety, there are warning signs, where appropriate, worded in the language of the in-migrant workers.[35] Foreign workers must enter the unemployment insurance fund, but after two years of employment in Denmark, their membership in the fund becomes voluntary. Contributors to the unemployment fund are entitled to unemployment benefits after six months of membership. Under certain conditions, unemployed European Communities nationals may receive their accrued unemployment benefits three months after entry into Denmark.[36] Workers recruited from outside the European Communities are entitled to a return fare should they have no short term prospect of employment.[37] There are special courses in Danish for in-migrant workers. The courses are for 110 hours, are designed to provide the students with 1,000 words of basic Danish, and are free of charge.

Housing and Welfare

In spite of various clauses in the Danish tenancy legislation, in-migrants have difficulties obtaining good housing. The Danish Government makes grants available for housing construction on the condition that a fixed proportion of the housing will be let to the in-migrant workers and their families, both indigenous and foreign. Many large enterprises built housing for their foreign workers. Foreign workers are entitled to the same housing subsidies as are Danes.[38]

All forms of social services and health care are available to in-migrants and Danes alike and all in-migrants are covered in case of sickness. After six weeks from the date of registration, they are eligible for benefits.[39] In-

[35] Denmark: Ministry of Social Affairs. *Betaenkning nr. 761 om Udenlandske Arbejderes Sociale og Samfundsmaessige Tilpasning her i Landet.* (Social and Societal Adjustment of Foreign Workers in Denmark). Copenhagen: Statens Trykningskontor. 1975. P. 7.

[36] Denmark: Ministry of Social Affairs. *Fremmedarbejder i Danmark.* Copenhagen: Ministry of Social Affairs, Information Section. 1974. Pp. 29-30.

[37] Conference of European Ministers of Labor. *Situation of Migrant Workers in Europe.* Report from a Conference held in Rome in November, 1072. Strassbourg: Document CMT (72) 6. 1972. P. 11. Mimeo.

[38] *Ibid.* P. 10; Denmark: Ministry of Social Affairs. *Betaenkning nr. 761 om Udenlandske Arbejderes Sociale og Samfundsmaessige Tilpasning her i Landet.* (Social and Societal Adjustment of Foreign Workers in Denmark). Copenhagen: Statens Trykningskontor. 1975. P. 15.

[39] Nordisk Utredningsserie. *Nordisk Kommunal Rösträtt och Valbarhet* (Voting eligibility in Scandinavia). Report NU 1975:4. Oslo: The Nordic Council of Ministers. 1975. P. 59.

migrant parents are eligible to receive child allowances after one year's stay in Denmark. In most cases, however, these benefits are granted sooner. Nationals of the Nordic countries, or of the European Communities treaty countries are entitled to these allowances soon after entry; citizens of Greece and Turkey after a six month stay. Refugees are also treated favorably. To be eligible for old age, invalid, or survivor's pension, it is necessary to be a Danish citizen. Hence, except nationals of the Nordic and the European Communities countries, the rights of aliens to such pensions are limited. Proposals to improve the pension regulations are pending.[40] In-migrants may deduct from their Danish taxable income payment tendered to their dependents outside Denmark.

Education and Related Services

All children in Denmark have a right to general education. The Danish policy is that foreign children should be integrated with children their own age and in classes conducted in Danish. Introductory classes where Danish is taught by bilingual teachers are arranged in areas showing a heavy settlement of foreign workers.[41] Adult education programs are open equally to in-migrants and Danes, but in-migrants seem to make little use of them. Only a few in-migrants take advantage of the free Danish language courses.[42]

Governmental financial support to in-migrants' associations has been rather limited until recently. The Ministry of Social Affairs subsidizes national associations while local clubs receive support from the municipalities. Grants to libraries to acquire books in foreign languages are under consideration.[43] The most notable service to in-migrants, the Interpreter Center, was established in the Ministry of Social Affairs in 1971. Services are available to in-migrants, employers, and other governmental agencies; they are free of charge and the interpreting is conducted over the phone. The Danish government subsidizes a newsletter in five languages. The Danish Broadcasting Company occasionally provides programs in in-migrants' languages.

[40] Denmark: Ministry of Social Affairs. *Betaenkning nr. 761 om Udenlandske Arbejderes Sociale og Samfundsmaessige Tilpasning her i Landet* (Social and Societal Adjustment of Foreign Workers in Denmark). Copenhagen: Statens Trykningskontor. 1975. Pp. 8-11.

[41] Conference of European Ministers of Labor. *Situation of Migrant Workers in Europe.* Report from a Conference held in Rome in November, 1972. Strassbourg: Document CMT (72) 6. 1972. P. 12. Mimeo; Denmark: Ministry of Social Affairs. *Betaenkning nr. 761 om Udenlandske Arbejderes Sociale og Samfundsmaessige Tilpasning her i Landet* (Social and Societal Adjustment of Foreign Workers in Denmark). Copenhagen: Statens Trykningskontor. 1975. P. 25.

[42] Denmark: Ministry of Social Affairs. *Betaenkning nr. 761 om Udenlandske Arbejderes Sociale og Samfundsmaessige Tilpasning her i Landet* (Social and Societal Adjustment of Foreign Workers in Denmark). Copenhagen: Statens Trykningskontor. 1975. Pp. 17, 24-25.

[43] *Ibid.* Pp. 5, 29.

Civil Rights

By and large, in-migrants are accorded the same rights and have the same obligations as Danish nationals. In the trade unions, in-migrant workers have the same rights as Danes. With the exception of European Communities nationals working in Denmark, aliens need special permission to own real estate, including condominium apartments, unless the immigrants have been in Denmark for at least five years. No alien is eligible for jobs in civil service nor is he required to do military duty. Regional and municipal voting rights for all aliens have been proposed from 1978, but the proposal has not yet been acted upon.[44] Decisions on naturalizations are made in each case by the Parliament; Nordic nationals may obtain Danish citizenship after three years residence.[45]

NORWAY

Migration Policy: Goals and Administration

The Government of Norway initiated a Committee in October, 1970 to examine the problems associated with in-migration and to propose policies and practical measures to deal with the increased number of aliens working in Norway. The Report issued from the Committee served as a basis for the governmental special Statement concerning guidelines for an in-migration policy. The Statement was endorsed by the Norwegian Parliament in March, 1974,[46] as was the second Statement in May, 1976.[47]

It is the aim of the Norwegian government that international cooperation, contacts and exchanges in regard to labor migration meet with the least possible restrictions. Norway cannot completely separate itself from the rest of the world. However, being a small country Norway cannot receive many in-migrants despite the heavy population pressures elsewhere. For those in-

[44] Conference of European Ministers of Labor. *Situation of Migrant Workers in Europe.* Report from a Conference held in Rome in November, 1972. Strassbourg: Document CMT (72) 6. 1972. Pp. 9-11. Mimeo; Denmark: Ministry of Social Affairs. *Betaenkning nr. 761 om Udenlandske Arbejderes Sociale og Samfundsmaessige Tilpasning her i Landet* (Social and Societal Adjustment of Foreign Workers in Denmark). Copenhagen: Statens Trykningskontor. 1975. P. 27.

[45] Nordisk Utredningsserie. *Nordisk Kommunal Rösträtt och Valbarhet* (Voting eligibility in Scandinavia). Report NU 1975:4. Oslo: The Nordic Council of Ministers. 1975. Pp. 77-78.

[46] Norway: Norges Offentlige Utredninger. Statement No. 39, 1973-1974. The Parliament. 1974.

[47] Norway: Norges Offentlige Utredninger. Statement No. 107, 1975-1976. The Parliament. 1976.

migrants Norway accepts, conditions must be created to make them equal to Norwegians. Norway does not expect to base her in-migration policies on a temporary need for labor. As a matter of fact, Norway imposed a temporary in-migration ban in February, 1975. Admission policies, until 1970, were quite liberal.

Norway has no central authority to handle in-migration and has no plans to establish one. However, a consultative body, and an interministerial coordinating committee have been set up to deal with matters of in-migration. Otherwise, in-migrants are handled administratively by the same branches of the government serving Norwegians.

In-Migration Regulations

Citizens of Denmark, Finland and Sweden do not need work permits in Norway. Foreign seamen on Norwegian ships engaged in overseas trade, similarly, are not required to have a work permit, but they need special permission from the police if they are signing up in Norway. Since February 1, 1975 there has been a ban on granting work permits. Exceptions apply to persons married to a Norwegian national or to a person already holding a work permit; aliens of Norwegian origin or persons with very close connections to Norway, refugees, scientists, artists, "key" workers essential for industry or commerce, and trainees are also excepted from the work permit ban. The in-migration ban does not apply to persons needing only a residence permit. Family reunions can thus take place on the condition that satisfactory housing is available.

An initial work permit is granted for a particular job with a particular employer for a specified period, which is normally one year. Application must be made through a Norwegian embassy or consulate in the applicant's home country or the country of his legal residence for the preceding six months. The applicant must have a firm job offer and an employment contract for at least one year. He must be able to read and write in his mother tongue and, if need be, pass a medical examination. His employer is responsible for securing suitable housing. After the first year, a work permit may be granted for another year, but the restriction on employer is lifted at this point. After the first two years, work permits may be granted for an indefinite period of time. No requirement is attached to permit renewals in regard to housing. Normally, no enterprise in Norway is allowed to have more than 25 percent of its work force alien.

Employment

A holder of the initial work permit may count on being allowed to stay in Norway. The permit may be refused only on grounds unrelated to the general employment situation. Efforts are taken that foreigners do not cluster in low paid jobs. In-migrants who have been earning less than 75 percent of the stipulated basic amount ($1,800 in 1976) either in the preceding calendar year or on an average during the last three years, are entitled to unemployment compensation.[48]

In-migrant workers should undergo job orientation. However, well organized orientation programs by the employer in collaboration with the trade unions apply only to workers recruited abroad collectively and there are not many such workers. Thus, job orientation tends to vary substantially from employer to employer.

In-migrant workers and their family members are entitled to 240 hours of instruction in Norwegian and in civics. The courses are free of charge, are being offered evenings and are usually organized by the Workers Educational Association or the University Extension Program.[49] The Directorate of Labor arranges vocational training courses, also free of charge.

Housing and Welfare

The employer wishing to hire foreign workers must secure housing for them. The housing must be inspected and approved by the local health authorities, and the lease must be signed for one year. On the whole, in-migrants encounter a similar housing situation as do Norwegians. In Oslo, for example, the municipality assists in-migrating Norwegian youth and foreign in-migrants in searching for housing.

A comprehensive system of social security is provided by the National Insurance Scheme. The Scheme is obligatory. It covers all persons domiciled in Norway irrespective of citizenship. The insurance covers costs in case of illness and death, injury and childbirth, and provides unemployment compensation, disability, old age and survivors' pension. An insurance period of at least 40 years is normally required to qualify for the full basic and the supplementary pensions. To receive any pension at all, a minimum insurance period of three years is required. Family allowance is paid for all children under 16 years of age who are domiciled in Norway. Foreign workers are entitled to a limited tax deduction per dependent supported outside of Norway.[50]

Social welfare agencies have, in principle, the same responsibilities toward

---

[48] The National Insurance Institute. *Social Insurance in Norway.* Oslo: The National Insurance Institute. 1976. P. 20.

[49] *See* note 25.

[50] Norway: Norges Offentlige Utredninger. *Innvandringspolitikk.* Report No. 1973:17 by the Committee of October 16, 1970 on immigration of labor policies. Oslo: Universitetsforlaget. 1973. Pp. 12-17, 22.

domiciled aliens as toward Norwegians. Nevertheless, social conditions of in-migrants have not been solved as yet in a satisfactory manner. The lack of demonstrable equality was adduced in support of the in-migration ban issued in 1975. In-migrants are known for underutilizing various social services. One of the reasons for this may be their lack of language skills.

Education and Related Services

Education in the nine year basic school is compulsory for all children aged 7 to 16 years who are domiciled in Norway. Various municipalities organize introductory schooling for in-migrants' children. The courses are taught in the children's native languages. There are also supplementary courses in Norwegian for the children. Recently, a few separate schools were established for children of Americans working in Norway's oil industry.[51]

The Norwegian government supports religious organizations serving in-migrant workers and public monies go to in-migrants' associations for cultural activities. A major library in Oslo began to build up its collection of literature in some of the languages of in-migrants. An Information Office for Foreign Nationals was established in 1970. It is an affiliate of the County Labor Division for Oslo and Akershus and its function is to dispense advice and assistance to in-migrants. An interpreter service was established at the same office in 1975 to assist immigrants as well as authorities, organizations and other parties dealing with immigrants.[52] The state offers limited support to the press reaching the immigrants.

Civil Rights

Aliens in Norway enjoy the same basic human rights and have the same obligations as Norwegians. In principle, foreigners do not have an unlimited right to enter, to stay and to work in Norway, nor can they own real estate without governmental approval. With certain exceptions, they are not excluded from holding civil service jobs. They are equal to Norwegians in their rights to join trade unions and to hold an office there. It was recently proposed that aliens who have resided in Norway for at least three years be granted voting rights in local municipal elections as of 1979. Aliens are not

[51] Ole-Petter Opsand. "Research on the Social and Educational Situation of Immigrant Children". Paper read before the Third Nordic Seminar on Migration Research, Espoo, Finland, May, 1976. 1976. Mimeo.

[52] Norway: Norges Offentlige Utredninger. Statement No. 107, 1975-1976. The Parliament. 1976. P. 70.

required to serve in the military. As a rule, seven years' residence (three years for Nordic nationals) is required to obtain Norweigan citizenship.[53]

FINLAND

Migration Policy: Goals and Administration

Finland is a country of emigration. The outflow of Finns reached its new peak in the years 1969 and 1970, causing the country's population to decline. In November, 1970, the government of Finland set up an Emigration Commission to examine problems relating to out-migration, return migration and emigrants' conditions abroad. The Commission was to work out policy proposals on migration. Ministries concerned with out-migration issues are represented in the Commission; furthermore, representatives of the trade unions and the employers associations, the Finnish associations in Sweden, and the civic associations maintaining contact with Finns abroad are represented on the Commission. The Commission issued four Reports between 1972 to 1976. The Reports proposed a number of practical measures as well as some guidelines for a migration policy.

Out-migration policy is viewed as a general social policy. The Commission has worked out the following *desiderata* of migration policy: 1) every Finn must be assured a job or livelihood in Finland; 2) every Finn contemplating emigration must be given complete and reliable information on the alternatives open to him, upon which he can base his decision; 3) Finns living abroad must be guaranteed a possibility of return and a job at home; and 4) any Finn living abroad must be assured a chance to develop his or her identity. Finland must keep track of the living conditions of its emigrants and make sure they do not lack the necessary means to enjoy their own culture and to maintain a lively contact with their own country.[54]

Out-Migration

The 1954 Agreement establishing the Common Nordic Labor Market stipulates cooperation to ensure that workers are recruited to the greatest possible extent through the public employment service system. In practice, however, most Finnish migrants bypassed the official work recruitment

[53] Nordisk Utredningsserie. *Nordisk Kommunal Rösträtt och Valbarhet* (Voting eligibility in Scandinavia). Report NU 1975:4. Oslo: The Nordic Council of Ministers. 1975. P. 77.

[54] Finland: Emigration Commission. *Siirtolaisasiain Neuvottelukunnan Mietintö I* (Emigration Commission, Report No. 1). Helsinki: Committee Report No. 1972:119. 1973.

channels. Finland and Sweden signed a supplementary protocol in April, 1973, to put into effect the principles agreed upon in 1954. This means that employers are now constrained to recruit their workers through the official employment service.

Thirty special officers of the employment service were designated to provide emigrants and returnees with information and advice, in addition to job placement. Great efforts are being made to inform the potential Finnish migrants about this new service available to them. An exchange of employment service officers between Sweden and Finland was initiated in 1971. Twice a year a group of Finnish employment officers work in local Swedish employment offices for four months at a time, while a group of Swedish officers serves in Finland. The main purpose of such an exchange is to make employment service officers familiar with the employment conditions in the other country and to be able to give first hand information to applicants. Furthermore, bilingual vacancy lists are distributed regularly to all participating employment offices.

The Finnish out-migrants are making an increasing use of the new employment service. In 1975, about 60 percent of the number of male job seekers, but only 20 percent of the number of female job seekers availed themselves of the public employment service.

Aware of the disadvantages to the country resulting from constant out-migration, the Finnish government is trying to formulate a policy which would hold out-migration down. Naturally, to restrict the freedom to migrate is out of the question. The country must direct its attention to measures making out-migration unnecessary. During recent years, a large number of measures have been taken in the field of economic, regional, industrial, and housing policies to improve the standard of living at home. During the 1970s, out-migration has been substantially slower than it was during the preceding decade.

Return Migration

A major objective of the Finnish migration policy is to guarantee return opportunities to Finns now living abroad. Everything should be done to facilitate their reintegration at home. Finns living abroad should be kept informed about employment opportunities at home. Information flow to Finns living in Sweden has been increased considerably. A periodical appearing since 1973 directed at job seekers and entitled, *Work in Finland*, is bilingual and published monthly. Once or twice a year another publication informs Finns in Sweden about housing conditions, social security provisions, taxation, education, and information on the costs of living in Finland.

The Finnish employment service is not in a position to provide financial aid to the returning migrants. However, returnees are entitled to the same moving allowance as are internal migrants in Finland. The subsidy granted under the Act of 1970 to facilitate regional mobility of labor applies in this case. To qualify, the returnee must have secured his job through the employment office and he must intend to resettle permanently in Finland. He also must have worked abroad for at least six months. The financial assistance consists of a reimbursement of travel costs to the new place of work, but only within Finland: an outfitting grant; family allowance; and a grant for moving personal effects and household goods.

Many returning migrants face difficult housing problems in Finland. They are now eligible to move into new housing partially financed by special funds earmarked for localities with labor shortage. There are income limits for eligibility, but in the case of returning migrants their higher earnings abroad are disregarded.

Returning migrants may incur financial losses because of the differences between Swedish and Finnish systems of social security. However, the transferability of credits improved considerably in recent years. Also, all migrants moving from one social security system into another are now better informed than was the case previously. Finns can obtain a tax service in Finland to help them claim eventual refund of taxes deducted from their incomes in Sweden.

Vocational skills of returning Finns do not necessarily meet the new Finnish requirements. Retraining and additional training are offered by many employers. The returning migrant may be referred to vocational training courses by the employment service. Both the cost of training and the living expenses of the trainee and his family are met by the state. The Ministry of Labor and the National Board of Vocational Education are jointly responsible for setting up vocational training programs. Courses vary in length from two weeks to eighteen months. Content of the courses is modular so that relatively short periods of training may suffice to equip the student with the requisite vocational skills. Courses are offered during the day in vocational training centers. These courses are primarily intended for the domestic unemployed and for those having a high risk of unemployment. Returnees from Sweden take such courses to "retool" themselves for the Finnish labor market.

Many Finns return home because their children face problems in school abroad. Since 1970, approximately two thousand Finnish children have been returning annually. Many of them experience language and reintegration problems at home. There are now special programs in Finland to help the school age children adjust to their new condition. Children with a good knowledge of Swedish are put into Swedish language schools in Finland where Swedish is the second official language.

Finns Abroad

The Finnish migration policy is to maintain close contact with Finnish emigrants and their descendants. A government sponsored civic association, the Suomi Society, was established in 1927 to foster cultural relations between Finns abroad and their home country. The Finnish government supports various cultural activities among Finns abroad by giving grants to the Finnish voluntary associations and the Finnish press abroad. "News from Finland" is a governmental publication started in 1975 to make Finns abroad aware of the changing situation at home. This newsletter is distributed to all Finns free of charge. There are also Finnish newspapers in Sweden, Australia, Canada, and the United States.

Aliens in Finland

There are few aliens domiciled and working in Finland. The official position of Finland on the recruitment of foreign workers from outside the Nordic countries is restrictive. Application for a work permit must be made from outside of Finland and prior to in-migrating. The regulations governing the issuance of work permits are analogous to those in other Nordic countries.

By and large, aliens enjoy basic rights and obligations equally with Finnish nationals. Thus far, aliens are not free to pursue political activities in Finland. As of 1976, the Nordic citizens with a legal residence in Finland are eligible to vote and to be elected in the municipal elections. They need to prove a two year residence up to voting registration. Aliens fall under the broad coverage of social security in Finland and they are eligible to receive old age pension after five years residence. They may not join the voluntary unemployment insurance, but after three years of stay, or sooner in certain cases, they qualify for the state operated unemployment benefits. Five years residence (three for Nordic nationals) is generally required to qualify for Finnish citizenship.

In 1976 the Finnish government initiated a Committee to review the aliens legislation and the governmental apparatus administering the aliens questions in Finland. The Committee's mandate is to study the situation of aliens in the Nordic countries and to put forth recommendations on that matter. Thus far there are no published reports on the findings of the Commission.

Evaluation

In principle, free mobility of labor within the Common Nordic Labor Market should be beneficial to all countries involved. In practice, this expectation has not been fulfilled. This is due largely to the fact that the inter-Nordic migration streams were not balanced and assumed greater proportions than envisaged in 1954. This was especially true about migration between Finland and Sweden. The disparities in the standard of living on one hand and the immobility of capital on the other may be seen as major contributors to this migratory imbalance.

Inter-Nordic migration of labor has given rise to significant social problems. It has also brought many positive results such as a closer cooperation in many fields of economic, social and cultural policy, a mutual understanding among the peoples and a wider variety of options for individual job seekers. On balance, the Common Nordic Labor Market has stood the test of time.

Nevertheless, the functioning of the labor market can be improved upon and efforts are being made in that direction. An example is the Nordic Cooperation Program in the Field of Labor Market Policy, adopted in November, 1975. It facilitates a closer cooperation among the Nordic countries by implementing principles of the 1954 Agreement. Another important new development is the establishment of the Nordic Investment Bank in Helsinki in August, 1976. The bank will facilitate mobility of capital among the Nordic countries. At the bilateral level, the supplementary Finnish-Swedish protocol of 1973 is a case in point, and so is the joint Committee on Industrial Cooperation set up by the Prime Ministers of Finland and Sweden in 1974.

A regular exchange of information on the status of migrations within the Common Nordic Labor Market countries has been found most valuable and has led to the establishment, in 1971, of a permanent subcommittee on migratory labor with the Nordic Labor Market Commission. Regulations on in-migration of non-Nordic nationals varied considerably over time. For instance, Sweden recruited workers actively during the 1960s until 1967. Denmark introduced a recruitment ban on non-Nordic nationals in 1970, except, of course, the nationals of the European Communities, starting with 1973. In Norway, the change in policy was gradual and a complete recruitment of labor ban was not issued until 1975. At the present time, immigration rules and their applications are essentially similar in all the Scandinavian countries. Nevertheless, a complete coordination of in-migration policies is still distant.

The Scandinavian countries were late in formulating their policies to integrate their in-migrants. However, once begun, their policies developed rapidly, notably in Sweden, and were informed by universalistic criteria of fairness and humanitarianism. A feature common to all Scandinavian in-migration policies is the positive valuation of family reunion and the in-migration of complete families. Another feature is the attempt to ensure the greatest possible equality of treatment and of opportunities for in-migrants and nationals alike. At the same time, in-migrants are encouraged to maintain their identity as peoples and to be politically self-assertive. In Sweden and Finland aliens have local voting rights. The Swedish immigrant and in-migrant policy may be counted as one of the most advanced in the world. In Sweden, the problems connected with the most primary needs of in-migrants have been solved to a large extent by appropriate action programs.

The present and future problems requiring solution are generally of a long term concern. Such as, what measures are needed to prevent special problems like semi-linguality or lack of identity from arising in the case of immigrants of the second and third generation? Or, how is the educational status of immigrant children to be improved in order for those who so desire to become genuinely bilingual? It would also be necessary to consider, in what way society should increase its support of the cultural activities of ethnic minorities, and determine what can be done to increase the influence of immigrants in politics and trade union activities. Another important question will be whether State initiatives can do anything to alter the attitudes of the general public to peoples of different origins, and in what ways economic cooperation can be developed among emigration and immigration countries to create alternative employment opportunities in the immigrants' countries of origin?[55]

The problems of return migration are pronounced only in Finland and, recently, there has been some return migration to Denmark. In Finland, there are issues still open. That is, how can effective alternatives to out-migration be created, and how can a country of origin get compensation for the investment made in the human capital leaving the country? Or, what should be done to ease returnees' problems of reintegration; in what form and to what extent should a country of emigration support the ethnic activities of its nationals and their descendants abroad? These and other questions present an intriguing challenge to the Finnish policy makers.

---

[55] Jonas Widgren. *The Position of Immigrants in Sweden.* Report for the UN Secretariat, May 26, 1974. Stockholm: Ministry of Labor. 1974. P. 2. Mimeo.

11

Switzerland*

HANS-JOACHIM HOFFMANN-NOWOTNY
University of Zurich

MARTIN KILLIAS
University of Zurich

Introduction

SWITZERLAND had remained an emigration country until the end of the nineteenth century. Today, however, the situation is reversed. At the end of 1976 there were 958,599 aliens registered in Switzerland excluding seasonal workers, border commuters, functionaries of the international organizations headquartered in Switzerland and their dependents. Of that number, 303,996 were residents on one year permits and 654,603 were residents with establishment permits, indicating that the latter have lived in Switzerland for at least ten years and are, de facto, domiciled there. In 1976, the number of aliens was lower by 105,927 as compared to the year 1974, when the maximum number of aliens was reached.

At the end of 1976 alien residents represented 15.3 percent of the Swiss population. Aside from Lichtenstein and Luxemburg, Switzerland had a higher proportion of resident aliens than any other country in Northwest Europe. Nonetheless, Switzerland does not have an immigration policy in the narrow sense of the word nor does the country consider itself an immigration country. In-migration policies in Switzerland were quite liberal in the past, but have become quite restrictive today.

* Translated from German by Daniel Kubat.

Population Mobility Prior to World War I

In the past, Switzerland's population was demographically robust. In relation to its economic power, Switzerland was highly overpopulated in the 18th century. In attempting to avoid the resulting problems, the authorities encouraged military emigration, a practice which had evolved in the 16th century and, had since been developed into an institutionalized form of exporting human beings. Estimates for the 18th century indicate that in contrast to some 50,000 civil emigrants, Switzerland sent out over 300,000 mercenaries, a considerable number for a population numbering about 1.7 million. A cursory calculation would suggest that about one-fifth of each cohort turning 20 years of age would thus be, at least temporarily, "lost". Immigration on the other hand was at that time completely negligible, probably due to the low economic attractiveness of Switzerland.

The notion of freedom of settlement had first been formulated in the Declaration of Human Rights (1789); it formed the basis for the freedom of migration. With the ideas of the French Revolution spreading, freedom of settlement found entrance in many constitutions of the early 19th century.[1] Several sociostructural factors may have caused or at least favored this development, among them a general boost of trade and traffic, and a tendential population surplus in many European countries which resulted in measures of systematic emigration to overseas countries. Since intra-European migration was slight, European states had no fear of undesirable side effects of this liberal migration policy.[2]

Swiss policy of settlement was not consistent during the first decades of the 19th century. After a period of considerable liberality during the Helvetian Republic (1799 to 1802) and the Mediation (1803 to 1814), there followed a relapse into the extreme policy of isolation previously experienced in the 18th century.[3] It was up to the cantons (a political administrative unit which answers directly to the Federal Government), to grant the right of settlement to foreigners, or for that matter, to citizens of other cantons. In 1827 the majority of the cantons concluded treaties of settlement with the Kings of France and of Sardinia-Piedmont-Savoy, which granted their respective citizens free settlement. These treaties were the starting point for the considerable immigration of Italians and Frenchmen during the subse-

---

[1] Josef Soder. "Die Aus- und Einwanderungsfreiheit", *Handbuch des Internationalen Flüchtlingsrechts*. W. Schatzel u Th. Veiter, eds. *Flüchtlingsrecht Vol. 1*. Fürst Franz Josef von Liechtenstein-Stiftung. Wien, Stuttgart: Braumüller. 1960.

[2] Andreas Hans Roth. "The Minimum Standard of International Law Applied to Aliens". Dissertation, Faculty of Law, University of Geneva. The Hague: Sijthoff. 1949; Josef Soder, *op. cit.*

[3] J. Langhard. *Das Niederlassungsrecht der Ausländer in der Schweiz*. Zurich: Orell Füssli. 1913.

quent decades.

The creation of the Swiss Federal Republic in 1848 brought along a uniform settlement policy. Prior to that, settlers were subject only to local restrictions based on preferences of a religious or ethnic nature. The Federal Constitution guaranteed, for the first time, the right of all Swiss nationals to settle anywhere within the country. With regard to the country's foreign residents, the new Swiss government entered into bilateral agreements with the neighboring, and later, with many other countries (21 in toto) regulating a mutual right to settlement.[4] As Switzerland remained an emigration country, such agreements were meant, primarily, to protect Swiss nationals abroad while the issue of foreign settlers at home remained unimportant.

Around the turn of the century the situation changed and Switzerland became an in-migration country. Most of the inflow was from the neighboring countries whose citizens were covered by the bilateral agreements. By the year 1914, foreigners represented 15.4 percent of Switzerland's population.[5] The newcomers tended to concentrate in large cantons and in urban areas. About three-fourths of them lived in the large German and French speaking cantons. The patterns of language distribution set at the beginning of the 19th century remained. The population distribution by proportion of language and ethnic groups in 1837 and in 1914 also remained about the same.[6]

Occupationally, foreigners were concentrated in construction and, in general, in lower status occupations. Among themselves, the French ranked the highest and the Italians the lowest.[7] According to the census of 1910, Germans, Italians and French foreign residents represented 39.7, 36.7 and 11.5 percent of all aliens respectively.[8] The strong differences in social level among the immigrant groups led to differing attitudes of the native population towards the members of the respective groups. Generally speaking, the immigrants were accepted most favorably in those regions of Switzerland which were culturally oriented toward their country of origin. Thus, cultural homogeneity permitted social mobility of foreigners, minimiz-

[4] Eduard von Waldkirch. "Die Grundsätze des Niederlassungsrechts der Fremden in der Schweiz", *Zeitschrift für Schweizerisches Recht*. Neue Folge, 42:56a-95a. Basel: Helbling & Lichtenhahn. 1923.

[5] Walter Bickel. *Bevölkerungsgeschichte der Schweiz seit dem Ausgang des Mittelalters*. Zurich: Buchergilde Gutenberg. 1947. P. 166.

[6] Walter Bickel. *Bevölkerungsgeschichte der Schweiz seit dem Ausgang des Mittelalters*. Zurich: Büchergilde Gutenberg. 1947; Rudolf Schlaepfer. "Die Ausländerfrage in der Schweiz vor dem Ersten Weltkrieg". Dissertation, Faculty of Philosophy I, University of Zurich. Zurich: Juvis Druck u. Verlag. 1969. P. 12.

[7] Walther Burckhardt. *Die Einbürgerung der Ausländer in der Schweiz. Schweizerisches Politisches Jahrbuch 1913*. Bern: K.J. Wyss. 1913; Rudolf Schlaepfer, *op. cit.*

[8] Hans-Joachim Hoffmann-Nowotny. *Soziologie des Fremdarbeiterproblems: Eine Theoretische und Empirische Analyse am Beispiel der Schweiz*. Stuttgart: F. Enke. 1973.

ing tensions normally attendant to a culturally mixed population.

Among the foreigners, only the Italians were working in greater numbers outside their "own" cantons. They began to represent "foreign elements" and during economic recessions became targets of scapegoating. For example, a "pogrom" of Italians took place in Zurich in 1896.[9] Thus, the concept of *Überfremdung* (overforeignization) now current dates back to the period before World War I and it enjoyed a wide currency even then.[10]

Surprisingly enough, discomfort about the high number of foreigners did not result in demands for a quota system or even a reduction of numbers, but all the pertinent plans aimed at the stronger integration of foreigners through naturalization.[11] Naturalization was, and still is, a matter of the local community *(Gemeinde)* and of canton. Thus, Swiss citizenship is a legal construction allowing free settlement within the country once granted by the Federal government but it is dependent on the local sponsorship which cannot be overridden.[12] The Federal government may stipulate only minimal conditions to be met prior to receiving the citizenship.

Before 1920 such conditions for naturalization were quite liberal. For instance, the Federal Act of 1876 required two years of residence; prior to that, there were no residence requirements. The cantonal governments were completely independent in laying down rules, and they were, in general, favorably disposed toward naturalization at that time.[13] The revision of the Alien Naturalization Act of 1903 retained most of the liberal provisions in order not to offend the already substantial settled alien community.[14] The chief worry of the Swiss at that time was that the number of naturalizations annually lagged far behind the number of new alien arrivals. Furthermore, the aliens showed a faster rate of natural increase than the Swiss.[15] The fact that the local governments were responsible for the welfare of their citizens functioned as a brake on naturalizations. To forestall a risk of economic dependency, many communities began to exact substantial cash payments from the candidates for naturalization.

A paradoxical situation emerged which remains Switzerland's dilemma today; a reduction in the number of foreigners in the country was pos-

[9] Viktor Willi. *Überfremdung - Schlagwort oder bittere Wahrheit?* Bern: Lang. 1970; Rudolf Schlaepfer, *op. cit.*

[10] Rudolf Schlaepfer. "Die Ausländerfrage in der Schweiz vor dem Ersten Weltkrieg". Dissertation, Faculty of Philosophy I, University of Zurich. Zurich: Juvis Druck u. Verlag. 1969.

[11] *Ibid.* 1969. P. 129.

[12] F. Fleiner and Z. Giacometti. *Schweizerisches Bundesstaatsrecht.* Zurich: Polygraphischer Verlag. 1949. P. 117. Reprinted, 1965.

[13] *Ibid.* 1949.

[14] *Ibid.* 1949. P. 191.

[15] Walther Burckhardt. *Die Einbürgerung der Ausländer in der Schweiz. Schweizerisches Politisches Jahrbuch* 1 91 3. Bern. K.J. Wyss. 1913.

sible only through the process of naturalization. Any other alternative, e.g. asking them to leave, was politically unthinkable. The Federal government was interested in franchizing the aliens. The local governments, on the other hand, felt they were dealing with the issue first hand and, in the majority of cases were reluctant to assimilate their residents politically. A notion of universal suffrage was not particularly ingrained in Switzerland.

The debate on naturalization was furthered by demands of a legal concept of *ius soli*. According to the "natural" law, those born in Switzerland should be given citizenship there. This would reduce the number of "foreigners", which was felt to be too high. The census of 1910 showed that 38 percent of the number of foreigners living in Switzerland were born there.[16] By the time this new view was to be translated into practice, World War I broke out, postponing Swiss attention on the issue until after the war, when the project was taken up again, but in a completely different political climate.

Before 1914, Switzerland attempted to solve the issue of too many resident aliens by naturalizing them and thereby effecting their integration into the country. Tendencies to close the borders, which emerged toward the end of World War I, cannot be said to have existed before the war.[17] As a population exporting country with its own nationals scattered abroad, bound by many bilateral agreements, Switzerland could not but remain liberal in matters of migration.

In any case, the "foreign" presence in Switzerland loses its ominousness when one realizes that, for one, a considerable number of foreigners were already born there and, for two, a great majority of them came from neighboring countries, fitting quite well into the cultural matrix tripartite as it remained.

The end of the World War I increased the interest of national groups to define their identities and their political boundaries more clearly than before. Among the unanticipated consequences of national self-determination was a distrust of foreigners. Each and every state sought national purity, a tangible consequence of which was the de facto abrogation of traditional freedoms to settle. Exchanges of border populations were not uncommon and were conducted on a large scale even though Switzerland remained exempt from such crass forms of nationalism. Abroad, and especially overseas, restrictive immigration policies became common, led largely by the United States.[18]

---

[16] F. Fleiner and Z. Giacometti, *Schweizerisches Bundesstaatsrecht*, Zurich: Polygraphischer Verlag. 1949. Reprinted, 1965; Salis and W. Burckhardt. *Schweizerisches Bundesrecht*. 6 Volumes. Frauenfeld: Huber. 1930.

[17] Rudolf Schlaepfer. "Die Ausländerfrage in der Schweiz vor dem Ersten Weltkrieg". 1969.

[18] Andreas Hans Roth. "The Minimum Standard of International Law Applied to Aliens". Dissertation, Faculty of Law, University of Geneva. The Hague: Sijthoff. 1949; Josef Soder.

As of November 21, 1917 it became very difficult to enter Switzerland as an alien. This was a measure to stop the heavy influx of war deserters and draft evaders who, it was felt, were putting Switzerland's neutrality into jeopardy. Later on, the border control was replaced by an internal aliens registration system. Even though transit through Switzerland remained unimpeded, work and residence permits were issued only in exceptional cases. The Federal Regulations of November, 1921 completed and operationalized the alien registration system by entrusting its administration to the Aliens Registration Police Authority *(Fremdenpolizei)* to monitor the movement of aliens within Switzerland.[19]

Paralleling restrictions on persons, Federal Regulations of July 8, 1919 announced a curtailing and a close supervision of foreign capital in Switzerland. The main purpose of the regulations was to avoid Swiss corporations falling under foreign control. The Regulations later became incorporated into the Swiss Civil Code of 1936.[20]

Under the new practice even aliens originally protected by a treaty of settlement were denied the right of domicile for the sole reason of *Überfremdung* (overforeignization). The new legislation was introduced as a temporary measure due to the war. However, it was here to stay. The contradictions between the current practice and the treaties concluded before 1914 could no longer be ignored. The prevalent opinion was that the treaties should be revised or canceled. In September, 1918 France gave notice of cancellation of its settlement treaty with Switzerland. Switzerland followed suit with notice of cancellation to Germany and Italy.[21] Despite the notices of cancellation, the parties involved agreed that the settlement treaties should remain in force until one party asked for cancellation to come into effect at short term notice.[22] To conclude new treaties proved to be more difficult than expected, and the old treaties have remained in force to this day.[23]

"Die Aus- und Einwanderungsfreiheit", *Handbuch des Internationalen Flüchtlingsrechts.* W. Schatzel u Th. Veiter, eds. *Flüchtlingsrecht Vol. 1.* Fürst Franz Josef von Liechtenstein-Stiftung. Wien, Stuttgart: Braumüller. 1960.

[19] Max Ruth. *Das Fremdenpolizeirecht der Schweiz.* Zurich: Polygraphischer Verlag. 1934.

[20] Peter Forstmoser and Arthur Meier-Hayoz. *Einführung in das schweizerische Aktienrecht.* Bern: Stampfli. 1976. P. 84f; Arthur Meier-Hayoz und Peter Forstmoser. *Grundriss des Schweizerischen Gesellschaftsrechts.* Bern: Stampfli. 1974. P. 119.

[21] Ernst Delaquis. "Im Kampf gegen die Überfremdung". A speech before the Legal Society in Bern. *Zeitschrift des bernischen Juristenvereins,* 57:49-69. Bern: Stampfli. 1921. P. 59.

[22] Max Ruth. *Das Fremdenpolizeirecht der Schweiz.* Zurich: Polygraphischer Verlag. 1934. P. 12.

[23] Max Ruth. *Das Fremdenpolizeirecht der Schweiz.* Zurich: Polygraphischer Verlag. 1934; Eduard von Waldkirch. "Die Grundsätze des Niederlassungsrechts der Fremden in der Schweiz", *Zeitschrift für Schweizerisches Recht.* Neue Folge, 42:56a-95a. Basel: Helbling & Lichtenhahn. 1923; P. Petitmermet. "Les Principes à la Base du Droit d'Établissement des Étrangers en Suisse", *Zeitschrift für Schweizerisches Recht.* Neue Folge, 42:97a-185a. Basel: Helbling &

Major Legislations on Aliens' Settlement

The Federal Act of March 26, 1931 *(Bundesgesetz über Aufenthalt und Niederlassung der Ausländer)*, ANAG and its Implementation Regulations of May 5, 1933, ANAV, became effective as of January 1, 1934. It provided that: 1) the Federal policing of aliens remain at the discretion of the officers of the Aliens Registration Police Authority. The Act itself offered only procedural guidelines; 2) aliens do not have a natural right to stay and to settle and their permits need not be renewed; 3) before issuing a permit, the duty of the Aliens Registration Authority was to consider the cultural and economic needs of the area, the proportion of aliens already resident, and the labor market conditions;[24] and 4) it established three classes of aliens: (a) those who have lived in the country for at least ten years; (b) annual permit holders; and (c) seasonal workers.[25]

The isolationist policy began when the War was nearly over and naturalization of foreigners became all but impossible. The data from the 1930 census show that of the domiciled aliens, 40 percent were born in Switzerland and an additional 10 percent grew up there. Only 20 percent of all foreigners have lived in Switzerland for fewer than ten years.[26] With the increasing restrictions on in-migration and settlement, the number of naturalizations continued to decline throughout the 1930s.[27] Unfortunately, the isolationist mood in Switzerland had an adverse effect on the reception of refugees leaving their countries at that time and later during World War II.[28]

Isolationist tendencies were not specific to Switzerland. They were part of a trend begun after World War I. In the Swiss case, the isolationism emerged after the proportion of the number of foreigners in the country started to decline. In 1914, aliens represented about 15 percent of the Swiss population, in 1920 about 10 percent and in 1941 their numbers were only slightly above 5 percent of the total population of Switzerland.[29]

The assumption that the number of aliens present in Switzerland had no direct influence on xenophobe tendencies seems to be born out by the

---

Lichtenhahn. 1923.

[24] Permits were limited to one locale. In case of change, a new permit was needed. ANAG, Art. 16, Sec. 11; ANAV, Art. 8, Sec. 1.

[25] Max Ruth. *Das Fremdenpolizeirecht der Schweiz.* Zurich: Polygraphischer Verlag. 1934.

[26] Max Ruth. "Das Schweizerbürgerrecht", *Zeitschrift für Schweizerishces Recht.* Neue Folge, 56:1a-156a. Basel: Helbling & Lichtenhahn. 1937.

[27] Walter Bickel. *Bevölkerungsgeschichte der Schweiz seit dem Ausgang des Mittelalters.* Zurich: Büchergilde Gutenberg. 1947. P. 220.

[28] Carl Ludwig. "Die Flüchtlingspolitik der Schweiz in den Jahren 1933 bis 1955". A report to the Bundesrat and the respective Local Council. (Bundeskanzlei) n.d. P. 372f.

[29] Walter Bickel. *Op. cit.* 1947. P. 214.

historical development.[30] The xenophobe tendencies setting in after 1917 occurred not with an increase, but rather, with a decrease in the number of the foreign population.

Switzerland has a history of grass roots movements demanding a restriction of in-migration and asking for an exportation of in-migrants. Even though these movements have the sentiments of many people, they failed thus far to be confirmed at the polling station. On the other hand, legal restrictions as they were being issued, do betray that the public sentiment was not being disregarded.

A structural explanation of isolationism and discrimination against foreigners rests on several points. Initially, the Swiss had a good reason to feel smug and self-satisfied after the War. A philosophy of "small is beautiful" was proclaimed where previously the smallness of the country surrounded by four empires gave rise to an inferiority feeling. The empires had fallen apart and foreign deposits in the Swiss banks gave the country economic security and an international prestige. Then, too, low status groups in Switzerland became politically fragmented by various left of center ideologies. Strike frequency was above average in the years 1918 to 1920.[31]

The legitimacy of large unions had been weakened.[32] A particularism in interpersonal relationships among the workers led to pronounced differentiations along the ascriptive lines, such as language and ethnicity. Also, the occupational stratification accentuated the ascriptive differentiation and the power of internationalism and working class loyalty was too weak to overcome such segmentation.

On the whole, however, the forces for or against isolationism remained sufficiently weak so that an occasional legal regulation of in-migrants was sufficient to assuage both camps. Furthermore, the restrictive policies were in keeping with the situation abroad; any domestic action was tempered by a concern for the opinion abroad.[33] The official policy after 1917 can be summarized as the way of least resistance. The policy of isolation served to fulfill nationalistic demands, without endangering economic interests or inducing sanctions on an international level, such as could be placed, for instance, against Swiss residents in foreign countries.

The legal framework defining the rights of foreigners in Switzerland has changed little. ANAG was revised on October 8, 1948, supplemented by the

---

[30] Hans-Joachim Hoffmann-Nowotny. *Soziologie des Fremdarbeiterproblems: Eine Theoretische und Empirische Analyse am Beispiel der Schweiz.* Stuttgart: F. Enke. 1973. P. 95.

[31] Arbeitsgruppe für die Geschichte der Arbeiterbewegung. *Schweizerische Arbeiterbewegung.* Zurich: Limmat Verlag. 1975.

[32] *Ibid.*

[33] Eduard von Waldkirch. "Die Grundsätze des Niederlassungsrechts der Fremden in der Schweiz", *Zeitschrift für Schweizerisches Recht.* Neue Folge, 42:56a-95a. Basel: Helbling & Lichtenhahn. 1923.

necessary ANAV implementation rulings as of March 1, 1949. The legal state of affairs concerning the rights of foreigners is, at the moment, in a transition stage. With the statute law, numerous regulations have been issued by the Federal government which have not yet been incorporated into the Swiss Civil Code.

The original intent of the alien legislation was to counter unemployment by restricting inflow of aliens; hence, the close cooperation between *Fremdenpolizei* and the cantonal employment bureaus. However, there was a rapidly growing need for workers immediately after the War. The admission restrictions were too cumbersome and they were bypassed by the authorities on the assumption that workers would enter Switzerland for a limited period, and would be out-rotated later.

The eased admission practices did not increase chances for aliens' integration in the land. Most aliens who were in Switzerland before 1945 were domiciled there and thus exempt from all restrictions save that of franchise. On the other hand, the aliens entering after 1945, were subjected to the new regulations, meaning that the number of persons being legally discriminated against has increased substantially. For instance, aliens on annual permits were not allowed to bring their dependents the first year of their stay. Those subject to special bilateral treaties waiving this provision were, of course, exempt.

The Swiss in-migration policy after 1945 maximized the import of foreign workers, but minimized their chances of integration into the Swiss society. In view of the Swiss social stratification system, an illustration in the case of Italians may show the built-in difficulties of social integration of aliens.

A regularized situation of Italians in various Swiss enterprises ran counter to the traditional and "natural" stratification and created friction between Swiss nationals and their "guest" workers. Even though the former often achieved social mobility because of less desirable jobs being left to the foreigners, such mobility was spurious with reference to other Swiss.[34] When foreign workers were contractually made equal to the Swiss, a certain amount of resentment was generated.

After 1960, there were political attempts to articulate the danger of *Überfremdung*. Thus far, there were five referenda on this issue, and a fourth and fifth were proposed in March, 1977.[35]

[34] Hans-Joachim Hoffmann-Nowotny. *Ibid.*

[35] The first referendum was launched in the canton of Zurich by the Democratic Party. Its platform was a ceiling on aliens not to exceed 10 percent of the population. In the spring of 1968, assured of the 50,000 signatures needed, the organizers nonetheless canceled the request to safeguard national unity. The second "initiative" took place in 1970 known as "Schwarzenbach-Initiative". Dr. James Schwarzenbach, Chairman of National Action, urged the voters to calm and restraint, again to safeguard national unity. The referendum was defeated narrowly, with a voter participation of 75 percent.

The "stabilization" policy, pursued by the Swiss Federal government seemingly independent of the political climate, means that starting in the late 1960s, the inflow of foreign workers was regulated to replace only those leaving. Finally, on July 9, 1975, a new policy came into effect providing for a decrement in the foreign labor force over time. The stabilization policy was accompanied by restrictions imposed on aliens who wished to own real estate in Switzerland. A precedent for such regulations had been set during the 1930s.[36]

The crux of the Swiss restrictive policy is the regulation restricting movement of aliens in the country. In 1968, when the restrictive legislation reached its peak, the status quo of the annual permit holders was frozen for five years. That meant that an alien coming to Switzerland to work could not change job, occupation, or residence (canton) for the next five years without losing his permit, which was tied to the alien's status at the time of entry. Regulations issued in the years 1970, 1971 and 1973, reduced the minimum stay for the job to one year, and occupation and canton stay to three. Certain employments were exempt, such as those in the field of health care and the tourist industry. The 1975 Regulations reduced all minimum stays to one year for all annual permit holders. These limits are federal but local or cantonal governments may raise them. The permit holders have no right to have their permits extended.

All in all, the latest regulations represent a certain liberalization and an improvement of the status of foreign workers in Switzerland. Additional improvement can be seen in the fact that spouses of Swiss nationals are exempt from alien permit regulations and are set equal to the domiciled alien population.

In matters of naturalization, on the other hand, the situation did not improve at all. The Federal Act of September 29, 1952, (Art. 15, Section 1) increased the number of years required for citizenship from six to 12 and a

---

The third initiative, again sponsored by National Action, was put to the vote on October 21, 1974. The platform was to have a ceiling of 12 percent aliens per canton, with a total ceiling of 500,000, which would mean a reduction of the alien population by about one-half in three years. It was defeated 2:1.

The fourth and fifth initiatives were voted on March 13, 1977. The fourth referendum was to limit the proportion of alien population to 12.5 percent of the Swiss population within the next ten years. The initiative was again launched by the conservative republicans headed by Schwarzenbach. The fifth referendum was to amend the Swiss constitution so that only maximum 4,000 naturalizations would take place annually. In the last few years naturalizations were taking place at a faster rate than previously. In 1976 alone, close to 10,000 aliens were naturalized in Switzerland. Both referenda were defeated at the polls. Voter participation was 44.6 percent. The fourth initiative was defeated in a result of 1,200,000 votes against 500,000 for the initiative. (*Frankfurter Allgemeine*, March 11, 1977; *Die Presse*, Vienna, March 15, 1977.)

[36] *Schweizerisches Bundesblatt*, 3:124ff. 1972.

TABLE 11:1

Growth of Switzerland's Population, Since 1960,
and the Proportion of Aliens in the Total Population[a]

Year	Population Total	Proportion Aliens in Percent
1960	5,429,100	10.8
1965	5,880,000	13.8
1966	5,953,000	14.2
1967	6,035,900	14.8
1968	6,115,000	15.3
1969	6,184,000	15.7
1970	6,269,800	15.7
1971	6,253,000	16.0
1972	6,310,200	16.4
1973	6,350,000	16.6
1974	6,375,500	16.7
1975	6,333,200	16.0

Note: [a] Estimated population of Switzerland in 1975 was 6.3 million.

Source: Statistische Jahrbücher der Schweiz.

ruling was added requiring a proof of assimilation.

Even though a few cities have increased their naturalization during the last few years, as a counter action to the *Überfremdung* movement, the majority of Swiss residents cannot hope to become citizens. The cash barrier, the denominational and language idiosyncrasies stipulated as conditions by many communities, all contribute to the difficulty of naturalization.[37] Any fundamental improvements in the status of aliens is hardly to be imagined in the near future. Although there is at present an initiative in this direction, its authors have, up to now, not succeeded in enlisting the support of the Labor Unions and the Social Democratic Party, since these organizations would probably have to face a loss of consensus with their basis, should they support the initiative.

The domestic political situation notwithstanding, the treatment of foreigners in Switzerland is under international pressure. The pressure comes primarily from agreements such as those with Italy or Spain on the

[37] Hans Schmid. *Die Ortsgemeinden im Kanton St. Gallen...* Zurich and St. Gallen: Polygraphischer Verlag. 1967; Rudolf Schlaepfer. "Die Ausländerfrage in der Schweiz vor dem Ersten Weltkrieg". Dissertation, Faculty of Philosophy I, University of Zurich. Zurich: Juvis Druck u. Verlag. 1969; Hans-Joachim Hoffmann-Nowotny. *Soziologie des Fremdarbeiterproblems: Eine Theoretische und Empirische Analyse am Beispiel der Schweiz.* Stuttgart: F. Enke. 1973.

TABLE 11:2

Aliens in Switzerland by Country of Citizenship
and by Proportion by Major Sending Countries, Since 1960

Countries		1960	1965	1966	1967	1968	1969
				Years			
Italy	N	346,223	454,657	483,653	509,930	522,638	531,501
	%	59	56	57	57	56	55
Germany	N	93,406	109,529	107,734	111,945	114,658	115,606
	%	16	14	13	13	12	12
Spain	N		77,343	78,442	81,450	87,724	97,862
	%		9	9	9	9	10
France	N	31,328	40,754	42,312	44,968	47,233	49,538
	%	5	5	5	5	5	5
Austria	N	37,762	39,824	39,459	40,617	41,911	43,052
	%	7	5	5	5	4	4
Others	N	76,020	88,136	93,387	101,670	118,978	134,236
	%	13	11	11	11	13	14
Total	N	584,739	810,243	844,987	890,580	933,142	971,795
	%	100	100	100	100	100	100

TABLE 11:2 (continued)

Aliens in Switzerland by Country of Citizenship
and by Proportion by Major Sending Countries, Since 1960

Countries		Years						
		1970	1971	1972	1973	1974	1975	1976
Italy	N	526,579	530,477	544,903	551,768	554,925	520,657	958,599
	%	54	52	53	52	52	51	100
Germany	N	115,564	114,223	114,106	111,411	110,507	109,563	
	%	12	14	11	11	10	11	
Spain	N	102,341	107,623	114,996	119,072	121,555	112,996	
	%	10	10	11	11	11	11	
France	N	51,396	52,276	53,137	53,024	53,000	51,885	
	%	5	5	5	5	5	5	
Austria	N	43,143	43,150	43,298	43,013	42,597	41,504	
	%	4	4	4	4	4	4	
Others	N	143,864	151,560	161,945	174,217	181,942	176,216	
	%	15	15	16	17	17	17	
Total	N	982,887	999,309	1,032,285	1,052,505	1,064,526	1,012,710	
	%	100	100	100	100	100	100	

Source: Statistische Jahrbücher der Schweiz

recruitment of workers, or the agreement with the Organization for Economic Cooperation and Development of which Switzerland is a member, or the agreement with the European Communities, of which Switzerland is not a member. All agreements concern themselves with discrimination because of race, or creed, or national origin and insist on equal treatment before the law.

Summary

Economically, the chances for integration have improved for the foreign workers in Switzerland, politically, they have not. There is no social group with enough political muscle which is in favor of political integration of aliens and which wishes to pressure the government for change. On the other hand, the newest Überfremdung initiative had asked for an annual ceiling of 4,000 naturalizations. Today's aliens in Switzerland number close to one million!

Switzerland does not consider itself an immigration country and its policies on in-migration and settlement must be understood from that point of view. Of course, Switzerland is not an isolated entity and cannot ward off international pressures which range from the regulation of working conditions to the social integration of its aliens. The sending countries are not likely to insist that their nationals become Swiss.

The residents of Switzerland consider themselves as belonging there and many of them were actually born there. Being deprived of their political rights is tantamount to being a minority in a country where overt discrimination is practiced. The more integrated Switzerland's residents become both economically and socially, the more likely they are going to feel that political integration is desirable. How this is going to happen remains to be seen.

Part IV

Countries of Out-Migration: Exportation of Labor to Northwestern Europe

12

Greece

THEODORE P. LIANOS
Athens School of Economics and Business

Recent Migrations of Greek Citizens

THE magnitude of migrations out of Greece has always been considerable. Official estimates of gross out-migration[1] are available from 1955 forward. During the period between 1955 and 1973 about 1,150,000 persons left the country. The significance of this number becomes apparent when it is translated into 13 percent of the Greek population.

A substantial proportion of Greek migrants have been attracted overseas. During the period under discussion, about 150,000 left for the United States, 80,000 for Canada and 160,000 left for Australia. From the countries in Europe, West Germany has attracted about 600,000 workers. Starting with 1960, migration of Greek workers to Northwestern Europe was principally, to the Federal Republic of Germany.

Although one would expect the proportion of return migrants to be higher from countries near Greece, the Greek situation appears "deviant". During the years 1968 until 1972, return migrants represented 16 percent of out-migrants to the United States, 30 percent in the case of Canada, 39 percent in the case of Australia and 30 percent in the case of West Germany.

---

[1] For statistical purposes, Greek official sources define, as migrants, those Greek citizens who leave the country for a stay abroad of at least one year. Gross out-migration refers to all persons leaving during the period. Statistical information reported here, was derived from the individual volumes of the annual *Statistical Yearbook*.

TABLE 12:1

Percent Distribution of Greek Out-Migrants[a] to
Germany, Belgium and Overseas, Between 1955-1973[b]

Year	Germany	Belgium	Overseas[c]	Other[d]	All	Out-Migrants N
1955	2	9	60	29	100	30,000
1956	2	8	52	34	100	34,000
1957	5	29	43	27	100	30,000
1958	8	3	53	36	100	25,000
1959	10	1	52	37	100	24,000
1960	45	1	35	19	100	48,000
1961	53	2	26	19	100	59,000
1962	59	5	24	12	100	84,000
1963	65	4	24	7	100	100,000
1964	69	1	21	9	100	106,000
1965	69	—	23	8	100	117,000
1966	52	—	36	12	100	87,000
1967	23	1	59	17	100	43,000
1968	40	—	48	12	100	51,000
1969	59	—	30	11	100	42,000
1970	70	—	26	4	100	93,000
1971	65	—	29	6	100	62,000
1972	62	—	29	9	100	43,000
1973	46	—	40	14	100	28,000

Notes: [a] Estimated population of Greece in 1976 was 9,100,000.

[b] Persons leaving the country for at least one year. Includes students, consular workers, governmental transfers and others.

[c] U.S.A., Canada and Australia.

[d] Residual category including nonworkers listed under [b].

Sources: Statistical Service of Greece. Statistical Yearbooks, respective years.

At such rates, Greeks abroad continue to increase. West German estimates of Greek workers present in the country in 1973 was 272,000.[2]

The economic conditions at home, characterized as they are by high unemployment, underemployment and a low per capita income, function as push factors for Greek out-migration. The often inefficient and overbureaucratized public administration contributes to a malaise of the Greek worker and makes it easy for him to leave home. Even though the official

---

[2] H. Werner. "Freizügigkeit der Arbeitskräfte und Wanderungsbewegungen in den Landerns der Europäischen Gemeinschaft", *Mitteilungen aus der Arbeitsmarkt- und Berufsforschung* (Nürnberg), 4:326-371. 1973.

TABLE 12:2

Cumulative Percent Distribution of Greek Out-Migrants,
by Major Age Groups and Proportion Male in Each Age Group,
for the Period 1955-1972

Age Groups	Proportion all Migrants	Proportion Male
0-19	22	50
20-39	66	62
40-64	11	58
65 and over	1	40
	100	
N	1,128,000	

Sources: Statistical Service of Greece. Statistical Yearbooks, respective years.

unemployment *(Census of 1961)* figures show "acceptable" levels of 6 percent, the difficult to measure underemployment with resulting low wages appears to be a key motive for out-migration.

The official unemployment figure at the time of the 1971 Census was reduced to about 3 percent. However, of all employed workers, 21 percent worked fewer than 20 hours preceding the census week and 26 percent worked fewer than 30 hours during the week in question.

In nominal terms, the per capita income rose from U.S. dollars, $236.00 in 1955 to $1,337.00 in 1972. However, in relation to West Germany, for instance, Greek values remained, throughout this period, only at 35 percent of German per capita values.

The disadvantaged Greek economy and the inefficient national administration combine to produce a chronically negative balance of payment and the resulting need for foreign exchange. Like other countries in a similar position, Greece welcomes the exportation of labor as a fast way to ease its financial situation.

The Pressure Groups and National Migration Policy

During the late 1950s, while there still was sizable unemployment and underemployment in Greece, the "economic miracle" in Northwestern Europe needed more and more manpower. Soon, labor began to migrate from Greece first to Belgium and then to West Germany. As the flow of out-migrants became quite substantial, a need for a national migration policy became apparent.

In the formulation of a national migration policy there were four groups which played a major role: the government itself; the parliamentary opposition; the employers' association; and the labor unions. At this time, the opinions of even those persons who were otherwise influential were not easily heeded unless they were channeled through an institution, e.g. a political party.

In the post-World War II period, Greece was committed to a policy of rapid industrialization and modernization implying, among other things, a de-emphasis on agriculture and an emphasis on rationalization of industry, both areas needing less and less of a still abundant supply of labor. From the government's point of view, out-migration presented a relief from the domestic labor pressures. At the same time, treating out-migration as an exportation of labor, some earnings could be foreseen arising from the remittances sent home. Finally, viewing out-migration as a temporary phenomenon and envisaging return migration, the government felt that the exportation of labor was an easy way to convert agricultural workers and unskilled industrial workers into a skilled labor force trained abroad and brought home at a later date when industrialization had advanced.

The parliamentary opposition, on the other hand, dwelled on the negative aspects of out-migration and kept blaming the government for not providing enough jobs at home. The opposition did not go so far, however, as to press for revoking the right to out-migrate freely.

Those political views portraying employers as wanting a large supply of labor at home to keep the unions weak did not apply in the Greek case. Rather, the employers' associations did not maintain any articulated position on out-migration. The employers, as a group, remained either lukewarm or ambivalent to the issue of migration. The president of the Federation of Greek Industries remarked, on one occasion, "it is difficult to say whether migration is a positive or a negative factor for the economic development of the country".[3] In a memorandum to the Ministry of Coordination, the president of the Chamber of Commerce and Industry noted that the "basic elements of a migration policy" should be the following: a) a minimum of occupational training of migrants, to be borne by foreign employers; b) permits of leave only to the unskilled workers who migrate to Northwestern Europe; c) an annual ceiling on out-migrants; and d) a discouragement of overseas migration which makes return migration less probable. That such recommendations are mostly pious wishes need not be emphasized.

Labor unions in Greece have viewed out-migration as resulting from the domestic conditions. The Secretary General of the General Greek Labor Federation noted, in an interview, "migration cannot and should not be stopped at the present time".[4] The unions viewed out-migration as a

---

[3] *Epoches*, June, 1965.   [4] *Ibid.*

TABLE 12:3

Greek Out-Migrants with Previous Work Experience by Proportion
of Migrants from Agriculture, and as a Proportion of All Out-Migrants,
Between 1955-1973

Year	Workers with Experience	Percent from Agriculture	Proportion of All Migrants
1955	9,200	72	31
1956	10,200	69	29
1957	6,100	57	20
1958	5,300	36	22
1959	7,000	40	30
1960	24,300	29	51
1961	31,400	14	53
1962	53,500	12	64
1963	61,800	12	62
1964	56,400	51	54
1965	58,200	49	50
1966	33,900	63	39
1967	12,200	48	28
1968	20,000	51	39
1969	46,100	71	50
1970	44,200	64	48
1971	24,500	59	40
1972	17,000	61	40
1973	10,000	48	36

Sources: Statistical Service of Greece. Statistical Yearbooks, respective years.

temporary phenomenon and presumed the return of most of the migrants to Europe. In addition, they wanted to see the conditions of their nationals abroad regularized and improved. In the long run, the only solution to the situation at home was economic development.

Greek Migration Policy

The migration policy de facto followed by Greece is reflected in the bilateral agreements with countries admitting Greek workers, in the consular support Greek nationals enjoy while out of the country on a work visa, and in the provisions made at home for the eventual return of Greek workers. Out-migration from Greece is far from being discouraged, return migration, thus far, is not being fostered and the preference is for out-migration to Europe, reflecting thus the attitude of the government as that of cautious ambivalence.

The Greek-German Agreement: Greece signed a bilateral agreement with the Federal Republic of Germany in March, 1960, governing the recruitment of Greek workers to work in Germany. The agreement is being administered jointly by the Greek Ministry of Labor and the German *Bundesanstalt für Arbeit* and the Unemployment Compensation Board represented in Greece by what is known as the German Commission.[5] The function of both parties to the agreement is to disseminate information about employment vacancies in Germany and, for the Greek counterpart, to supply the available workers. The German Commission provides a complete job description of each vacancy with corresponding information on the place of work, wages and benefits, the duration of contract and all the particulars. The Greek authorities then make a list of available workers with their occupational background and other relevant information. The final decision on hiring rests with the German employers and contracts are signed prior to departure.

The German employer covers the cost of travel from the Greek border but not the cost of return upon expiration of the contract. Greek workers may, if they so choose, remit all their earnings home; on the other hand, their requests to bring to Germany other members of their family are treated favorably.

Similar bilateral agreements were signed with France, Belgium and the Netherlands. These agreements have a limited political significance as few Greek workers out-migrate into those countries.

Social Provisions in West Germany: Greek workers and their families face a multitude of problems most of which are not directly related to their jobs. The problems range from simple ones such as properly addressing a letter, to major ones such as finding suitable housing or schools for their children. The division of social assistance in Germany is such that Greek residents fall under the care of the Evangelical Church, the Greek Orthodox Church and Greek consulates and the associations formed by the Greek residents themselves.

The World Council of Churches, which allocates segmented care to various ethnic groups and nationalities in Europe, designated the *Innere Mission* of the Evangelical Church as the main West European religious agency to provide services to the Greek communities. The Innere Mission, which has offices in 48 major German cities, runs the Greek Homes, organizes various national and cultural events, and retains its own staff of social workers to work with the Greek communities. The Mission also finances German

---

[5] In 1960, the full name of the German Federal Labor Office was: *Bundesanstalt für Arbeitsvermittlung und Arbeitslosenversicherung.*

language classes for the Greek nationals and provides settlement assistance to new arrivals. Despite this wideflung net of services, only about 20 percent of the Greeks in Germany request the services of the Mission and only 60 percent know of its existence.

The Greek Orthodox Church restricts its activities to the operating of Sunday schools while interest in the social aspects of Greeks living in Germany remains alien to the primarily religious orientation of the Church.

There are 14 consular offices and 22 offices of the Greek Ministry of Labor in Germany. The explicit role of the latter is to supervise and support Greeks employed in the Federal Republic of Germany. As of 1965, the total staff of the governmental agencies was only 38 to take care of some 184,000 Greek workers. By necessity, the offices are in major urban centers (22 cities), whereas Greek workers are dispersed in about 150 cities. This scatter of Greek labor makes it difficult to effect a consular care of the Greek nationals.

Starting with 1960, Greek workers began to form their own associations and communities. Throughout the decade, the communities offered their own German language classes and evening courses for illiterate coworkers, as well as undertaking school classes for the children.[6]

Greek Migration Policy: Evaluation

A brief sketch of the economic conditions in Greece in the postwar years and of the pressures on the government to face the issues of emigration suggests that the government's migration policy was to let things happen. Under the circumstances, it is only fair to say that as a short run policy on migration, it was the only feasible one. When sizable out-migrations began to take place around 1960, the situation at home was bad and it had been so for about a decade. One cannot seriously criticize any government for not being able to change a bad situation overnight. Economic development providing ample employment at home is a long process and at variance with ideological impatience for things to happen now.

An interpretation of out-migration suggests that the outflow of migrants can be reduced by encouraging labor mobility within Greece. Whether such widespread regional imbalance between demand and supply of labor exists in Greece is open to question. The fact that the internal migration in Greece in the decade between 1960 and 1970 involved about 600,000 persons, mostly from rural areas to the cities, need not necessarily attest to major regional imbalances but rather to the universality of rural-urban migration fueled by social as well as economic considerations. It stands to be repeated that there was no feasible migration policy that could reduce the volume of

[6] C. Matzouranis. *Greek Workers in Germany* (in Greek). Athens: Gutenburg. 1975.

out-migration in the short run, short of stopping the issuance of passports.

On the other hand, those responsible for the formulation of economic policies can be seriously criticized not for what they did, but rather for what they failed to do. There are two criticisms to be made. In the first place, out-migration was permitted to happen too haphazardly, without seizing the opportunity to transform the human labor capital into a pool of skilled labor. The skills would be learned abroad, but under a prior guidance at home. In the second place, no suitable provisions were made to attract those Greek workers back who, on their own initiative, acquired useful industrial skills abroad.

There was a proposal that "appropriate government services should be organized more systematically and should collaborate with their foreign counterparts to secure the employment of Greek emigrants in sectors which will offer better specialization and more useful experience". It has been also suggested that the government should provide migrants "with all possible assistance in maintaining strong links with their home country".[7] Indeed, the failure of the government migration policy is not that it does not keep labor at home, but rather, that it fails to attract their own nationals back home.

An explanation of this failure allocates the blame to the poor public administration and inefficient government machinery already referred to. To devise and implement a plan to achieve the desired results already delineated, will require knowledgeable, skillful and determined public administrators who, in the Greek civil service, are few and far between.

Recent Developments in the Greek Labor Market

The magnitude of Greek out-migration to primarily West Germany has been considerable between the years 1960 and 1972. The years of 1967 and 1968 were the years of an economic recession in Germany with the corresponding abatement of the migratory flows.

Starting with 1972, the employers in Greece began to complain about labor shortages, suggesting that a further economic development of the country is being threatened. The Greek employers strongly supported a policy of importation of labor from African and Asian countries. This paradoxical situation, namely exportation of their own labor and importation of alien labor to Greece, indicates that something is decidedly wrong with the Greek migration policy. Greece has, currently, a stock of about 3,000,000 workers in Western Europe and the employers in Greece are

---

[7] X. Zolotas. *International Labor Migration and Economic Development.* Athens: Bank of Greece. 1966.

TABLE 12:4

Estimated[a] Number of Greek Immigrants Abroad as of 1971

Countries	Number
Europe Total	311,000
W. Germany (1972)	272,000
Belgium	9,000
Switzerland	8,000
Sweden	7,000
Holland	2,000
Others	13,000
Overseas Total	400,000
Australia	200,000
Canada	90,000
U.S.A.	80,000
Africa	20,000
Others	10,000

Note: [a] Unpublished data.

Source: H. Polyzos. *Report on Migration and Migration Policy*. Athens. No date.

pressing for an importation of labor from abroad.[8]

Officially, no work permits have been issued to foreign workers in Greece. Unofficial estimates for the years 1974 and 1975 indicate at least 20,000 foreign workers in Greece, most of whom are from Pakistan. However, after a summer action in 1975 whereby the foreign workers' visas were summarily canceled, the workers are leaving Greece in significant numbers. Furthermore, the joint activities of the Ministry of Labor and the German Commission have ceased because of the labor importation stoppage in the Federal Republic of Germany in the fall of 1973.

Prospects

Whereas it remains to be seen whether the economic situation in Western Europe will improve enough to restimulate an outflow of Greek workers, presently, the situation is stalemated. Most of the Greek workers already in Germany have been there for more than five years. Given their earning power and their habituation to a standard of living which would be difficult to match at home, a major flow of return migrants is not expected in the near future.

[8] Theodore P. Lianos. "Flows of Greek Out-Migration and Return Migration", *International Migration* (Geneva), 13:119-133. 1975.

At the same time, the economic situation at home is not so bad that a major outflow of Greek labor to Northwestern Europe is not to be expected in view of the new policy, of the labor importing countries like West Germany and France, to invest in the labor exporting countries directly. Actually, this new policy, more proposed than implemented, would bring Greek nationals back, as their employers, investing in Greece, will prefer a Greek labor force already trained abroad.

13

The Iberian Peninsula

MARIA BEATRIZ ROCHA TRINDADE
The New University of Lisbon

History

EMIGRATION from the Iberian peninsula dates to the time of the discoveries. Emigration has been pervasive over the centuries and has become part and parcel of the national consciousness also acting as a valve for demographic pressures. Differing from each other in destination, in composition of the emigrating populations, in the timing of different migration streams, and in the motivation for leaving their respective countries, Portuguese and Spanish emigrants have, nonetheless, many things in common. These two peoples share parallel historical trajectories of emigration.

Varied as the out-migrations of the Spanish and the Portuguese may have been over time, an analysis of the several phases of emigration suggests a common cultural and social pattern based on the parallel evolution of the respective social, economic and political structures. The geographical location alone and the long history of seafaring had determining influences on these two peoples.

It is the venturing into uncharted seas and continents by those two peoples and the riches brought back, although soon squandered, which may explain the neglect of the industrial development at home and the falling behind of industrializing Europe. This economic backwardness, in turn, predisposes the population of the Peninsula to out-migration today.

The psychological attitude on the Peninsula was similar to that of repeated gold rushes, but without much to bequeath when the time came. The

Peninsula thus became a mere supplier of the international markets — a role which has suffered a decline — resulting, ultimately, in the economic dependency on the rest of the industrialized world.

The one product which came from the Peninsula in great abundance was men. Men, willing to work, who finding no employment at home, had to leave for other places, namely for Africa and the Americas: the Portuguese largely migrated to Brazil and the African coast while the Spaniards emigrated to Spanish America.

The mass migrations overseas from Europe around the turn of the century took the population of the Peninsula in tow. The emigration from Spain to the Hispanic Americas was strong, reaching a peak in the annual figures with over 150,000 entries registered for 1920. There was a decline in the 1930s, but after World War II, the flow of emigrants resumed. In 1970, the flow was again reduced, and only 7,800 persons were registered.[1]

For Portugal, Brazil has always been the main country of immigration. Between the years 1901 and 1960, close to seventy percent of the entire number of Portuguese emigrants left for Brazil. Starting with the 19th century, the United States also attracted immigrants from the Peninsula. It was primarily the emigrants from the Azores and Cabo Verde who established settlements in Massachusetts, Connecticut and Rhode Island, which continue, even today, to attract Portuguese emigrants.[2]

The two wars, the Great Depression in America, and the increasing restrictions at home undercut the flow of emigrants from the Peninsula overseas. On the other hand, alternate out-migrations were starting to take place in Europe. At the beginning of World War I the Ministry of Agriculture in France established the *Office National de la Main d'Oeuvre Agricole* to recruit the needed agricultural workers for the war economy, principally from Portugal and Spain. Between 1915 and 1918, about 150,000 Iberian workers were brought to France through this organization alone. In spite of a high return migration rate, which is understandable for this kind of migration, the total of Spanish persons in France was estimated at about 350,000 in 1918. This number then decreased gradually until 1936. Whereas, until that time, the migrant population was predominantly male and young, its demographic composition changed dramatically with the onset of the Civil War in Spain. An inflow of refugees consisting of women, children, the elderly, and later on, of political exiles, brought into France a population dissimilar to the originally recruited agricultural work force and, numerically, superior to the original migrants. World War II occasioned a reverse flow of population leaving France which reduced the resident Spanish population significantly.

---

[1] *Emigración y Justicia Social*, 1971.
[2] Joel Serrão. *A Emigração Portuguesa*. Lisbon: Livros Horizonte (2nd Ed.). 1974.

TABLE 13:1

Spanish Legal Emigration to Europe 1962-1976,
by Volume and Sex[a]

Year	Number	Percent Males
1962	65,336	79.3
1963	83,728	79.1
1964	102,146	82.1
1965	74,539	79.7
1966	56,795	75.8
1967	25,911	77.2
1968	66,699	79.7
1969	100,840	83.8
1970	97,657	84.4
1971	113,702	87.0
1972	104,134	86.3
1973	96,088	89.4
1974	50,695	91.9
1975	20,610	—
1976	12,055	—

Note: [a] Estimated population of Spain in1974 was 35,224,000. Estimated population of Portugal in 1975 was 8,845,000.

Sources: Instituto Español de Emigración. *Emigración Española Asistida, Estadistica del Año 1974*, Madrid; Gabinete de Estudios del Instituto Español de Emigración. *Informe sobre la Emigración Española*. January, 1977. Madrid.

After the war, however, the economic reconstruction of Europe produced widespread shortages of labor, offering the migrants from the Peninsula new work opportunities. The outflow of emigrants overseas remained strong, but the European migrations provided additional outlet for the Peninsular population. After 1957, and particularly since 1959, a major shift in migration currents took place for the Spanish; the traditional emigration to the Hispanic Americas declined, and the bulk of out-migration became continental. That is, it became largely directed to the countries of the European Economic Community (primarily France), but also moved to Switzerland and Austria and, Scandinavia. The new Spanish in-migrants to France were notably similar in their demographic make-up to the migrants of the 1930s as they were young and predominantly male. These migrants then began to outnumber the Italians who, until then, and together with the East Europeans, were the most numerous group in France. In 1974, however, the newest in-migrants to the country, the Portuguese, gained a numerical ascendancy in France.

As compared to Spain, the Portuguese emigration to Europe has not been a result in a shift of migration preferences, and Portuguese emigration overseas continued to be stable. For the Portuguese, the intra-European migration represents an additional outlet; starting in 1961, the Portuguese migration to Western Europe grew and by 1966, it attained a yearly maximum of about 86,000 persons. France, then, remained the main destination of these migrants.

Intergovernmental Agreements on the Exportation of Labor

In the case of emigration from the Iberian Peninsula, until recently, the intervention by the State took the form of a response to the spontaneous development of emigration. This is to be expected, given the intrinsic contradictions among the governmental, administrative and national policies. The most fundamental objective of any government is to create conditions which would not force its citizens to emigrate; conditions which are, so it seems, not achievable in the forseeable future. Further, there is the fact that emigration may be beneficial to the country in the short run even though the country is losing its population, and personal freedom of movement should be honored even though the national sovereignty is based on the principle of nationalistic allegiance.

Such a situation leads necessarily to a somewhat ambiguous attitude which is reflected in the respective emigration legislation. For instance, in the case of Portugal, there has been a continuous change in administrative institutions regulating emigration. The first emigration department to operate on a national scale, the *Commisariado Geral dos Serviços de Emigração*, was succeeded, in 1947, by the *Junta de Emigração*, which was responsible to the Ministry of the Interior.

The volume of Portuguese emigration during the decade of the 1960s aroused public attention and was amply discussed and highlighted as a national problem by the media. Thus, emigration became a controversial social problem of national proportions since the total population was decreasing and the emigrants represented a drain on talent and national resources. Those controls which the government indirectly imposed to stem emigration proved inefficient and encouraged a clandestine emigration which was fueling the clandestine immigration internationally.

The complexity and urgency of the problem required a national body to deal with it and not simply a single governmental department. In August, 1970, the Junta de Emigração was transformed into the *Secretariado Nacional de Emigração* placed under the Presidency of the Council of Ministers.

The revolution of April 25, 1974 resulted in a greater emphasis being proclaimed in the area of human rights, including the respect for political and ideological individual freedoms. This included the notion of the free movement of labor.

In the meantime, however, the European economic crisis was having its impact, the most significant one being the restrictions the members of the European Communities were imposing on labor from nonmember states.

Thus, in Portugal, the issue was switched away from regulating emigration, to measures and provisions protecting the rights and integration of the Portuguese workers abroad, especially in Europe. The switch is reflected in the statement of the Secretary of State for Emigration, "Our emigration policy will consist in assisting Portuguese communities already established abroad to provide support for them and to ensure their close ties to Portugal".[3] Since 1975, the Department of State for Emigration is responsible to the Ministry of Foreign Affairs.

In Spain, the *Consejo Superior de Emigración* had been established since 1907, answering to the Ministry of Government. Its functions were to coordinate the Juntas de Emigración set up at various ports of embarkation to regulate labor contracts and transportation of emigrants.

In 1924, a new *Dirección* was established under the Ministry of Labor, Commerce and Industry. The Juntas were also added to some Spanish consulates in the receiving countries, a Junta Central, having its seat in Madrid.

This administrative system was replaced in 1956 by the *Instituto Español de Emigración* falling under the Ministry of Labor, but with members of other governmental portfolios having their voice in the role of the Instituto.

Until the beginning of this century, emigration from Spain, like that from Portugal, was a matter of individual initiative. The controls imposed at first were those directed to the transatlantic emigration. They dealt with conditions and procedures for leaving through seaports and regulated contracts for sea passages.

In Portugal, emigration was regulated by Decree No. 44,427, of June 29, 1962, acknowledging the principle of free emigration. The provisions for emigration, however, that governed the issuing of passports were cumbersome enough to represent effective brakes to an unrestrained emigration. In 1974, the passport issuing was simplified making the whole pre-emigration procedure simpler.[4]

The cornerstone of the present emigration policy in Portugal is Article 44 of the Constitution of April, 1976, whereby, "To all [citizens] is granted the right of emigrating or leaving the national territory, and the right of returning to it", Article 14 of the Constitution reads, however, "Portuguese citizens who are, or reside, abroad enjoy the protection of the State for the exercise

---

[3] *Diário de Notícias*, 1976.
[4] A. Saragga Leal. *L'Évolution de l'Émigration Portugaise*. Lisbon: 1973.

TABLE 13:2

Legal Emigrants from Spain in 1974 by
Country of Destination and by Proportion Male

Destination	Number	Percent Males
Europe Total	50,695	90
Switzerland	42,029	95
France	5,601	16
The Netherlands	2,338	93
Other Europe	727	57
Outside Europe	4,586	53

Sources: Instituto Español de Emigración. *Emigración Española Asistida Estadística del Año 1974*, Madrid; Gabinete de Estudios del Instituto Español de Emigración. *Informe sobre la Emigración Española*. January, 1977. Madrid.

of their rights, and are liable to the duties which are not incompatible with their absence from the country".

The Spanish emigration law of June, 1971 is akin to the Portuguese emigration legislation, but it distinguishes between repatriation, a situation arising from a failed attempt at living abroad as an emigrant, and return, a voluntary return to the home country viewed as a normal completion of the migration cycle.

To guarantee the security of workers abroad, both Spain and Portugal entered into agreements with several labor importing countries of the European Communities. These agreements strive to normalize and streamline labor relations and to assure job protection of the workers in the host countries. [5]

Spain retains five bilateral agreements which are still in force with;[6] 1)Belgium (as of November 28, 1956); 2) The Federal Republic of Germany (as of March 28, 1966); 3) France (as of January 25, 1961); 4) the Netherlands (as of April 8, 1961); and 5) Austria (as of May 2, 1962).

At this point, the Spanish government sought to replace bilateral agreements with member countries of the European Communities with a multilateral agreement applying to Spain the benefits of labor mobility enjoyed by the workers of the European Communities.[7] A similar conven-

[5] Francisco Sanchez Lopez. *Emigración Española a Europa*. Madrid: Confederacion Española de Cajas de Ahorros. 1969.

[6] Instituto Español de Emigración. *IV Congreso de la Emigración Española*. Oviedo, Gijon y Santiago de Compostela. October. Proceedings. 1971.

[7] Filipe Vasquez Mateo. *La Nueva Emigración a Iberoamerica*. Madrid: Instituto Español de Emigración. 1968.

tion, known as the Madrid Act, already existed between Spain and the Hispano-American Republics (Law of May 30, 1965).

The bilateral agreements between Portugal and other European countries still in force include:[8] 1) the Netherlands (as of November 22, 1963); 2) France (as of December 31, 1963), this was modified as of July 23, 1971 stipulating the annual quota of entries for Portuguese of 65,000; 3) the Federal Republic of Germany (as of March 17, 1964); and 4) Luxemburg (as of May 20, 1970), this was amended in 1975 introducing clauses against job discrimination.

There is no bilateral agreement with Switzerland, which accepts Portuguese workers on a seasonal basis, e.g. for fruit and beetroot harvesting. The stay of these workers does not exceed 9 months per year.

Finally, both Spain and Portugal have entered in a number of ad hoc agreements with the receiving countries, mostly to protect the welfare and health of their respective populations. In Portugal, these special agreements are administered and supervised by the *Caixa Central de Seguranca Social dos Trabalhadores Migrantes*, responsible to the Ministry of Social Affairs. Spain has similar agreements with Italy, France, Belgium, the Federal Republic of Germany, Switzerland, Austria, Denmark, the Netherlands, Luxemburg, and Portugal.

To further multilateral agreements, the Portuguese Department of State for Emigration has signed an agreement with ICEM, the Inter-Governmental Committee for European Migrations.[9] Spain joined ICEM already in 1956. Both Portugal and Spain, as well as many other countries are currently plagued with high unemployment at home. Since the unemployment is essentially structural, a supra-national placement system, such as ICEM can alleviate the problem only modestly.

Consular Support of the Nationals Abroad

The development of out-migration, especially into the various countries of Western Europe, required a reassessment of emigration policies by the sending countries. Ever since the economic situation in the host countries deteriorated enough to present problems of social welfare and assistance to the in-migrants (the question of legal immigration into most West European countries is quite complex), both the Iberian countries created institutions to support their nationals abroad. The creation of such institutions was pioneered by Spain and followed later by Portugal.

[8] Secretariado National de Emigração, 1975.

[9] ICEM is an autonomous body founded in Brussels in 1951; its seat is now in Geneva. Its purpose was to coordinate the placement of postwar refugees. Since its inception, over two million persons were placed through its offices.

The Instituto Español de Emigración is the main institution to care for the nationals abroad. Its activities are reflected in its increasing budget.[10] One of the Instituto's activities is to set up and coordinate delegate bodies, *agredadurias laborales*, abroad which protect the Spanish nationals, especially those employed. These bodies cooperate closely with the local consulates.

The program of the *Asistencia Social*, a home based welfare organization, reaches abroad as well and takes care of those in need of repatriation or with other social needs.

The Law of July 21, 1971 (Law 33/1971) encourages direct creation of associations and centers with the purpose to strengthen the Spanish identity abroad and to allow the emigrants to maintain strong ties with their home country.

Other governmental agencies, falling for instance under the Ministry of Education and Science, pursue cultural and educational activities among the Spanish nationals abroad, following a formalization of such activities, starting in 1969. The *Consejo Escolar Primario para la Education de los Emigrantes Españoles* enlarged its functions abroad by adding adult classes.

Only after 1970 did Portugal develop a true program of support of its nationals abroad, especially in Europe. The official activities are connected to the establishment of the Secretariado National de Emigração in 1970. Its purpose is summarized in the later promulgated Decree-Law No. 402/70, stating, "This [government] has recognized the urgent need of intensifying measures designed not only to create conditions for settling in the country . . . but also to discipline and route migration currents . . . and set up a whole network of support to emigrants wherever they are".[11]

Instituto de Emigraçaõ Portuguese was initiated in 1974. Clearly inspired by its Spanish counterpart. Its functions include the coordination of the activity of the delegates of the Department of State for Emigration who act as liaison persons to the emigrant communities abroad. Furthermore, the Instituto undertakes technical and financial support of various projects designed to facilitate the emigrants' stay abroad, and to tie them to their home country. Unfortunately, a continuity of immigration policies was not vouchsafed by the changeover in the governments in Portugal.

The exportation of labor was numerically significant for both sending countries on the Peninsula. However, since 1973, their labor force has ceased to be welcome and sought after, since the energy crisis had its repercussions in the West European economy.

Whereas the Portuguese intra-European movements in 1973 still mounted

[10] *Diario da Republica,*, No. 117, la serie, May 5, 1976. In 1971 alone, the budget represented about 90 million pesetas, that is about 1.3 million dollars.

[11] *Diário do Governo*, 1974.

TABLE 13:3

Marital Status of Spanish Legal Emigrants by Sex,
Leaving in 1974

	Single	Married	Other
Male	18,855	21,542	168
Female	1,670	2,451	49
Total	20,525	23,993	217

Sources: Instituto Español de Emigración. *Emigración Española Asistida Estadistica del Año 1974*, Madrid; Gabinete de Estudios del Instituto Español de Emigración. *Informe sobre la Emigración Española*. January, 1977. Madrid.

close to 100,000 persons, this number dropped to 44,451 in 1974 and to 25,619 in 1975. In Spain, the number of assisted emigrants was 96,008 in 1973 as compared with 104,134 one year earlier. Not only was there a sharp drop in the number of those who out-migrated for the first time, but there is a good possibility that a massive return migration will occur.

This situation requires the sending countries to promote an active understanding of their nationals abroad and to appeal to the humanitarian and social consciences of the host countries so that a massive return migration does not take place. In the case of Portugal, the recent decolonization policy made it become a host country to former residents in the colonies, thus complicating the labor situation far more than is the case in Spain. The political systems of the two countries also tend to differ, making it difficult to coordinate the activities concerning their nationals abroad.

In Spain, the most noticeable change in the approach to the problem of emigration is the emphasis on return migration.

A recent enactment of January 25, 1975 by the Ministry of Labor[12] is specifically directed to emigrants who contemplate returning home. The regulations foresee the payment of documentation expenses, travel and subsistence during the return period, medical assistance, reduction of military duty, and a free importation of property acquired abroad. It also foresees allocation of assisted housing for the returnees, as well as payment of unemployment subsidies to workers over 40 years of age.

In Portugal, on the other hand, the internal problems created by a considerable surplus of manpower are not unrelated to the decolonization situation. Therefore, an effective introduction of a policy parallel to that of Spain is not likely to occur. Fortunately, there has not been a significant

[12] G.G. Passigli. "Report on Spanish Emigration", *Workshop on The Comparative Study of the Re-Integration Policy of Five European Labor Exporting Countries*. Berlin: Wissenschaftszentrum. 1975.

The Politics of Migration Policies

TABLE 13:4

Occupational Background, by Sex, of Spanish Legal Emigrants,
Leaving for Three Main Receiving Countries in 1974

Economic Sector	Sex	Switzerland	France	Netherlands
Primary	Male	6,136	1,672	294
	Female	63	102	
Secondary	Male	32,409	2,391	1,745
	Female	564	406	
Tertiary	Male	1,091	110	126
	Female	243	151	
Not	Male	96	67	189
	Female	1,427	102	

Sources: Instituto Español de Emigración. *Emigración Española Asistida Estadistica del Año 1974*, Madrid; Gabinete de Estudios del Instituto Español de Emigración. *Informe sobre la Emigración Española*. January, 1977. Madrid.

stream of return migrants to Portugal in recent years. The future is always uncertain, however, especially if some of the host countries resort to labor rotation policies.

The Portuguese Department of State for Emigration has sponsored a survey of Portuguese residents in the Federal Republic of Germany to discover the potential return migrants: only about one-third of the respondents had definite plans to return. This was in March, 1976.

One of the reasons some countries encourage emigration of their nationals and some fail to discourage it, is the hope for remittances sent home. For Portugal, the remittances were the most important source of foreign currency during this decade. The remittances also have an important place in Spain's balance of payments.

Recently, Portugal has experienced a drop in this form of revenue, related to the political uncertainty at home, so that the approximately one billion U.S. dollars remitted home in 1974 dropped considerably.

The Instituto Español de Emigración has indicated that there was a decline of fifty percent in 1975 as compared to the year previous in the receipts of the *Banco de España*.[13] In January, 1976 the emigrants' remittances came to about 40 million dollars compared to January, 1975 when about 60 million dollars were remitted.

To retain the fiduciary confidence of their nationals abroad, both governments initiated programs allowing foreign currency accounts at home.

[13] Instituto Español de Emigración. *Boletín Informativo*, No. 94, April, 1973.

In Portugal, this took place in 1976 by the Decree-Law No. 729 H/75, Order in Council 138/76.[14] In Spain, such an arrangement had existed since 1970 (Decree No. 3259/70, of October 29, 1970).

In both the preambles to the respective decrees the principle is stressed of preparing for the return of emigrants. In the introduction to the Spanish decree it is noted, "The need to facilitate the social promotion of our emigrants for their return and to ensure for them the enjoyment of the results of their effort...a quick and safe way of placing their savings..."' The preamble to the Portuguese decree similarly remarks, "...the gradual integration of emigrants who wish to return to their home country requires a considerable investment effort...conditions enabling emigrants who send their savings to Portugal to be protected against any hazards that may jeopardize them".

Such formal provisions, however, do not go far toward an institutional support of reintegration of the returnees. The fact that the distances in Europe are not large, "commuting" between one's place of work and one's home country, however sporadic, makes it unnecessary either to return or to stay abroad. More likely than not, those migrant workers may live out their lives wandering about. This is more likely to happen as the policies for their reintegration are vitiated by the economic difficulties at home, and the policies from home to keep them tied to their mother country make it difficult for them to integrate in the countries where they live.

Occupational Characteristics of the Out-Migrants

The uneven socioeconomic development of European countries, coupled with an uneven demographic growth, produced two blocs whose labor needs seem to have been complementary during the third quarter of this century.

The "receptor bloc" of Northwestern Europe enjoyed an unprecedented economic prosperity and full employment allowing its nationals to move upward the occupational scale vacating lower level positions to be filled by migratory labor from the "donor bloc".[15]

The role of in-migrating labor played in various countries was, partly, a function of the timing of their arrivals and partly their occupational background. The established mold allowed for self-continuation even though the original condition may have changed.

While maintaining similar characteristics of their emigration patterns, Spain and Portugal occupied different positions in the occupational

---

[14] *Diário do Governo*, Dec. 22, 1975.

[15] Stephen Castles and Godula Kosack. *Immigrant Workers and Class Structure in Western Europe*. London: Oxford University Press. 1973.

TABLE 13:5

Portuguese Legal Emigration to Europe,[a] 1960-1976

Year	Number to Europe	% to Europe	% Male	% in Families
1960	3,744	12	54	50
1961	5,984	18	58	41
1962	8,985	27	59	39
1963	16,821	43	64	37
1964	37,658	68	69	34
1965	70,467	79	66	39.
1966	85,677	71	60	49
1967	82,885	90	52	56
1968	52,796	66	41	59
1969	42,353	60	58	45
1970	43,261	65	65	34
1971	28,180	56	58	40
1972	33,691	62	51	42
1973	57,267	12	65	32
1974	17,419	40	52	55
1975	5,395	22	49	57
1976	2,687	15	—	—

Note: [a] The major receiving countries only: W. Germany, France, Netherlands, Luxemburg, United Kingdom, and Switzerland.

Sources: Secretaria de Estado de Emigração. *Boletim anual*, 1975. Lisbon; Instituto de Emigração, D.S.I.E.A.E. 1976. Lisbon. Provisional data for 1976.

integration abroad. The Spanish workers have a longer tradition of entering the Northwest European labor market and thus were able to "corner" some better occupations in the trades, than the later arriving Portuguese. The inevitable occupational mobility allowed the "bonne" in France to fall to a Portuguese after that occupational niche had been vacated by a Spanish woman; the present Spanish workers in industrial occupations left the less desirable construction work to the Portuguese "macon". Whether the Portuguese will later be replaced by the unskilled labor coming from North Africa is a matter of economic development in Europe.

The occupational background of the out-migrants from the Peninsula is primarily industrial, more so for the Spanish than for the Portuguese. In 1974, for instance, 14 percent of Portuguese showed occupational backgrounds in the primary economic sector, 22 percent in the secondary sector, 7 percent in the service occupations and 58 percent showed no previous economic activity. The last figure, for the most part, includes dependents.

TABLE 13:6

Legal Emigrants Aged 10 Years and Over, by Employment Held
in Portugal Prior to Leaving, by Principal Economic Sectors, 1960-1975

Year of Emigration	No. of Emigrants	Proportion of Emigrants in Sectors			
		Primary (Agriculture)	Secondary (Industrial)	Tertiary (Service)	No reported employment
1960	25,028	32.9	11.1	7.4	48.6
1961	27,463	33.5	14.5	8.4	43.6
1962	27,591	30.0	18.2	8.5	43.3
1963	32,994	28.2	27.3	6.8	37.7
1964	48,288	28.4	31.1	7.0	33.5
1965	75,152	25.8	30.2	7.7	36.3
1966	97,725	27.2	22.2	6.4	44.2
1967	70,567	24.9	14.5	4.5	56.1
1968	59,728	20.9	9.2	5.0	64.9
1969	57,040	27.8	17.6	7.3	47.3
1970	57,587	25.5	29.0	9.0	36.5
1971	40,260	19.2	24.1	9.5	47.2
1972	42,041	16.2	25.7	8.7	49.4
1973	66,690	15.9	36.5	11.0	36.6
1974	31,698	14.4	21.6	6.5	57.5
1975	18,052	13.1	13.4	12.9	60.6
1976	17,454	—	—	—	—

Sources: Secretaria de Estado de Emigração. *Boletim anual*, 1975. Lisbon; Instituto de Emigração, D.S.I.E.A.E. 1976. Lisbon. Provisional data for 1976.

For the Spanish men, there were half as many with agricultural and extraction industries background as with industrial occupations background in France, the major receiving country. This ratio is even higher for men working in Switzerland where many skilled trades are supplied by the Spanish.

Of course, the occupational structures at home show corresponding differences, Spain being more similar to the occupational distribution in Western and Northern Europe than Portugal, whose population is still heavily agricultural.

In a way, the forces of modernization are catching up with the peoples on the Peninsula. Once seafarers and discoverers and builders of empires, now they contribute anonymously to the economic growth of the industrialized countries thus strengthening the understanding between the peoples.

14

Italy[*]

FRANCESCO CERASE
University of Rome

New Pressures and Trends in Italian Migration Policies

ITALY is a country of emigration. In the one hundred years following the unification of Italy, approximately 27 million Italians left their homeland and, in all likelihood, at least one-half of them settled abroad permanently.[1]

These migratory flows have been intimately linked with the development of Italian society. In the 1880s the agricultural crisis precipitated a great exodus. The forces of industrialization starting at that time and accelerating until World War I stimulated heavy migrations. The policy of colonization and the military expansion of the fascist regime stimulated population resettlements. Finally, the new freedom of movement initiated after World War II encouraged new migrations.[2]

However, in the course of time, migratory flows ceased to be a national

---

[*] Since this paper was written, Italy has gone through a serious economic recession. In the midst of it migration has again tended to become a rather forgotten issue, as seemingly more urgent problems have come to the fore. Viewed in the present perspective many of the proposals discussed above turn out to be more wishful expectations of a given historical moment than policies which are actually being implemented.

[1] L. Bertelli, G. Corcagnani and G.F. Rosoli, eds. *Migrazioni.* Catalogo della Biblioteca del Centro Studi Emigrazione di Roma. Rome: Centro Studi Emigrazione. 1972; A. Golini and G. Caselli, eds. *Bibliografia delle Opere Demografiche Italiane (1966-1972).* Rome: Instituto di Demografia, University of Rome. 1973.

[2] *Il Ponte*, 30:11-12, 1974; F. Barbagallo. *Lavoro ed Esodo nel Sud 1861-1971.* Naples: Guida. 1973; Francesco P. Cerase. *Sotto il Dominio dei Borghesi.* Sottosviluppo ed emigrazione nell'Italia Meridionale 1860-1910. Rome: Carucci. 1975.

phenomenon and became regionalized and, primarily, confined to the south of the country.[3] It is estimated, that about 80 percent of all Italian emigrants of today come from the South.[4] The more than 500,000 southerners who emigrated during the last five years, migrated mostly to Northwestern Europe with the result that their return rate and turnover is high.[5]

The recent attention to the problems of Italian emigration has brought forth a new awareness of its extent and a social concern that such massive emigration must have its causes in the socioeconomic imbalances in the Italian regions.

A major impetus forcing reassessment of the traditional thought about emigration came from the National Conference on Emigration, organized in Rome, February, 1975. The reports at the Conference brought to public attention the new trends and the sociopolitical forces operating in policy making with respect to migration.

The basic fact remains that migration constitutes a national problem. Defined as such, it requires a commitment on the part of the entire country and, above all, it calls for the articulation of a new model for Italian socioeconomic development.

The implications of migration, until now presumed to be an individual matter, assume a sociological character. That is, the actions of individuals are understood to stem from the structural arrangements of a society no longer able to take care of all its citizens. The traditional *assistenza* and *tutela*, from the beginning the only concern of Italian migration policies, assume a new meaning indicated in the collective responsibility the country has toward its nationals.

The dilemma of the Italian emigration policies is that men should be free to move, but should their move result from adverse conditions at home, their freedom to stay is being abridged. The postwar Italian governments have not really been able to overcome this dilemma. Despite an increasing awareness of the real causes of emigration, the urgent need to find an immediate solution to the massive unemployment through emigration took precedence.[6]

[3] The "Regions" in Italy are administrative subdivisions intermediate to the municipalities and the cental government. Sicily, Calabria, Basilicata, Apulia, Campania, Abruzzi, and Molise are the Italian south.

[4] E. Vercellino. *Aspetti e Problemi dell'Emigrazione Italiana*. Rome: Conferenza Nazionale dell'Emigrazione. Ministero degli Affari Esteri. 1974.

[5] *Studi Emigrazione*, 1974; E. Publiese and G. Mottura. "Mercato del Lavoro e Caratteristiche dell'Emigrazione Italiana nell'Ultimo Quindicennio", Agricoltura, Mezzogiorno e Marcato del Lavoro. Bologna: Il Mulino. 1975; R. Lenzi and A.M. Birindelli. *Aspetti e Problemi dell'Emigrazione Italiana con Particolare Riguardo a Quella nell'Ambito CEE*. Rome: CISP. In press; *Richerche e Studi Formez*, 1976.

[6] P. Cinnani. "La Scelta del Governo Italiano nel Secondo Dopoguerra", *Il Ponte*, 30:1342-1358. 1974.

TABLE 14:1

Percent Distribution of Italian Emigrants to Europe and Elsewhere Abroad
by Major Receiving Countries in Europe, by Proportion Male to Europe and to Elsewhere, 1965-1975[a]

Year	Germany	Switzerland	France	Other	All Europe	% Male	All Elsewhere	% Male	All Emigrants N	%[b]
1965	32	37	7	7	82	80	18	52	282,643	100
1966	26	35	6	6	74	78	26	54	296,494	100
1967	21	39	7	6	73	75	27	54	229,264	100
1968	24	38	6	6	73	74	27	54	215,713	100
1969	26	38	6	6	76	73	24	55	182,199	100
1970	28	35	6	7	76	72	24	54	151,854	100
1971	32	35	5	6	79	71	21	55	167,721	100
1972	31	36	6	6	79	72	21	54	141,852	100
1973	33	35	5	6	80	70	20	55	123,802	100
1974	30	34	6	8	78	—	22	—	112,020	100
1975	30	33	7	8	78	—	22	—	92,588	100

Notes: [a] Estimated population of Italy in 1974 was 54,000,000.
[b] May not add to 100 due to rounding.

Sources: For the years 1965-1973, Consiglio Nazionale dell'Economia e del Lavoro, 1976; for 1974, Ministero Affari Esteri, 1975; Emigrazione filef, 1976, VIII, n. 11-12.

The Italian government entered into bilateral and multilateral agreements on migration with many European countries to safeguard the employment and welfare of its nationals abroad. The agreements were meant, on the one hand, to link helping the nationals and looking-after the nationals with a general principle of fundamental human rights and, on the other hand, the agreements were meant to secure an outlet for the Italian surplus labor.

The agreements among the numbers of the European Economic Community, of which Italy is a member, guarantee a free movement of labor, in principle. The situation affecting Italian workers abroad is not free from ambiguities,[7] although the Charter of the European Community is sufficiently clear. It states that the member states have a prior claim on the available job vacancies over workers from nonmember states. The de facto implementation of the equal opportunity clauses, however remains hazy.

Because of the difficulties in monitoring the treatment of indigenous and immigrant workers in matters of salary and related benefits, the employers, if they can get away with it, tend to employ workers not protected by the European Communities agreements. This results in a direct disadvantage to the Italian emigrants. The Italian Minister of Labor presented a memorandum of protest dealing with the *Politica dell'impiego nella CEE*, to the meetings of the Council of Ministers for Social Affairs of the European Economic Community, June 24, 1971, in which he denounced the failure to effect the principle of priority employment.[8]

Italian Workers in Switzerland

In Switzerland, there are distinctive problems for Italian workers. There are three types of Italian workers in Switzerland: the resident; the seasonal; and the *frontaliere*. The most precarious situation exists for the seasonal worker even though he spends most of his time in Switzerland.

Italian policy has been directed mainly toward achieving equality of treatment of both the Italian and Swiss workers with respect to salary, accident insurance, social welfare and medical care. In addition, the Italian government pursues the policy, 1) that Italians be allowed to bring their families, 2) that they be allowed a greater job mobility and 3) with regard to the seasonal workers, that their status may be changed to resident status.

After some protracted negotiations an agreement was reached between Italy and Switzerland in 1964, covering some of the above points discussed.

[7] V. Briani. *Il Lavoro Italiano in Europa*. Ieri ed oggi. Rome: Ministero Affari Esteri. 1972; E. Vercellino. *Aspetti e Problemi dell'Emigrazione Italiana*. Rome: Conferenza Nazionale dell'Emigrazione. Ministero degli Affari Esteri. 1974.

[8] V. Briani. *Op. cit. Aspetti e Problemi dell'Emigrazione Italiana all'Estero nel 1974*. Rome: Ministero Affari Esteri. 1975.

However, soon thereafter, the Swiss National Council introduced restrictive norms regarding immigration to accommodate the internal anti-alien pressures. What has become known in Switzerland as the *Überfremdungsgefahr* (a danger of too many foreigners in the country) has become the slogan militating against the permission intergovernmental agreements regarding migrant labor.[9]

In such cases, Italy finds itself to be the weaker bargaining partner. There are, however, reasons for this. Initially, of course, there have been no effective organizations operating on the local level to represent Italian workers, any more than there has been any true cooperation between Italian consular authorities and the resident Italian communities.[10] Secondly, an economic policy genuinely directed to eliminate the structural causes of emigration has never been pursued.

There is, thus, a situation of a double bind for the Italians working in Europe. Italy, as a country, lacks the necessary political muscle to look after its own nationals abroad and, when economic recessions occur, Italian workers are returning to regions in Italy which have little to offer. Recently, a realization of these facts led to a number of movements to remedy the situation of the Italian migrant and the returnee.

Regions as Pressure Groups

The general movement to do something about the situation of emigration is being spearheaded by the Regions, in their administrative capacities. The various actions and, primarily, legislative formulations, are spurred on by the realization that continuous out-migration was an inappropriate solution to the regional economic and social woes. More often than not, heavy out-migration produces populations which are demographically top heavy, containing high old-age dependency ratios and general economic stagnation and social decay.

As a response to the prevailing conditions, practically all southern Regions are introducing articles into their statutes to remedy the situation by deemphasizing out-migration. For example, Article 4:2 of the Statutes of the Molise Region reads: "The Region will attempt to stop the depopulation of its territory, to put an end to emigration, to avoid the phenomenon of social disintegration ensuing from it, to foster return of those who have emigrated".

[9] C. Calvaruso. *Sottoproletariato in Svizzera*. Rome: Coines. 1971; Centro Studi Emigrazione. *La Svizzera dopo Schwarzenbach*. Rome: CSE. 1970.

[10] The consular offices answer directly to the Ministry of Foreign Affairs, whereas questions of emigration and social welfare are handled by separate Ministeries in Rome, surely two different traditions of administrative practices. This issue, too, was hotly debated at the National Conference on Emigration.

Or, Article 8 of the Statutes of the Campania Region reads: "The Region recognizes as one of its objectives the solution of the emigration problem and shall eliminate this phenomenon and repatriate its citizens". Or, Article 16, of the Statutes of the Apulia Region reads: "The Region sees in the phenomenon of mass emigration something which hinders greatly the civil development of the Apulian community; it shall seek, within the framework of its planning, to overcome the conditions which have made migration necessary;...it shall promote measures for looking after the interests of people who have emigrated from the Region".[11]

The implementation of such ambitious plans, however, becomes another question. In the field of legislation, the Regions can invoke Articles 117 and 118 of the Italian Constitution which grant to the Regions the right to promulgate and administer laws pertaining to "social welfare, health and hospital care" and to "professional development and aid to education". Such provisions could then be applied, to the returning migrants, in particular.

In fact, however, Regional policies shift depending on the time perspective. As long term policies, the intent is there to address the problem of the structural causes of out-migration. Such programs must occur, however, within a framework of a broad and coherent national economic program and, in particular, by taking advantage of the European Social Fund. Dating back to the Treaty of the European Economic Community, Article 123, of March 25, 1957, the Fund is meant to promote within the Community "possibilities for work and for geographic and professional mobility of workers". The powers of the Fund were later specified by the Council's decision of February 1, 1971, allowing direct aid to improve "personal work situations".[12]

These and other new initiatives to affect policies on out-migration were discussed at the first Regional Conference on Emigration held in July of 1973 in Perugia, and were later proposed by the Regional representatives to the National Conference on Emigration.[13]

What was proposed is that the new alternative for economic development is to be based on integration of agricultural production and the industrial processing of produce to overcome the crises besetting the Italian agriculture. In other words, this new combination of food processing and agriculture

[11] Ministero Affari Esteri. *Guida Pratica delle Norme Statali e Regionali Applicabili sul Territorio Italiano nell'Interesse del Citadino Emigrato.* Rome: Ministero Affair Esteri. 1976.

[12] ISFOL.. *Fondo Sociale Europeo. Quanderno di Formazione.* Rome: ISFOL.. 1975.

[13] The gist of the proposals is that the search for a new model of national development must be informed by the notion of replacing the criterion of a maximum productivity by that of a maximum employment. The fact is that emigration is not restricted to unskilled workers, but includes educated persons as well who are unable to find employment in the depressed regions of the South.

will cease to be "an income drain in the direction of the industrial sector and will foster a process of aggregation of income within the agricultural sector. This will insure an increase in agricultural income no longer based on policy of protection of prices, but dependent, rather, on a just reintegration to the agricultural sector of sectors with high added value such as the processing and distributive industries."[14]

Many regions, however, were able to initiate short and middle term measures serving to improve the lot of the potential, or of the returning migrant and his family. That is, some of the measures sought to guarantee the educational placement of children of return migrants, to help returning workers through the payments of unemployment benefits, to reimburse the return trip, occupationally to retrain migrants upon return, and to provide for various family allowances. In addition, the Regions financed studies and offered research grants for the study of emigration. Various Regions also created Regional Councils on Emigration to deal with the issues of emigration and, in particular, return migration. Through the institutions of Regional Councils of Emigration the emigrants acquired an additional political voice.

The laws and the individual articles of the statutes represent, no doubt, a step forward. Most of them are, however, ad hoc legislations and fail to tackle the root of the problem, which is being defined as the structural inequality inherent to the Italian south. Such structural inequalities, however, are difficult to tackle without the complete cooperation of the central government and, above all, without its serious attempt to enforce any form of national economic planning.

For this reason the effectiveness of the Regions was reduced to a simple social assistance on one hand and to a ritualism of promulgating policies on emigration on the other. This does not mean that legal provisions, dealing with the whole question of emigration, should not be initiated nor does it mean that the problems of returning migrants should not be examined and resolved. It means, rather, that whatever help there is must be put in a context which "does not simply reduce the Region to the position of dispenser of benefactions", but, rather, the help must be viewed from a perspective of a farsighted planning stressing an ample employment at home.[15]

Labor Unions as Pressure Groups

Italian labor unions underwent a phase of "self-criticism" in the matter of

---

[14] Regione dell'Umbria. *La Questione dell'Emigrazione e la Politica delle Regioni per un Nuovo ed Alternativo Modello di Sviluppo in Italia.* Rome: Conferenza Nazionale dell'Emigrazione. Mimeo. 1975. P. 17.

[15] F. Pittau. "Regioni ed Emigrazione", *Dossier Europa. Emigrazione.* Rome: Centro Studi Emigrazione. 1976.

TABLE 14:2

Percent Distribution of Italian Returnees from Europe and from Elsewhere, by Major Countries of European Stay, by Proportion Male of All European Returnees and All Returnees from Elsewhere, 1965-1975

Year	Returnees from Europe				All Europe	% Male	% All Elsewhere	% Male	All Returnees	
	Germany	Switzerland	France	Other					N	%
1965	35	47	8	6	96	82	4	53	196,376	100[a]
1966	38	46	8	6	98	81	3	55	206,486	100
1967	34	48	8	7	96	77	4	55	169,328	100
1968	29	49	9	8	95	75	5	54	150,027	100
1969	26	44	8	7	85	73	15	58	153,298	100
1970	26	39	8	7	79	72	21	55	142,503	100
1971	28	40	7	8	82	71	18	56	128,572	100
1972	30	38	7	8	82	70	18	55	138,246	100
1973	30	38	6	7	81	69	19	55	125,168	100
1974	30	38	6	8	83	—	17	—	116,708	100
1975	30	41	5	7	83	—	17	—	122,774	100

Note: [a] May not add to 100 due to rounding.

Sources: For the years 1965-1973, Consiglio Nazionale dell'Economia e del Lavoro, 1976; for 1974, Ministero Affair Esteri, 1975; Emigrazione filef, 1976, VIII, n. 11-12.

their attitudes to emigration only a few years ago. Prior to that, their posture was indifferent and, occasionally, hostile toward emigrants, who abandoned the collective "struggle" for the selfish interests of self-advancement.

In recent years, however, the Italian Federation of Labor has proved to be the one social force most effective in promoting new migration policies to safeguard the interests of Italians abroad.

Labor unions have stated, on more than one occasion, that a problem of emigration is "a problem of the entire working class and of the entire Italian and European union movement which must address itself to the problem through its manifold organizations and commit itself to solving it by calling on all workers whether migrant or not".[16] It means that labor unions face "this fundamental crux of the working condition in a new and different manner, as an integral part of the entire complex of problems of the union movement and of employment, of collective bargaining and economic development, of a serious policy of reform, of a new type of collaboration and integration, on the union level, on the international level, and on the level of the European Common Market community".[17]

These are, then, the new objectives of the federated Italian labor unions. It is important to examine, however, the direction in which they are actually moving, the results they are registering, and the obstacles they are encountering.

A recent analysis summarizes the steps undertaken by the labor unions to promote a migration policy at the national level: 1) to seek an increasingly direct participation in all decisions which affect migrant workers and their families; 2) to demand an increasing responsibility for defining a national employment policy incorporating the issue of migration; and 3) to create an information system of data on those social and governmental institutions that deal with emigrants and return migrants.[18]

On the international level, the unions may be noted to be aiming, on the one hand, to utilize the European Social Fund to contribute directly to the development of the Regions and, on the other hand, to establish ties with the unions in the countries of Italian immigration.

The unions have their difficulties in transcending issues limited to specific contingencies and cases at home, and they are not in a position to organize workers abroad with respect to specific places of work and to specific work relations. Their domestic influence on the national policies of migration is being vitiated by the traditional bureaucratic inertia of the national government. Abroad, on the other hand, the Italian unions are more likely to find a generic response among other labor unions, where a modest

---

[16] E. Vercellino. *Aspetti e Problemi dell'Emigrazione Italiana*. Rome: Conferenza Nazionale dell'Emigrazione. Ministero degli Affari Esteri. 1974. Pp. 231-232.

[17] *Ibid*. P. 206.

[18] C. Calvaruso. *Sindacati ed Emigrazione*. Rome: Coines. 1974. P. 32.

TABLE 14:3

Percent Distribution of All Italian Emigrants to Europe
and of All Returnees from Abroad, by Major Age Groups, 1965-1973

Age Groups	1965 Eur[a]	1965 Ret[b]	1966 Eur	Ret	1967 Eur	Ret	1968 Eur	Ret	1969 Eur	Ret	1970 Eur	Ret	1971 Eur	Ret	1972 Eur	Ret	1973 Eur	Ret
Less Than 14	5	4	7	5	8	8	9	10	10	12	11	14	12	14	11	15	12	15
15-29	51	46	49	45	41	43	45	40	41	34	38	31	39	31	36	30	35	29
30-39	26	28	25	27	25	26	25	26	26	27	26	26	24	26	25	25	25	25
40-49	12	13	13	14	13	14	14	15	16	16	16	17	16	17	17	17	17	17
50 and over	6	9	7	9	8	10	8	10	8	16	9	13	9	13	11	13	11	14
Total[c]	100	100	100	100	100	100	100	100	100	100	100	100	100	100	100	100	100	100
N to Europe	232,421		219,353		166,697		158,462		139,140		115,114		133,132		111,908		98,970	
N Returnees	196,376		206,486		169,328		150,027		153,298		142,503		128,572		138,246		125,168	

Notes: [a] Emigrants to Europe.
[b] All Returnees.
[c] May not add to 100 due to rounding.

Sources: For the years 1965-1973, Consiglio Nazionale dell'Economia e del Lavoro, 1976; for 1974, Ministero Affari Esteri, 1975; Emigrazione filef, 1976, VIII, n. 11-12.

beginning has been made by the establishment of the European Confederation of Unions. A true cooperation at the shop level, though, is quite a way off in the future.

There is no doubt that the best strategy for the Italian unions to follow is to interest migrant workers in the unions of countries of immigration. In the immediate future the unions will be most effective through their pressure to pass specific legislative measures favoring migrants at home and through the shop level organization of workers abroad. At the shop level, the unions play a decisive role both in formulating specific objectives pertaining to wages, working conditions, and related matters. At the same time, they endeavor to link these objectives to a more general strategy of advancing the workers' movement in the countries of in-migration.

Particularly significant in this context is the role played by the unions in bodies such as the *Comitato Consultivo degli Italiani all'Estero* and in the *Comitato Nazionali d'Intesa*. The latter, the National Committee for Coordination is made up of all political organizations of Italian emigrants abroad. The fact is that some of the members represent the Catholic Church, and thus the involvement of the Church in questions of emigration has acquired a renewed intensity reflected in a number of pronouncements by the Church on that matter.

New Organizations of Italian Migrants Abroad

It is through bodies like those just mentioned that Italian migrants can now advance their own interest and thus directly affect governmental policies. Largely as the result of a recommendation by the National Council for Economy and Labor, the Council of Italians Abroad is being considerably restructured to include a larger representation of migrants through their local communities abroad, the labor unions, and emigrant associations in Italy. It has been organized according to the areas of the world and the kinds of problems. It meets at regular intervals throughout the year.[19]

The existence of such bodies as well as the debate which goes on within them shows that the developments discussed thus far are intimately connected to the grass roots. It is the migrants themselves who are today requesting greater participation in the decision process regarding matters that concern them.

The stereotype of the Italian migrant set at the turn of the century is becoming increasingly invalid. Today, more often than not, the migrant has

---

[19] Presently (Spring, 1977) there is a new law under discussion to replace this body with the Consiglio Italiano dell'Emigrazione (Italian Council for Emigration) through which the interests of migrants will find a more direct voice.

TABLE 14:4

Percent Distribution of Italian Workers Emigrating to Europe and Elsewhere by Major Economic Sectors of Employment Prior to Leaving, and by Proportion of All Emigrants, 1970-1973

| | Economic Sectors | | | | | | N All[a] Workers | | % of All Emigrants | |
| | Agriculture | | Industry | | Services | | | | | |
Years	Eur.	Else.	Eur.	Else.	Eur.	Else.	Eur.	Else.	Eur.	Else.
1970	13	15	69	60	19	26	88,193	16,569	77	45
1971	13	14	70	63	18	23	98,633	16,265	74	41
1972	12	15	69	59	19	27	84,021	13,139	75	44
1973	11	12	69	61	20	28	72,559	11,071	73	45

Note: [a] Each row adds to 100 alternately in first six columns. Deviation due to rounding.

Source: For the years 1965-1973, Consiglio Nazionale dell'Economia e del Lavoro, 1976.

a more definite notion and awareness of what structural conditions have pushed him out of his country; therefore, also more often than not, he is looking for explanations of what social forces are responsible for this. He is more receptive to appeals which call for direct action and, he is more likely to claim his own rights as a worker and as a human being.

In no way, perhaps, has this new awareness become more evident than in the request of migrants to be directly responsible for what is to be done to safeguard their own interests. The old concept of assistance, the *tutela*, is currently being replaced by a more highly articulated concept of social rights. For instance, a position from the Comitato Nazionale d'Intesa in Switzerland clarifies that the concept of *tutela* can no longer be seen as one of simple assistance, but must be understood as a guarantee that, in the case of migrants, the fundamental rights, which the workers' movement has succeeded in ensuring both in the home country and in the countries of immigration, must be respected. This requires that necessary legislation be passed to initiate full economic and social parity with indigenous workers. It also requires a thorough revision of Italian economic policy that would end the weakening of small scale industry and the progressive decay of agriculture and would initiate the overhauling of the system of production capable of multiplying jobs and of guaranteeing for all, including migrants who may return, stable and respectable jobs in their homeland.

15

Turkey

DANIEL KUBAT *
University of Waterloo

Turkish Out-Migration Since 1960

DEMOGRAPHICALLY, Turkey is the fastest growing country of all the principal labor suppliers to Northwestern Europe. The present population of about 40 million includes a net addition of about 10 million since the last census in 1965. The eastern regions of Turkey are the least hospitable to human habitation, but they are the fastest growing in population. The pronatalist tradition in Turkey is difficult to curb while the age of first marriage for women remains 18 years, and lower in the more rural and eastern regions. The pronatalist attitude is also fostered by the influence the military establishment has on the nation.[1]

Turkey has a substantial supply of manpower. Naturally, the majority of the available work force has only a limited industrial experience; a substantial proportion of Turkish population in the working age categories is still employed in agriculture.

To get Turkey out of industrial and agricultural backwardness, the government has embarked upon a vigorous campaign of industrialization and mechanization of agriculture. An unanticipated consequence of the latter is the displacement of about eight subsistence farming families per

---

* It is necessary that the co-author of this chapter, a resident of Istanbul, remain anonymous.

[1] Lewis S. Anderson. *Turkey*. New York: The Population Council. Country Profile Series. January, 1970.

new tractor introduced. The net result of the mechanization of agriculture is an army of about one million rural population displaced annually. Since Turkey is already adding about one million to its population annually, these two forces combine to provide an enormous surplus of manpower which the country cannot absorb alone.[2]

One of the options available to Turkey since about 1960 has been to export labor abroad. At the end of 1975, Turkey had sent over 800,000 workers to Northwestern Europe, about 80 percent of which went to the Federal Republic of Germany.

For whatever reasons, the Turks did not develop extensive informal networks to secure jobs abroad without official assistance. The unofficial Turkish migrations also appear to be more subject to fluctuations in the European economy than are the official migrations regulated by work contracts. Nonetheless, starting abruptly in 1973, the official recruitment of Turkish workers subsided considerably so that in 1975 only about 4,500 Turks out-migrated to Europe. This is a negligible number which is easily lost in the larger number of returnees.

Regulation of Manpower Migration

Turkey entered into a number of bilateral agreements with several labor importing countries to facilitate a regulated recruitment of Turkish manpower and to safeguard the social protection of Turkish nationals abroad. Usually two separate agreements were signed, one detailing the recruitment of labor and the other regulating social insurance payments and their transferability, medical care and similar social welfare measures.

The agreements were with the following countries: Federal Republic of Germany (labor: October 30, 1961, amended September 1, 1964; welfare: April 30, 1964); France (labor: April 8, 1965; welfare: no agreement); Austria (labor: May 15, 1964; welfare: October 12, 1966, amended February 3, 1967 and October 1, 1969); the Netherlands (labor: August 10, 1964; welfare: April 15, 1966, amended June 14, 1967); Belgium (labor: July 16, 1964; welfare: July 4, 1966); United Kingdom (labor: no agreement; welfare: June 1, 1961); Sweden (labor: signed March 10, 1967 but never activated; welfare: no agreement); Denmark (labor: no agreement; welfare: signed November 13, 1970 effective two months later); Switzerland (labor: no agreement but recruitment privately through Turkish employment bureaus; welfare: May 1, 1969); Australia (labor: October 5, 1967; welfare: no agreement); and Lybia (labor: January 5, 1975; welfare: no agreement).

The agreements cover some basic rights of Turkish workers. Some of the features of the agreements include: medical examination by teams from the

2 *Ibid.*

TABLE 15:1

Out-Migration of Turkish Workers Abroad by Number of Legal
Out-Migrants, by Proportion Male and by Number Registered
in West Germany, for the Years 1961 through 1976[a]

Year	Number Recruited	Proportion Male	Number in W. Germany (December)
1961	1,476	95	5,193
1962	1,185	95	15,318
1963	30,328	92	27,144
1964	66,176	94	69,211
1965	51,520	78	121,121
1966	34,410	72	157,978
1967	8,947	64	137,081
1968	43,204	74	139,336
1969	103,975	81	212,951
1970	129,575	85	327,985
1971	88,442	86	424,374
1972	85,229	78	497,296
1973	135,820	80	599,000
1974	20,211	93	571,000
1975	4,419	91	522,669
1976	—	—	515,830

Note: [a] Estimated Population of Turkey in 1975: 40,000,000.

Sources: Turkish Employment Service, *Annual Lab or Reports:* Bundesarbeit für Arbeit. Ausländische Arbeitnehmer — Beschäftigung, Anwerbung, Vermittlung, Erfahrungsbericht 1972/73. Nürnberg, 1974; Die Beschäftigungslage Ende Dezember 1974 und Ende März 1975 im Bundesgebiet und den Landesarbeitsamtbezirken. Nürnberg, 1975; ANBA, 1976, No. 10, p. 1100; 1977, No. 9, p. 1212.

receiving countries (excepting Lybia); right of the receiving countries to select the workers according to their occupational skills (excepting Lybia); age limits on applicants for jobs; written contract prior to departure (excepting Australia); guarantee of fair and prevalent wages without a contract prior to departure (only Australia); recruitment of skill levels without specifying persons; recruitment of pre-specified persons (excepting Lybia); equal treatment principle (excepting Lybia); free flow of remittances (excepting Lybia); joint grievance committees (excepting Belgium and Lybia); and additional paid holidays for Turkish workers (only Belgium).

The welfare agreements have been tailored to the measures prevailing in the respective receiving countries.

TABLE 15:2

Percent Distribution of Turkish Workers in West Germany,
by Major Sectors of Employment, for the Years 1963-1975

Years	Mining and Related	Industry[a]		Construction	Other	Total	
		Heavy	Light			Percent	N
1963	13	43	16	16	18	100	32,962
1964	15	40	15	22	10	100	85,172
1965	12	41	19	19	10	100	132,777
1966	10	40	24	18	11	100	160,950
1967	8	37	25	17	14	100	131,309
1968	7	41	27	16	11	100	152,905
1969	6	43	26	16	10	100	244,335
1970	7	45	24	15	10	100	353,898
1971	7	41	25	16	11	100	453,145
1976	4	72		8	16	100	515,830

Note: [a] Light industry has a heavy concentration of Turkish women workers.

Sources: Bundesanstalt für Arbeit. Ausländische Arbeitsnehmer. Nürnberg, various years.

The percent distribution of all Turkish workers abroad at the end of 1975 was: 80 percent in West Germany; close to 7 percent in France; 4.5 percent in Austria; 3 percent in the Netherlands; and 2 percent in Belgium with the other countries totalling less than 5 percent and no country having more than one percent of the entire number of Turkish workers abroad. The total is estimated at about 815,000.[3]

The Ankara Agreement

In the 1960s, the Turkish government discovered that out-migration had lessened considerably the unemployment situation at home and, perhaps more importantly, the remittances sent home considerably relieved the chronically negative balance of payments. Such a positive experience with out-migration encouraged the state planning office to include regularly the outflow of labor into the Turkish Five Year Plans.

The Turkish optimism toward the export of labor was also fueled by the legal history of what is known as the Ankara Agreement, signed September 12, 1963. According to this Agreement, free movement of workers applying to member states of the European Communities was to be extended to Turkish nationals by December 1, 1976. At the time of the signing of the Agreement there were six member states of what was then the European Economic Community (the Federal Republic of Germany, France, the Benelux countries and Italy). Since that time, Ireland, the United Kingdom and Denmark have gained a full membership status in the European Communities.

Turkey has always been interested in becoming a member of the European Communities, primarily to find a steady market for its labor. The Ankara Agreement provided for a three-stage integration of Turkey, beginning in 1973 and ending in 1995. The desired clause of free movement of workers could take effect in the 12th year from the signing of the Agreement.

Certain political developments, not unrelated to the current economic recession in Europe, as well as the fact that the new members of the European Communities must ratify all agreements, led to a possible rescheduling of the Turkish integration so that the Ankara Agreement must now be renegotiated.

Politics Abroad

The migration policy pursued by Turkey since 1963 was predicated on the anticipated membership in the European Communities. The Five Year Plan of Turkey, ending in 1977, included exportation of labor in its calculations of manpower needs[4] and projected exports totaling about 350,000 workers by the end of the plan — a figure later found to be too optimistic.

The recent realization of economic limitations of the receiving countries as well as the protracted negotiations around the Ankara Agreement has brought about some loss of governmental enthusiasm for the whole issue of membership in the European Communities. There are several reasons why this loss of enthusiasm has taken place.

Initially, Greece was also pressing for a full membership status and relations between the two governments have been strained for some time now. Turkey feels that it plays second fiddle to Greece in terms of the sympathies of the Communities and, that too many political concessions would have to be made in exchange for the membership.[5] Beyond this, however, Turkey feels that its NATO commitments which benefit the Communities are disproportionately heavy and that the payoffs in terms of priorities for its labor export are small.

A third consideration is that since the Ankara Agreement was signed, close to eighty other countries were conferred the "favored nation" status by the Communities, thus making the value of such a status doubtful. In addition to this, Turkey did not succeed in marketing its agricultural products in Europe as expected, and the country's industry is, as yet, in no position to compete successfully. On the other hand, the Agreement forced Turkey to lower some protective tariffs for industrial goods from Europe beginning in 1976, an additional disadvantage to Turkish industrial development.

The final consideration in this "loss of enthusiasm" is that the Turkish workers abroad are unprotected once they change their contractually ascribed jobs. The negotiated measures originally expected to take effect in the beginning of 1974, to extend protection of equal treatment in employment, are still outstanding and the bilateral agreements do not cover workers who relocate on their own.

Turkey's situation on the international labor market is, thus, unfavorable since the workers from nonmember states of the Communities do not enjoy the guarantees of work protection which workers from member states do.

Politics at Home

The pressures at home to keep exporting labor remain considerable. Turkey is a latecomer to the international flow of labor. The country's labor out-migrated chiefly through official channels, and the "culture of out-migration" characterizing some other nationals does not seem to have taken in Turkey. This means, that once the official channels for out-migration are shut, little private out-migration through friendship networks takes place.

---

[5] Kamran Inan, in *Milliyet*, March 14, 1976.

In 1963, Turkish agriculture employed about 12 million persons. This figure represented about three-fourths of Turkey's entire labor force. The mechanization of agricultural production already referred to added to the growing army of unemployed. By 1973, Turkey was estimated to have about two million unemployed. This figure represents 12.5 percent of the country's population between 15 and 64 years of age including those in the armed forces and those working abroad. To recalculate the unemployment rate on the actual labor force would yield values substantially higher.

The pressure on the government to seek outlets for the country's labor force abroad is thus considerable. It is not surprising that the goals of the Turkish migration policy were and are to export as many nationals abroad as possible disregarding any possible negative effects such a policy may come to have.[6] The current Five Year Plan foresees 1.8 million persons between 15 and 64 years of age as surplus labor beyond and above the liberally calculated absorption capacity at home and abroad.[7]

In addition to the sheer demographic pressure, the fiscal obligations of the government are such that it welcomes workers' remittances as a major substitute to exporting goods. Remittances represented about 14 percent of foreign currency earned by Turkey in 1964 but that figure rose to close to 70 percent at the beginning of this decade. In absolute figures, in 1971 about 1.2 billion Turkish Lira (470,000,000 U.S. dollars) were remitted home and about the same nominal amount in 1975. The devaluation of the lira, however, lessened the value earned. Also, 1972 registered a sharp decrease in the remittances received. Not all the reduction in the remittances were brought about by the economic distress in Europe.

It is only now, however, that the Turkish government is presented with the problem of how to utilize best the imported capital. The individual preferences of account holders are to misinvest their capital along traditional lines into small agricultural holdings, small businesses or building lots; or, worse yet, in imported durable goods.

In addition to the problem of how money is spent at home, there is the question of how to repatriate the five or so billions in U.S. dollars presumably hoarded by Turkish workers abroad. The reluctance to remit money home stems from the relatively high inflation rate in Turkey, which was 20 percent in 1974 and 17 percent in 1975.

In an attempt to attract the money of its nationals, Turkey has introduced a new banking regulation effective April 1, 1976 which allows Turkish nationals to deposit foreign currency in Turkish banks and to maintain a foreign currency account. The interest paid on such accounts is 7 percent, a

---

[6] S. Paine. *Exporting Workers, the Turkish Case.* Cambridge, England: Cambridge University Press. 1974.

[7] State Planning Office, DPT 1272.

rate competitive, for instance, with the German banks. There are, thus far, no limitations on the accounts.[8] This measure was supplemented by an agreement between the Turkish Central Bank and the Dresdner Bank in Germany. The agreement permits the Central Bank to open an account with the Dresdner Bank in which Turkish citizens abroad deposit their money which is then credited to their foreign currency accounts in Turkey. The general trust Turkish workers have in German banks helps the government to repatriate hard currency home. The catch is, however, that the Central Bank may institute controls on the disposal of money by the individual account holders.

The uncertain status of the Turkish workers abroad and the uncertainties of economic and currency nature at home encourage the workers to actions which assumed political character.

In December, 1975, the Committee for Cooperation was founded in Bavaria, West Germany, where there are about 200,000 Turkish workers. The aim of the Committee was to safeguard the interests of Turkish workers abroad. To demonstrate its political seriousness, the Committee asked their countrymen not to remit money home until the government settled certain issues of social security provisions for returnees and, above all, introduced steps to improve the schooling situation of children returning home.[9]

New organizations of workers are springing up in Turkey. These are union cooperatives where individuals pool their resources to start new, or to bolster ailing enterprises run by and for the primary benefit of returnees. Their political weight is not to be underestimated.

Issues in Return Migration

The return migration although not heavy at the moment generates new political pressures. It is a result of two influences: 1) workers are returning from abroad because their employment, or their employability, was terminated; and 2) some of the workers found that they cannot, or did not wish to adapt to life abroad; or they did not plan to stay in the first place.

At first, movement of the surplus peasant population to cities made the urban population potentially mobile. Migration abroad occurred primarily as organized transfers of workers and often in large groups. Under such conditions the problems of migrant adaptation are exacerbated since their integration into their host society is hindered by the lack of institutional support for an effective integration. Additionally, the housing and general provisions for the foreign workers are centered on their employment,

[8] Ersoy Caner, in *Milliyet*, May 14, 1976.
[9] A. Cemal, in *Cumhuriyet*, May 15, 1976.

contractually often defined as for a specified period of time. The fact that most of the workers overstay their first work contracts produces only belated efforts at some sort of social integration.

It is also important to note here, that the cultural visibility of Turkish workers abroad makes it difficult for them to develop friendship cliques with their co-workers. This is the more difficult as the friendship pattern of industrial workers are kinship and neighborhood, but not work oriented.

The ties to the home country are usually meant to militate against an effective integration[10] and such ties are fostered by the government itself. The Turkish government is not, however, in a position to take good consular care of its citizens. The Turks are dispersed all over Europe and, in West Germany alone, they are found in many more cities than Turkey could possibly have consular representation.

One of the major efforts of the consular representation of Turkey is to assure adequate schooling for the children of their citizens. Such issues are handled through the respective educational agencies and cover provisions for allowing Turkish children to have some tutoring in their mother tongue.

The other major function of the Turkish consulates is to intervene on behalf of Turkish workers in case of apparent discrimination in employment. However, due to a careful position of the Turkish government in such matters, the consular officials receive little direct support from the home office.

Even though there are direct and indirect obstacles to an integration of Turkish workers in their host countries, their return home is not being encouraged. Not only is the economic situation at home difficult at the moment and may remain so for the time being, but the returning workers are not likely to become fully reintegrated at home either. That is especially notable when their stay abroad has been prolonged. The stay of Turkish workers abroad exceeds, on the average, five years.

The main victims of the uncertainty as to where one belongs are the children of migrants. While in West Germany, for instance, they are enrolled in German schools where, for reasons of language and a different and perhaps difficult curriculum, they have fallen back. When they return, they have fallen back with respect to the Turkish curriculum, especially where the command of written Turkish has been weakened. From this, one can speculate about the "turned off" youth and the radicalization of the marginal groups.

---

[10] S. Pflegerl. "Aetiologie und Veränderung des Migrationsmotins als Grundlag des Reintegrationsproblems: Dargeshellt am Beispiel der Türkie". Report before the International Workshop — Conference on Migration Policies and Research, Committee on Migration, International Sociological Association, Vienna, 1975 (Mimeo); Gastarbeiter zwischen Integration und Abstossung: Die Sozialisation der Gastarbeiter im Aufnahmland. Munich and Vienna: Sergend und Volk (1977).

The stay abroad taught Turkish workers certain rudiments of politics through voluntary associations. Such are then imported back home where they are being organized and led mostly by return migrants. What they are bringing home is a new perspective on matters in their own country and their observations of worker participation in decision making encountered abroad.

This new thinking among Turkish returnees is reflected in particular in the creation of the already referred to union cooperatives; in May, 1975 these organizations numbered approximately 28, with about 30,000 members in toto. The cooperatives employ now about one thousand officials and their disposable capital is valued at about 30 million U.S. dollars.

Concerns and Prospects

In a thorough assessment of the situation in Turkey, Susan Paine[11] lists the impact of out-migration on the Turkish socioeconomic conditions at home: a) out-migrants from the agricultural areas do not represent the landless proletariat, so to speak, but, rather, they represent small and medium income farmers. Upon return, savings from abroad are reinvested into the farm which may well increase its efficiency, but which also contributes to local unemployment; b) it would appear that the departure of skilled or semi-skilled workers from Turkish industrial plants diminishes the total number of employees instead of providing for a simple turnover; c) most of the return migrants are of urban origin and return to the cities; the imported capital raises land and real estate prices with profits going primarily to the sellers and their intermediaries; and d) most of the out-migrants come from the richer parts of Turkey and those from the poorer parts tend to resettle elsewhere in the country thus maintaining, and even increasing, the regional differences which began the chain migrations.

There is no doubt that Turkey's hand is being forced in regard to migration policy. Given the demographic situation at home, Turkey must export labor. At the same time, due to the weak negotiating position of Turkey vis à vis labor importing countries, Turkey cannot proceed too firmly to safeguard the interests of its nationals abroad despite the increasing reports about job discrimination against Turkish workers. The originally anticipated scheduled return of Turkish workers[12] did not take place. Turkish migrants

[11] S. Paine. *Op. cit.*

[12] Gunther Beyer. "Migration from the Mediterranean Basin to Central, West and North Europe", *Emigration from Mediterranean Basin to Industrialized Europe*. F. Angelli, ed. Rome: University of Rome, Institute of Demography. 1976. Pp. 13-19; R.E. Krahenbuhl. *Emigration and the Labor Market in Turkey*. Report for the OECD Manpower and Social Affairs Committee: Paris: OECD. 1969.

abroad, left to their own devices learn rudimentary political self-protection. After their return, given their new political skills in pressuring and given their collectively impressive fiscal power, they are able to gain a preferred treatment, slowing down, however indirectly, the democratization processes normally accompanying modernization.

The question remains whether the one million or so Turkish nationals abroad will be able to stay there in face of the cloudy economic forecasts. Should they stay, one of the reasons behind a massive exportation of labor, namely the inflow of hard currency, may be choked off by deposits abroad. Should they return, and in great numbers, their accommodation at home may bring about those political changes the Turkish government may not entirely welcome.

16

Yugoslavia

IVO BAUČIĆ
University of Zagreb

Yugoslav Migration Policies after World War II

THE first economic migrants from Yugoslavia were registered in the immigration countries of Europe as early as 1954, but it was only in 1962 that political institutions and governmental administration revealed their position on out-migration. At that time about 50,000 Yugoslav workers had already left the country.[1]

A public discussion of out-migration or external migration started in Yugoslavia at a time when a relatively large number of Yugoslav citizens had already been employed abroad. No doubt, the numerous instances of illegal border crossings and illegal employment abroad past the expiration of Yugoslav tourist or business visas prompted a discussion of out-migration and exerted a strong influence on the formation of Yugoslav migration policy.

No detailed analysis of the development of Yugoslav migration policies exists thus far. The present discussion is informed mainly by observations made in the course of research on migration and by a familiarity with the social , political and economic development of Yugoslavia since the end of the war.

---

[1] Ivo Baučić. "Die Auswirkungen der Arbeitskräftewanderung in Jugoslawien", *Ausländerbeschäftigung und internationale Politik*, R. Lohrmann and K. Manfrass, eds. Munich and Vienna: Ouldenbourg. 1974. Pp. 171-206.

The migration policy adopted by a country depends largely on specific policy measures adopted in regard to national social and economic development. In the case of Yugoslavia, it is extremely difficult to relate migration policy to social and economic development policies because Yugoslavia was the first, and to this day the only, socialist country in the world which permits free labor migration of its working age population to the countries of Northwestern Europe.

Thus, forging its own migration policy, Yugoslavia was not able to compare its own experiences with those of other countries with similar political systems. Furthermore, Yugoslav migration policy had to be adapted to the migration policies of the labor importing countries. These have always been in a position to determine the shape of not only their own migration policies but of the policies of the sending countries as well. Their superior bargaining position was abetted by the permanently huge supply of foreign manpower on one hand, and by an understanding of the labor markets at home and abroad on the other. The immigration countries have a great advantage over the emigration countries. They control the selection of foreign workers, their entry and their residence. They are in the enviable position to accept only as many workers as they wish and only those with qualifications as suits their needs. Aside from this, the labor importing countries may resort, ultimately, to a repatriation of workers they no longer need.

Yugoslav migration policies reflect not only socioeconomic development at home but also the development of Yugoslav foreign policy. Furthermore, the situation of both the Yugoslav and West European labor markets entered into the policy formulation as did the aspirations of Yugoslavs already abroad and those at home wishing to migrate.

Counting from about 1945, Yugoslavia had three distinct and consecutive migration policies. From 1945 to about 1962, Yugoslavia's migration policy was a restrictive one. The official standpoint toward out-migration was negative. The second policy, which lasted for about nine years, was positive toward out-migration. There was public discussion of migration, and employment abroad was not discouraged. The third, and present, migration policy dates back to about 1972. The positive evaluation of out-migration was subjected to a critical reassessment. An attempt was made to control and channel migration flows.

During the time that the postwar policy on migration was in force, the government tried to constrain all potential out-migrants. During the time that the second migration policy was adhered to, the official policy was aimed at enabling as many workers to go abroad as there were candidates. In the third, the present period, the official policy is aimed at selective employment abroad, i.e., at sending abroad the surplus of the unemployed agrarian population from Yugoslavia's underdeveloped regions. One of the

TABLE 16:1

Yugoslav Workers in Europe, Registered Yugoslav Workers in
West Germany, Registered Workers in Yugoslavia as Working Abroad
and the Proportion of Workers Returning, Since 1954[a]

Year	Estimated In Europe[b]	Registered In Germany	Registered As Abroad	Proportion Returning
1954	3,000	1,801	—	—
1955	3,500	2,085	—	—
1956	4,000	2,297	—	—
1957	4,500	2,778	—	—
1958	10,000	4,846	—	—
1959	15,000	7,310	—	—
1960	18,000	8,826	—	—
1961	30,000	—	—	—
1962	50,000	23,608	—	—
1963	90,000	44,428	—	—
1964	115,000	53,057	7,019	16.2
1965	140,000	64,060	38,019	13.6
1966	210,000	96,675	84,159	16.1
1967	220,000	97,725	93,825	66.2
1968	230,000	99,660	145,231	26.9
1969	420,000	226,290	247,266	13.7
1970	550,000	388,953	358,421	19.1
1971	660,000	469,173	419,385	13.5
1972	760,000	471,892	465,439	16.1
1973	830,000	514,000	526,770	16.7
1974	820,000	445,000	523,214	134.0
1975	790,000	430,000	518,197	254.7
1976	750,000	390,000	495,571	559.9

Notes: [a] Estimated population in Yugoslavia in 1975: 21,000,000.
[b] Mid-year estimates from various sources archived in the Center for Migration Studies, University of Zagreb.

Sources: I. Baučić. "Die Auswirkungen der Arbeitskräftewanderung in Jugoslawien". *Ausländerbeschäftigung und internationale Politik*. R. Lohrmann and K. Manfrass, eds. Munich/Vienna: Ouldenbourg. Tables 1 and 14; files of the Center for Migration Studies, University of Zagreb.

goals of the new policy is to balance the number of workers leaving with the number of those returning.

It should be kept in mind that Yugoslavia underwent a complete change in political and socioeconomic system after the war. The fight against fascism and the revolution which took place at that time ended the already obsolescent capitalist system which had been extremely reactionary. Also, the economic underdevelopment of Yugoslavia as well as the multinational character of the country must be remembered. After the war, Yugoslavia was one of the least developed countries in Europe.

Prior to the war, an estimated one million and one-half Yugoslavs were living abroad. After the war, Yugoslavia needed all of its manpower to reconstruct, to develop and to industrialize. The postwar efforts brought full employment. During this period, Yugoslavia attempted to bring back emigrants from abroad, especially those from overseas. Unfortunately, there are no data on the return migration which immediately followed the war. It is generally known, however, that a part of the returning migrants found it difficult to reintegrate into the new Yugoslav society and left the country again after a short stay.

After the break off of political and economic ties in 1948 with the USSR and the other socialist countries in Eastern Europe, Yugoslavia continued to restrict emigration of its citizens. At this time, travel to Western Europe was made extremely difficult if not impossible. The majority of Yugoslavs who sought employment in Western Europe prior to 1954 crossed the border out of Yugoslavia illegally, joining the political refugees who left after the war.

After 1954, an ever increasing number of Yugoslav citizens stayed abroad seeking employment. Their travel was made possible by obtaining a business visa or an exit permit to visit relatives. Declaring themselves political refugees, they were able to find economic opportunities in Western Europe.

Unemployment as a motive to leave Yugoslavia was extremely rare until the mid-1950s. The governmental strategy of full employment paid off in that jobs were freely available. However, after Yugoslavia adopted a new policy aimed at the country's participation in the international division of labor, the internal economy gradually changed to a more capital intensive economy accompanied by the higher productivity of labor. The result of the rationalization of production was an increase in the number and the rate of unemployed. In 1958, there were already 132,000 unemployed and the unemployment rate increased to 5.2 percent of the labor force.

In 1962, Yugoslav migration policy underwent significant changes. In an effort to include Yugoslavia in the international division of labor, the government began to look on out-migration as a means to this end. The transition from a restrictive policy to a policy encouraging Yugoslav workers to seek work in the countries of Western Europe occurred rapidly. In 1963, several Yugoslav employment agencies started to cooperate with German employers to recruit workers demanded by German industry. By 1964, employment agencies all over the country introduced special employment services for Yugoslavs willing to work abroad. By 1962 a special amnesty law was passed to enable all those who left Yugoslavia illegally to change their status from that of political emigrant to that of economic out-migrant.

Thus, in the early 1960s employment abroad was accepted as a necessity. In a sense, this was unavoidable given the current level of socioeconomic development at home. The government felt that exportation of labor represented a temporary solution and saw employment of Yugoslav workers abroad as a temporary measure. Starting with 1963, the National Bank of Yugoslavia began to register foreign exchange income from migrants' remittances as a special item in its accounting. By 1965, Yugoslavia had entered into bilateral agreements with Austria and France to regulate the employment of Yugoslav workers in these countries and to formalize their legal and social status. Similar agreements were concluded in 1969 with Sweden, Germany, the Netherlands, Luxemburg and, overseas, with Australia. A closer look at the texts of these agreements as well as at their implementation demonstrates beyond any doubt that Yugoslavia was in a weak position from the start as a negotiating partner; not strong enough to ensure effective equality of treatment for the country's citizens. The agreements were entered into when Yugoslavia fostered a mass employment of its workers in the countries of Western Europe. Furthermore, a great number of Yugoslav workers were already employed in these countries prior to and thus, not covered by such agreements. On the other hand, the labor importing countries remained in a position to: a) continue importing Yugoslav workers without any specific agreement; b) disregard existing agreements at their own convenience; and c) interpret and implement them to suit their own interests.

Yugoslavia's positive stance toward employment abroad by nationals became obvious after the economic reform of 1965 as a consequence of which the total number of employed decreased the following year by 2.2 percent and the proportion of unemployed rose to 7.2 percent as compared to 6.4 the year previous.[2] Foreign employers were thus in a position to "skim off" a number of qualified Yugoslav workers by offering them better jobs. That was accomplished through various foreign employment agencies cooperating with the Yugoslav employment agencies and through direct contact with potential job seekers. For instance, the census of 1971 lists close to 50 percent of Yugoslav workers abroad who had had work experience at home.

To curb the out-migration of skilled labor, the Yugoslav employment agencies attempted to channel information about employment abroad to job seekers from the less developed regions, namely those in the central and southeastern parts of Yugoslavia. This is the region which had a surplus of underemployed agrarian population. These efforts paid off, especially during the years 1969 and 1972 when the demand for Yugoslav workers was high,

[2] *Statistical Yearbook of Yugoslavia*, 1966.

TABLE: 16:2

Yugoslav Workers Abroad According to Yugoslav Census of 1971
and the Registration by Percent Distribution
in the Various Receiving Countries

Country	Census		Registration	
	N	%	N	%
W. Germany	411,503	61.2	436,500	55.2
Austria	82,957	12.3	90,000	11.4
France	36,982	5.5	39,500	5.0
Switzerland	21,201	3.2	25,000	3.2
Sweden	16,359	2.4	22,500	2.8
BENELUX	7,358	1.1	11,000	1.4
Other Europe	20,509	3.1	22,500	2.8
EUROPE	596,869	88.8	647,000	81.8
Australia	40,168	6.0	60,000	7.6
Canada	13,579	2.0	41,000	5.2
U.S.A.	16,368	2.4	33,000	4.2
Other	4,924	0.7	9,500	1.2
TOTAL	671,908	100.0	790,500	100.0

Note: [a] The Yugoslav Census data are arrived at through inquiries with neighbors and relatives.

Sources: I Baučić. "Die Auswirkungen der Arbeitskräftewanderungen in Jugoslawien". *Ausländerbeschäftigung und internationale Politik*. R. Lohrmann and K. Manfrass, eds. Munich/Vienna: Ouldenbourg, Table 3.

particularly in Germany.

Whereas Yugoslavia was able to increase its export of surplus agricultural population during these years, the drain on skilled manpower did not diminish. Yugoslav citizens were able to get passports and exit visas without much difficulty starting with 1965. By 1967, exit visas were freely granted for repeated travel and without any indication of country of destination. Starting in 1968, exit visas were being issued for a period of two years without any restrictions on the number of trips, country of destination or purpose of travel. Whenever the holder of such a visa had its validity extended, the validity of the passport was also extended. Passports issued for the purpose of employment abroad did not differ from ordinary passports issued to tourists or businessmen. There was no mention of the purpose of the trip. For this reason, an accurate registry of Yugoslav workers departing abroad does not exist. There is the Yugoslav census of 1971, which included nationals abroad, and there are data sources in the registration records of the receiving countries. Those leaving Yugoslavia through the offices of

Yugoslav employment agencies are being statistically intercepted, but they represent an estimated 50 percent of the total out-migration of workers.

The New Policy

The migration policy of the period between the years 1962 and 1972 supported by broadly held views that out-migration has many positive consequences for the sending country proved to be too optimistic. It is true that both the individual migrant and the country derived some benefits. The remittances home alone shored up the chronically negative balance of payments.

After a dramatic increase in the number of Yugoslav workers employed abroad,[3] observations and research began to show the negative consequences of out-migration. Some of the negative features of an unrestrained out-migration may be listed as: unfavorable social and legal status of Yugoslav workers abroad reflected in their increasing alienation; irrational use of savings remitted home (buying of imported consumer goods); difficulties of replacing skilled workers at home; inadequate provisions for return migrants; and increasing emigration of whole families representing a permanent loss to Yugoslavia.

Such findings and realizations induced a gradual change in the political attitudes toward out-migration by the early 1970s. Even though such critical views had been expressed in the years past, now they were being uttered by various political organizations and by governmental bodies.

The Presidium of the League of Communists of Yugoslavia and the Presidium of the Socialist Federal Republic of Yugoslavia held a joint session on February 5, 1973, to discuss the social, economic and political issues of out-migration. The resolution resulting from this session emphasized that out-migration of Yugoslav workers may have to continue into the future but that the number of out-migrants will be reduced howbeit gradually. Furthermore, new conditions are to be created to encourage the return of especially professional and skilled manpower. This will be achieved by combining public funds with migrants' savings. Finally, employment abroad will be regulated in accordance with the interests of the national economy.

Migration policy and the status of Yugoslav workers abroad were discussed at the Federal Conference of the Socialist League of Yugoslavia, the central organization of all social and political associations in the country. The recommendations released on February 15, 1973, called for political, informational, cultural and educational efforts among Yugoslav workers abroad. The need to reduce the number of persons emigrating permanently

---

[3] 1968: 230,000; 1969: 420,000; 1970: 550,000; 1971: 660,000; 1972: 760,000; 1973: 830,000. Files of the Center for Migration Studies, Zagreb.

and the necessity to create conditions favorable to the return of migrants were also stressed.

On June 8, 1973, the Government of Yugoslavia promulgated a Law on the Basic Conditions for Temporary Employment and Protection of Yugoslav Citizens Abroad. In accordance with it, only employment agencies are allowed to act as mediators in the employment of Yugoslavs abroad. The Federal Employment Bureau collects new job offers from foreign employers and coordinates returns from abroad. The most significant provision of the Law is the obligation of the Republics and autonomous Provinces of Yugoslavia to reach an Agreement expressing the foundations and conditions for organized employment of Yugoslav citizens abroad and for their return from temporary employment abroad. The Agreement was reached in mid-1974. The Law also requires that, in accordance with the Agreement, the Federal Employment Bureau and the employment agencies of the individual Republics and autonomous Provinces must establish a joint and detailed plan for employment of Yugoslav citizens abroad specifying, for instance, the number, occupations, skills level, and regions from which the manpower should be drawn. The most important part of the Agreement is that which stipulates provisions for return migrants and for their reintegration into the national economy.

Thus, the new Law together with the Agreement (which has the force of law) form the core of the new migration policy in Yugoslavia. An implementation of the new policy will depend on the development of a new economic and social order in Yugoslavia (changes in tax structure, customs regulations, banking procedures, etc.). The efficacy of migration as a tool for a more rapid development of Yugoslavia will require understanding and help from countries of in-migration as well. Only concerted actions and harmonized migration policies among the sending and receiving countries will bring this about.

Concerns and Prospects

At present, the narrow national interests of the economically stronger and better organized partners influence the international migration. Economic growth of the less developed countries is being impeded and economic cooperation among sending and receiving countries is meager. To determine the optimal development of European migration from the point of view of their positive influence on future economic integration in Europe, the beneficial aspects of migration must come to the foreground.

As long as extreme regional differences in economic and social development exist, motivation for migration will also exist and no doubt, there will be population movements for years to come. The spatial mobility of population is one of the most visible characteristics of contemporary society. No matter how negative the effect of specific migrations, spatial movement of people remains basically a favorable factor in the optimal use of natural, technological and human resources.

Nonetheless, in the case of Yugoslavia, the numbers of migrant workers will be reduced if and when the conditions for return and the conditions for stay improve at home. Migration cannot and should not be the only path to an accelerated economic development. The transfer of capital and technology from economically more developed countries can contribute equally toward a better utilization of labor surpluses.

As far as the sending countries are concerned, new migrants should be recruited mainly from the surplus of young agricultural workers and they should be trained in industrial jobs before leaving. The training and experience in countries of destination can be harmonized with the needs of the home countries where the migrants will, hopefully, spend the greater part of their active life.

The economic gains stemming from migration should be distributed more fairly so that the migrants' country of origin may benefit as well. Both countries should contribute to an economic reintegration of return migrants. In particular, the sending countries must do much more than they are doing now, they must welcome the returnees to the planning of local, regional and sectoral economic development. In addition to taking advantage of the knowledge and skills acquired abroad, it is of special importance to effect a more productive use of migrants' savings remitted from abroad.

If the migration agreements will emphasize worker rotation in the future, some of the out-migrants will want to stay abroad a long time or permanently. That should remain their free choice. The interchange of persons between different countries can only be beneficial to the community of nations.

It is impossible to consider international migration apart from other issues mankind is facing and apart from other forms of international exchange and cooperation. Therefore it is essential that the migration of workers be viewed not only as a component of an international labor policy, but also as a part of coordinated plans for the demographic and regional development of both receiving and sending countries.

Considering the fact that we live in one world, in a limited space with limited resources, migration must form an integral part of an active and harmonized international policy for the optimal use of raw materials, physical energy and human labor.

References

General References

BEIJER, G., "Modern Pattern of International Migratory Movements". In, *Migration*. J.A. Jackson, ed. Cambridge: Cambridge University Press (1969). BÖHNING, W.R., "Migration of Workers as an Element in Employment Policy", *New Community*, 3:6-25. 1974. DUMON, M.W.A., "Family Migration and Family Reunion", *International Migrations*, 14:53-83. 1976. GIRARD, ALAIN, "Postface". In, *Les travailleurs étrangers en Europe Occidentale*. Ph. J. Bernard, ed. Paris: Mouton (1976). Pp. 407-414. HANDLIN, OSCAR, *The Newcomers*. Cambridge: Harvard University Press (1959). ICEM, "Intergovernmental Committee for European Migration. Second Seminar on Adaptation and Integration of Permanent Immigrants. Geneva, November, 1975. Recommendations", *International Migrations*, 14:19-49. 1976. RICHMOND, A.H., "Sociology of Migration in Industrial and Post-industrial Societies". In, *Migration*. A.J. Jackson, ed. Cambridge: Cambridge University Press (1969). Pp. 238-281; "Les migrations internationales et la conjoncture presente". In, *L'émigration du basin mediterranean vers l'Europe industrialisée*. Franco Angelli, ed. Rome: University of Rome, Institute of Demography (1976). SMITH, T. LYNN, *Fundamentals of Population Study*. Chicago, Philadelphia, New York: Lippincott (1960). VAN PRAAG, PHILIP, "Quelques considerations conçernant les relátions entre variables démographiques et variables politiques", *European Demographic Information Bulletin*, 8:2-21. 1977.

Chapter 1: Australia

AUSTRALIAN INSTITUTE OF POLITICAL SCIENCE, *How Many Australians?* Sidney: Angus and Robertson (1971). BORRIE, W.D., *Population and Australia. First Report of the National Population Inquiry*. Canberra: Australian Government Printing Office (1975). IMMIGRATION PLANNING COUNCIL, *Australia's Immigration Programme for the Period 1968 to 1973*. Report. Canberra: Australian Government Printing Office (1968). PRICE, CHARLES, "Introduction". In, *Australian Immigration: A Bibliography and Digest, Part I*. Charles Price and Jean Martin, eds. Canberra: Australian National University Press (1976); *Australian Immigration. Research Report No. 2 to the National Population Inquiry*. Canberra: Australian Government Printing Office Service (1975a); "Australian Immigration: 1947-73", *International Migration Review*, 9:304-318. 1975.

Chapter 2: Canada

BOYD, MONICA, "Immigration Policies and Trends: A Comparison of Canada and the United States", *Demography*, 13:83-104. 1976. BRETON, RAYMOND, JILL ARMSTRONG AND LES KENNEDY, *The Social Impact of Changes in Population Size and Composition: Reactions to Patterns of Immigration.* Ottawa: Information Canada GP* (1974). CORBETT, D.C., *Canada's Immigration Policy.* Toronto: University of Toronto Press (1957). DEPART-MENT OF CITIZENSHIP AND IMMIGRATION, *Citizenship, Immigration and Ethnic Groups in Canada: A Bibliography of Research Published and Unpublished Sources 1920-1958.* Ottawa: Queen's Printer (1961). DEPARTMENT OF MANPOWER AND IMMIGRATION, *Highlights from the Green Paper on Immigration and Population.* Ottawa: Information Canada (1975); *Immigration Policy Perspectives.* Volume 1. Ottawa: Information Canada GP (1974); *The Immigration Program.* Volume 2. Ottawa: Information Canada GP (1974); *Immigration and Population Statistics.* Volume 3. Ottawa: Information Canada GP (1974); *Three Years in Canada.* Ottawa: Information Canada GP (1974); *Immigration, Migration and Ethnic Groups in Canada: A Bibliography of Research 1964-68.* Ottawa: Information Canada (1970). EPSTEIN, LARRY, *Immigration and Inflation.* Ottawa: Information Canada GP (1974). GREEN, ALAN G., "Is Foreign Labour Complementary or Competitive (in terms of skills) with Native Borne Labour? The Canadian Case, 1911-41", *International Migration*, 6(1):371-375. 1974. HAWKINS, FREDA, *Immigration Policy and Management in Selected Countries: A Case Study of Immigration Policy and Management and Their Implications for Population Growth in the United States, Australia and Israel.* Ottawa: Information Canada GP (1974); *Canada and Immigration: Public Policy and Public Concern.* Montreal and London: McGill-Queens University Press (1972). HENRIPIN, JACQUES, *Immigration and Language Imbalance*, Ottawa: Information Canada GP (1975). KALBACH, WARREN E., *The Effect of Immigration on Population.* Ottawa: Information Canada GP (1975). KANTNER, ANDREW, WENDY DOBSON AND HERVÉ GAUTHIER, *Canada. Country Profiles Series.* New York: The Population Council (1974). KUBAT, D. AND D. THORNTON, *A Statistical Profile of Canadian Society.* Toronto: McGraw Hill-Ryerson (1974): *Canadian Immigration Policy (The White Paper).* Ottawa: Queen's Printer (1966); *Citizenship, Immigration and Ethnic Groups in Canada: A Bibliography of Research Published and Unpublished Sources 1962-64.* Ottawa: Queen's Printer (1964); *Citizenship, Immigration and Ethnic Groups in Canada: A Bibliography of Research Published and Unpublished Sources 1959-61.* Ottawa: Queen's Printer (1962). KUBAT, DANIEL, LEO DRIEDGER, FRANK F. FASICK, WARREN E. KALBACH, *German Nationals in Canada: Their Intentions to Naturalize.* Report to the Secretary of State. Waterloo: University of Waterloo, Department of Sociology (1976). PARAI, LOUIS, "Canada's Immigration Policy, 1962-1974", *International Migration Review*, 9(4):449-477. 1975; *The Economic Impact of Immigration.* Ottawa: Information Canada GP (1974). RAWLIK, GEORGE, "Canada's Immigration Policy, 1945-1962", *Dalhousie Review*, 42:287-300. 1962. RICHMOND, ANTHONY H., "Black and Asian Immigrants in Britain and Canada: Some Comparisons", *New Community*, 4:501-516. 1976; "Immigration, Population and the Canadian Future", *Sociological Focus*, 9:125-136. 1976; "The Green Paper — Reflections on the Canadian Immigration and Population Study", *Canadian Ethnic Studies*, 7:5-21. 1975; "Canadian Immigration: Recent Development and Future Prospects", *International Migration*, 13:163-180. 1975; *Aspects of the Absorption and Adaptation of Immigrants.* Ottawa: Information Canada GP (1975). TIENHAARA, NANCY, *Canadian Views on Immigration and Population: An Analysis of Post-War Gallup Polls.* Ottawa: Information Canada GP (1975). TIMLIN, MABEL F., "Canadian Immigration Policy: An Analysis", *International Migration*, 3:52-72. 1965.

* Entries designated with GP refer to the Canadian Immigration and Population Study Reports. There were four main reports and a host of research papers.

Chapter 3: New Zealand

DEPARTMENT OF STATISTICS, *New Zealand Population and Migration.* Wellington: Government Printing Office (1974); *New Zealand Official Yearbook.* Wellington: Government Printing Office. Annual. IMMIGRATION ADVISORY COUNCIL, *Review of Immigration Policy.* Wellington: Government Printing Office (1974). INTER-DEPARTMENTAL COMMIT-TEE ON POPULATION QUESTIONS, *New Zealand Population Policy Guidelines: To Assist the Formulation of a Population Policy for New Zealand.* Report to the Government. Wellington: Government Printing Office (1975). MC INTYRE, W. DAVID AND W.J. GARDNER, eds., *Speeches and Documents on New Zealand History.* Oxford: Clarendon (1971). O'CONNOR, P.S., "Keeping New Zealand White, 1908-1920", *New Zealand Journal of History,* 2:41-65. 1968. ROY, W.T., "Immigration Policy and Legislation". In, *Immigrants in New Zealand.* K.W. Thompson and A.D. Trilin, eds. Palmerston North: Massey University (1970). Pp. 15-24. SINCLAIR, KEITH, *A History of New Zealand.* London: Penguin (1959); "Why Are Race Relations in New Zealand Better than in South Africa, South Australia or South Dakota?" *New Zealand Journal of History,* 5:121-127. 1971.

Chapter 4: The United States of America

COALE, ANSLEY J., "Alternative Paths to a Stationary Population". In, *U.S. Commission on Population Growth and the American Future. Demographic and Social Aspects of Population Growth.* Charles F. Westoff and R.E. Parke, Jr., eds. Vol. 1 of the Commission Research Reports. Washington, D.C.: U.S. Government Printing Office (1972). Pp. 591-603. GIBSON, CAMPBELL, "The Contribution of Immigration to the United States Population Growth: 1790-1970", *International Migration Review,* 9(2):157-177. 1975. KEELY, CHARLES B., "Effects of the Immigration Act of 1965 on Selected Population Characteristics of Immigrants to the United States", *Demography,* 8:157-169. 1971; "Immigration Composition and Population Policy", *Science,* 185:587-593. 1974; "Effects of U.S. Immigration Law on Manpower Characteristics", *Demography,* 12:172-191. 1975. KEELY, CHARLES B. AND ELLEN PERCY KRALY, "Recent Net Alien Immigration to the U.S.: Its Impact on Population Growth and Native Fertility". Read before the Population Association of America meetings. April, 1977. Mimeo. LIPSET, SEYMOUR M., *The First New Nation.* New York: Basic Books (1963). STODDARD, ELLWYN R., "A Conceptual Analysis of the 'Alien Invasion': Institutionalized Support of Illegal Mexican Aliens in the U.S.", *International Migration Review,* 10(2):157-189. 1976. TOMASI, SILVANO M. AND CHARLES B. KEELY, *Whom Have We Welcomed? The Adequacy and Quality of United States Immigration Data for Policy Analysis and Evaluation.* New York: Center for Migration Studies (1976). U.S. BUREAU OF THE CENSUS, *Census of Population 1970, Vol. 1, Characteristics of the Population, Part 1, United States Summary, Section 1.* Washington, D.C.: U.S. Government Printing Office (1972); *The Statistical History of the United States.* New York: Basic Books (1976). U.S. DEPARTMENT OF COMMERCE, *Statistical Abstracts of the United States 1957.* Washington, D.C.: U.S. Government Printing Office (1957). U.S. HOUSE OF REPRESENTATIVES, *Amending the Immigration and Nationality Act and for Other Purposes.* Report No. 745, 89th Congress, 1st Session, August 6, 1965. U.S. SENATE, *Amending the Immigration and Nationality Act and for Other Purposes.* Report No. 748, 89th Congress, 1st Session, September 15, 1965. WARREN, ROBERT AND JENNIFER PECK, "Emigration from the United States: 1960-1970". Read before the Population Association of America meetings. April, 1975. Mimeo.

Chapter 5: The United Kingdom

BARKER, A., ed., *Strategy and Style in Local Community Relations.* London: The Runnymede

Trust (1975). CHEETHAM, JULIET, "Immigration". In, *Trends in British Society Since 1900*. A.H. Halsey, ed. London: Macmillan (1972). Pp. 451-508. DEPARTMENT OF EDUCATION AND SCIENCE, *Educational Disadvantage and the Needs of Immigrants*. London: Her Majesty Stationary Office, Cmnd 5720, March, 1974. DUMMETT, ANN, *Citizenship and Nationality*. London: The Runnymede Trust (1976). FOOT, PAUL, *Immigrants and Race in British Politics*. London: Penguin (1965). GERRARD, JOHN A., *The English and Immigration*. London: Oxford University Press (for the Institute of Race Relations) (1971). GARTNER, LLOYD P., *The Jewish Immigrant in England, 1870-1914*. London: Allen and Unwin (1960). HEPPLE, BOB, *Race, Jobs and the Law in Britain*. London: Penguin (1968). JACKSON, J.A., *The Irish in Britain*. London: Routledge and Kegan Paul (1963). KRAUSZ, E., *Ethnic Minorities in Britain*. London: Paladin (1972). MABEY, CHRISTINE, *Social and Ethnic Mix in Schools and the Relationship with Attainment of Children Aged 8 and 11*. London: Center for Environmental Studies. Research Paper No. 9 (1974). MAC DONALD, IAN A., *The New Immigration Law*. London: Butterworths (1972). MC INTOSH, N. AND DAVID J. SMITH, "The Extent of Racial Discrimination", *Political and Economical Plan: Broadsheet Series and Major Reports*, Vol. 40, Broadsheet 547. 1974. PATTERSON, SHEILA, *Immigrants in Industry*. London: Oxford University Press (1969); "Immigrants and Minority Groups in British Society". In, *The Prevention of Racial Discrimination in Britain*. S. Abbott, ed. London: Oxford University Press (for the Institute of Race Relations) (1971). Pp. 21-53. POPULATION PANEL, *Report of The Population Panel*. London: Her Majesty Stationary Office, Cmnd 5258, March, 1973. ROSE, E.J.B., ed., *Colour and Citizenship*. London: Oxford University Press (for the Institute of Race Relations) (1969). SHAH, SAMIR, *Immigrants in Employment, A Study of Home Workers in the Rag Trade in London's East End*. London: The Runnymede Trust (1975). SMITH, DAVID J., "Racial Disadvantage in Employment", *Political and Economic Plan, Broadsheet Series and Major Reports*, Vol. 40, Broadsheet 544. 1974; "The Facts of Racial Disadvantage", *Political and Economic Plan; Broadsheet Series and Major Reports*, Vol. 42, Broadsheet 560. 1976. SMITH, DAVID J. AND ANN WHALLEY, "Racial Minorities and Public Housing", *Political and Economic Plan; Broadsheet Series and Major Reports*, Vol. 41, Broadsheet 556. 1975. THOMPSON, E.P., *The Making of the English Working Class*. London: Gollancz (1965). ZUBRZYCKI, J., *Polish Immigrants in Britain*. The Hague: Nijhoff (1956).

Chapter 6: Austria

BEIRAT FÜR WIRTSCHAFT- UND SOZIALFRAGEN, *Möglichkeiten und Grenzen des Einsatzes ausländischer Arbeitskräfte*. Report to the Austrian Government. Vienna (1976). BUTSCHEK, F., "Wanderungen und ihre Folgen", *Europäische Rundschau*, 3:69-78. 1975. BUTSCHEK, F. AND E. WALTERKIRCHEN, *Aspekte der Ausländerbeschäftigung*. Monatsberichte des Österreichischen Instituts für Wirtschaftsforschung. Vienna (1974). GASTARBEITER-KREIS, *Gastarbeiter-Wirtschaftliche und Soziale Herausforderung*. Vienna: Europa Verlag and Österreichischer Wirtschaftsverlag (1973). GEHMACHER, E., "Die Soziale Problematik der Gastarbeiter". In, *Gastarbeiter in Österreich*. Proceedings of the Austrian Conference on Sozialarbeit conducted in 1971. Vienna: Europaverlag (1972). IFES, *Ökonomische und Soziale Kosten-Nutzen-Rechnung der Gastarbeiterbeschäftigung in Wein*. Report to the City of Vienna. Vienna: Institut für Empirische Sozialforschung (1972). PETER, ALEXANDER, *Die Beschäftigung Ausländischer Arbeitskräfte in Österreich*. Linz: Institut für Arbeitsmarktpolitik (1972). RAUTER, FRANZ, *Das Fremdarbeiterproblem in Innsbrucker Textil- und Bekleidungsbetrieben*. Innsbruck: Wagnersche Universitätsbuchhandlung (1972). SALTZBURGER INSTITUT FÜR RAUMFORSCHUNG, *Grenzen und Probleme der Beschäftigung von Gastarbeitern im Lande Salzburg*. Salzburg: SIR (1974). ÜDAG, *Das Österreichische Ausländerbeschäftigungsgesetz vom 20, März 1975: Geist und Ungeist einer Leistungsgesellschaft*. Vienna: Überdiözesane Arbeitsgemeinschaft für Gastarbeiter Fragen (1975). WERNER, HEINZ, "Freizügigkeit der

Arbeitskräfte und die Wanderungsbewegungen in den Ländern der Europäischen Gemeinschaft", *Mitteilungen aus der Arbeitsmarkt- und Berufsforschung*, 4:326-371. 1973. WOLFGANG, CHRISTIAN AND ELKE KINDSVATER, *Lohnarbeit am Beispiel der Gastarbeiter*. Frankfurt/ Main: Europäische Verlagsanstalt (1973).

Chapter 7: The BENELUX Countries

ALS, G., *La population du Luxembourg*. Luxemburg: Service Central de la Statistique (1975); *Luxemburg: Historic, Geographic and Economic Profile*. Luxemburg: Service Central de la Statistique (1976); "Les Migrations du bassin Méditerranéen vers le Luxembourg". In, *L'emigrazione del Bacino Mediterraneo verso l'Europa industrializzata*, F. Angelli, ed. Rome: University of Rome, Institute of Demography (1976). Pp. 221-238. BAGLEY, CH., "Immigration and Social Policy in the Netherlands", *New Community*, 1:25-28. 1971. BATON, P., *Coéducation d'enfants belges et étrangers*. Bruxelles: Institut de Sociologie de l'Université Libre de Bruxelles (1968). BEYER, G. AND J.J. OUDEGEEST, eds., *Some Aspects of Migration Problems in the Netherlands*. The Hague: Martinus Nijhoff (1952); *International Migration from and within Europe*. Liège: International Union for the Scientific Study of Population, Proceedings (1973). Pp. 425-437; "Migration from the Mediterranean Basin to Central, West and North Europe". In, *L'emigrazione del Bacino Mediterraneo verso l'Europa Industrializzata*. F. Angelli, ed. Rome: University of Rome (1976). Pp. 13-29. BOVENKERK, E., "Dutch Immigration Policy and the Myth of Return", *International Migration*, 13:147-150. 1975. BRAECKMAN, C., *Étrangers en belgique*. Bruxelles: Edition Vié Oeuvrière (1973). BRUYERE, J., "L'Immigration de main-d'oeuvre étrangère. En 1976, Nécessité ou Mésaventure"?,*Population et Fàmille*, 39:1-39. 1976. BUSSERY, M.H., "Incidence sur l'économie française d'une réduction durable de la main-d'oeuvre immigrée", *Economie et Statis-ique*, 3:37-45. 1976. CAMPIOLO, G., "Les étrangers en Belgique. Notes sur la littérature sociologique et quelques autres travaux", *Studi Emigrazione*, 13:219-234. 1976. CAPORALE, CH., "Coût et profit des migrations", *Revue de l'Action Populaire*, 184:37-50. 1965. CARON, A., "Migrant Workers in Belgium and Their Vocational Training", *Migration Today*, 7. 1966. DENIS, FR., "Toekomstbeeld der Immigratie in Belgie", *Maandblad Arbeid*, 6:465-478. 1965. DOOGHE, G., *DeBevolking in Belgie, Demografisch Overzicht*. Brussels: Centrum voor Bevolkings-en Gezinstudien. Technical Report No. 10. 1976. FINEAU, N., "Migration in Belgium", *Migration News*, 21(3):16-20. 1972; "Free Movement of Migrant Workers in Belgium", *Migration News*, 23(3):21-24. 1974. HEYDEN, H., "Diskussion über die Ausländerbeschäftigung im Europa", *Bundesarbeitsblatt*, 24(1):33-36. 1973. KAYSER, B., "Nouvelles politiques des pays européens d'immigration", *Studi Emigrazione*, 37:90-95. 1975. LÜSCHER, F., "Justice and Migration", *Migration Today*, 20:107-109. 1976. RAINTON, D., "The Social Role of the Dutch Police: With Special Reference to Minority Groups and Community Relations", *New Community*, 4:524-529. 1975/1976. SERVICE CENTRAL DE LA STATISTIQUE ET DES ETUDES ECONOMIQUES (LUXEMBURG) *Projections Démographiques 1974-2000*. Luxemburg: Ministère de l'économie national. Débats parlementaires sur le projet de budget 1975 (1975). Pp. 10. Mimeo. STEIGENGA, W., *Industrialization — Emigration. The Consequences of the Demographic Developments in the Netherlands*. The Hague: Martinus Nijhoff (1955). TER HEIDE, H., "Labor Migration from the Mediterranean Area to the Benelux Countries". In, *Population and Family in the Low Countries*. H.G. Moors et al., eds. Leiden: Martinus Nijhoff (1976). Pp. 132-148. TINBERGEN, J., "Investment, Balance of Payment and Welfare", Lecture, Utrecht, October 17, 1951. VAN DE KAA, D.J., "Demographic Change and Social Policy: A European Perspective". In, *Demographic Change and Social Policy*. M. Buxton and E. Craven, eds. London: Center for Studies in Social Policies (1976). Pp. 62-71. VAN DEN BRINK, T., "Some Quantitative Aspects of Future Population Development in the Netherlands". In, *Some Aspects of Migration Problems in the Netherlands*. G. Beyer and J.J. Oudegeest, eds. The Hague: Martinus Nijhoff (1952). Pp. 40-58.

VAN DER WINDT, K., "Bevolking en welzijn in Nederland. Eindrapport Commissie Muntendam", *Nederlandse Staatscourant*, 30:6-17. 1977. VAN PRAAG, PH., "Aspects économiques à long term des migrations internationales dans les pays de la C.E.E.", *International Migration*, 9:126-137. 1971. VERWEY-JONKER, H., ed., *Allochtonen in Nederland*. The Hague: Government Printers (second edition) (1973). WANDER, H., *Demographic Aspects of the Active Population*. Paper before the Seminar on the Implications of a Stationary or Declining Population in Europe. Strasbourg, Council of Europe. September (1976). Pp. 12. WERNER, H., "Migration and Free Movement of Workers in Western Europe", *International Migration*, 4:311-327. 1974.

Chapter 8: France

ADLER, S., *People in the Pipe-Line. The Political Economy of Algerian Migration to France 1962-1974*. Boston: Massachusetts Institute of Technology. September (1975). Mimeo. BONNET, J.C., *Les pouvoirs publics français et l'immigration dans l'entre deux guerres*. Lyon: Université du Lyon II, Centre d'histoire économique et sociale de la région lyonnaise (1976). CALVEZ, C., *Le problème des travailleurs étrangers*. Paris: Conseil économique et social. Avis et Rapport No. 7. 1969. CHEVALIER, L., *Problèmes Français de l'immigration*. Paris: Cours de Droit (1947). COMMISSARIAT GÉNÉRAL AU PLAN, "Notes sur les besoins d'amélioration de l'information statistique concernant la population étrangère en France", *CORDES*. Paris (1973). Mimeo. COMMISSION DE MAIN D'OEUVRE DU Ve PLAN, *Rapport général*. Paris: Documentation Française (1966). COMMISSION EMPLOI, *Rapport (Préparation du VIe Plan)*. Paris: Documentation Française (1972). Vols. I and II; *Rapport général (Préparation du VIIe Plan)*. Paris: Documentation Française (1977). COURGEAU, D., "Les départ hors de France, de travailleurs étrangers: un essai de mesure", *Population*, 23:609-624. 1968; *Étude interministérielle de rationalisation des choix budgétaires. Effects de l'immigration sur certains aspects du développment économique et social*. Paris: Documentation Française (1976). GANI, L., *Syndicats et travailleurs immigrés*. Paris: Editions Sociales (1972). GIRARD, A., "Attitudes des Français à l'egard de l'immigration étrangère", *Population*, 26:827-875. 1971. GIRARD, A., Y. CHARBIT, AND M.L. LAMY, "Attitudes des Français à l'égard de l'immigration étrangère, nouvelle enquête d'opinion", *Population*, 29:1015-1069. 1974. HERMET, G., *Les Espagnols en France*. Paris: Les Editions Ouvrières (1967). HUBER, M., *La population de la France pendant la guerre*. Paris: Presses Universitaires Françaises (1931). INED, *VIe rapport du la situation démographique de la France*. Paris: Institut National d'Études Demographiques. March. 1977. LANNES, X., *L'immigration en France depuis 1945*. The Hague: Nijhoff (1953). MARCZEWSKI, J., "Y-a-t-il eu un 'Take Off' en France?", *Cahiers de l'ISEA*, Series A.D., No. 1:69-94. 1961. MARKOWITCH, J.J., "L'industrie Française de 1789 a 1964", *Cahiers de l'ISEA*, Series A.F., No. 6. 1966. MAUCO, G., *Les étrangers en France. Leur rôle dans l'activité économique*. Paris: A. Colin (1932). MICHEL, A., *Les Algériens en France*. Paris: C.N.R.S. (1956); *La nouvelle politique de l'immigration*. Paris: Secretariat d'Etat (1977). NADOT, R., "Les effets de l'immigration sur la natalité en France depuis 1953", *Population*, Vol. 18. 1963; "L'immigration étrangère en France depuis la guerre". In, *L'exode rural, Suivi de deux études sur les migrations*, P. Merlin, ed. Paris: Presses Universitaires Françaises (1971). NIZARD, A., "La population active selon les recensements depuis 1946", *Population*, 26:9-62. 1971. POINARD, M., *L'émigration Portugaise et les retours*. Paris: OECD (1971). Rapport du groupe de travail sur l'émigration. 1971. *POPULATION*, "Démographie historique", 30:1-265. 1975. Special Issue. POUSSOU, J.P., "Les mouvements migratoires en France, et à partir de la France de la fin du XVe au'début du XIXe siècle: Approches pour une synthèse". In, *Annales de démographie historique*. 1970. PREFECTURE DE LA SEINE, *Les Portugais dans le départment de la Seine*. Enquête, July 1964. Service d'études et de recherches. 1965. Mimeo; *L'immigration des Espagnols dans le département de la Seine*. Service d'études et de recherches. 1967. Mimeo. ROBIN, R., "Bilan de

10 années de naturalisations (1962-1972)", *Revue Française des affaires sociales,* pp. 39-56. 1973. SAMMUT, CARMEL, "L'immigration clandestine en France depuis les circulaires Fontanet, Marcellin e Gorse". In, *Les travailleurs étrangers en Europe occidentale.* Ph.J. Bernard, ed. Paris: Mouton (1976). Pp. 379-397. SINGER-KEREL, J., "Conjocture économique et politique Française d'immigration 1952-1974". In, *Les travailleurs étrangers en Europe occidentale.* Ph. Bernard, ed. The Hague: Mouton (1976). Pp. 23-63. TAPINOS, G., *L'économie des migrations internationales.* Paris: Fondation nationale des sciences politiques (1974); *L'immigration étrangère en France (1946-1973).* Paris: Presses Universitaires Françaises (1975). TAPINOS, G., Y. MOULIER AND P. EWENCZYK, *La population Française à l'étranger et les flux d'immigration Françaises.* Paris: Fondation nationale des sciences politiques (1976). TRIPIER, M., "L'attitude des Français à l'égard de l'immigration étrangère: Note Critique", *L'année sociologique,* 26:179-188. 1976. TUGAULT, Y., "L'immigration étrangère en France: Une nouvelle méthode de mesure", *Population,* 26:691-705. 1971. ZEHRAOUI, A., *Les travailleurs Algériens en France. Étude sociologique de quelques aspects de la vie familiale.* Paris: Maspero (1971).

Chapter 9: Germany

AKDAG, E., "Türkische Arbeitnehmergessellschaften". Paper read before the 31st Konferenz für Ausländerfragen des kirchlichen Aussenamtes der evangelischen Kirche in Deutschland. Frankfurt, October, 1975. ARBEIT UND SOZIALPOLITIK, "Bonn Aktionsprogram für Ausländerbeschäftigung", Editorial feature. *Arbeit und Sozialpolitik,* 6-7:183. BORRIS M., *Ausländische Arbeiter in einer Grossstadt.* Frankfurt: Europäische Verlagsanstalt (1973). BRAUN, R., *Sozio-kulturelle Probleme der Eingliederung Italienischer Arbeitskräfte in der Schweiz.* Erlenbach and Zurich: Eugen Rentsch (1970). BUNDESANSTALT FÜR ARBEIT, Ausländische Arbeitnehmer—Beschäftigung, Anwerbung, Vermittlung, Erfahrungsbericht 1970. Nürnberg: Bundesanstalt für Arbeit (1971); *Repräsentativ-Untersuchung '72 über die Beschäftigung Ausländischer Arbeitnehmer im Bundesgebiet und ihre Familien- und Wohnungsverhältnisse.* Nürnberg: Bundesanstalt für Arbeit (1973). DODENBERDER, "Zwischenbilanz der Ausländerpolitik". Paper read before the Südosteuropa-Gesellschaft, Tutzing, Germany. Nov. 16, 1976. EPD-DOKUMENTATION, "Entwurf von Thesen zur Ausländerpolitik eines Ausschusses der Bundesregierung vom 23. Oktober, 1975", *epd-Dokumentation,* 5:4-10. 1976. ERNST, H., "Städte ohne Gettos", *Die Zeit,* No. 46:40. 1974; "Wende in der Ausländerpolitik?", *Arbeit und Sozialpolitik,* 6/7:181-186. 1973. FORCH, H., "Die Freiheitsrechte der ausländischen Arbeitnehmer in Detuschland". Dissertation, Law, University of Mainz. 1968. GÖRGL, E., "Empfehlungen und schulische Massnahmen". In, *Ausländerkinder in Deutschen Schulen.* Hermann Muller, ed. Stuttgart: Ernst Klett (1974). Pp. 99-112. GROSSMANN, W.,"Sozialisationsbedingungen und Bildungschancen Ausländischer Arbeiterkinder", *Gettos in unseren Schulen?,* 137:11-25. 1974. KANEIN, W., *Das Ausländerrecht und die wesentlichen fremdenrechtlichen Vorschriften: Kommentar.* Munich, Berlin: Beck (1966). LANGKAU, J. AND U. MEHRLÄNDER, *Raumordnungspolitische Steuerung der Ausländerbeschäftigung.* Bonn-Bad Godesberg: Bundesministerium für Raumordnung, Bauwesen und Städtebau (1976). LOHRMANN, R., "Politische Auswirkungen der Arbeitskräftewanderungen auf die Bundesrepublik Deutschland". In, *Ausländerbeschäftigung und internationale Politik.* R. Lohrmann and K. Manfrass, eds. Vienna: Oldenbourg (1974). Pp. 103-140; *Beschäftigung Ausländischer Arbeitnehmer in der Bundesrepublik Deutschland unter spezieller Berücksichtigung von Nordrhein-Westfalen.* 2nd Ed. Koln and Opladen: Westdeutscher Verlag (1972); *Soziale Aspekte der Ausländerbeschäftigung.* Bonn-Bad Godesberg: Neue Gesellschaft (1974); *Einflussfaktorer auf das Bildungsverhalten Ausländischer Jugendlicher.* Bonn: Neue Gesellschaft (1978). MILKE, K., "Rechtsprobleme der ausländischen Arbeitnehmer in der Bundesrepublik Deutschland". Dissertation. Faculty of Law. University of Würzburg. 1967. PRESSE UND INFORMATIONSAMT

DER BUNDESREGIERUNG, "Ausländerbeschäftigung weiter rückläufig", *Sozialpolitische Umschau*, Dec. 5, No. 201. 1975; "Zuwanderung von Ausländern stark rückläufig", *Sozialpolitische Umschau*, April 25, No. 67. 1975. SCHILDMEIER, A., *Integration und Wohnen*. Hamburg: Hammon (1975). STATISTISCHES BUNDESAMT, THE FEDERAL REPUBLIC OF GERMANY, "Wanderungen 1975", *Wirtschaft und Statistik*, 9:549-554. 1976; "Ausländer im Bundesgebiet", *Wirtschaft und Statistik*, 1:20-26. 1976. WERNER, H., "Freizügigkeit der Arbeitskräfte und die Wanderungsbewegungen in den Ländern der Europäischen Gemeinschaft", *Mitteilungen aus der Arbeitsmarkt-und Berufsforschung*, 4:326-371. 1973. ZIERIS, E., *Betriebsunterkünfte für ausländische Mitbürger Nordrhein-Westfalen*. Düsseldorf: Der Minister für Arbeit, Gesundheit und Soziales des Landes NRW (1972).

Chapter 10: The Scandanavian Countries

CONFERENCE OF EUROPEAN MINISTERS OF LABOR, *Situation of Migrant Workers in Europe*. Report from a Conference held in Rome in November, 1972. Strassbourg: Document CMT (72) 6 (1972). Mimeo. DENMARK: MINISTRY OF LABOR, *Betaenkning nr. 589 om udenlandske arbejderes forhold in Danmark (Conditions of Foreign Workers in Denmark)*. Report of a Commission. Copenhagen: Statens Trykningskontor (1971). DENMARK: MINISTRY OF SOCIAL AFFAIRS, *Fremmedarbejder in Danmark*. Copenhagen: Ministry of Social Affairs, Information Section (1974); *Betaenkning nr. 761 on udenlandske arbejderes sociale og samfundsmaessige tilpasning her i landet. (Social and Societal Adjustment of Foreign Workers in Denmark)*. Copenhagen: Statens Trykningskontor (1975). FINLAND: CENTRAL STATISTICAL OFFICE, *Statistical yearbook of Finland 1975*. Helsinki: Central Statistical Office of Finland (1976). FINLAND: EMIGRATION COMMISSION, *Siirtolaisasiain neuvottelukunnan mietintö I*. (Emigration Commission, Report No. 1). Helsinki: Committee Report No. 1972:119 (1973). MAJAVA, ALTTI, *Migration Research in Scandinavia*. Proceedings of the Nordic Seminar on migration research. Siikaranta, Finland. January, 1973. Helsinki: Ministry of Labor, Planning Division (1973); *Migrations between Finland and Sweden from 1946 to 1974: A Demographic Analysis*. Helsinki: Ministry of Labor, Planning Division (1975). Mimeo; *OECD Joint Project on Emigrant Workers, National Report on Finland*. Helsinki: Ministry of Labor and Paris: OECD Document CT/MIG/42 (1976). Mimeo. THE NATIONAL INSURANCE INSTITUTE, *Social Insurance in Norway*. Oslo: The National Insurance Institute (1976). NORDISK UTREDNINGSSERIE, *Utlänningspolitik och utlänningslagstiftning i Norden (Aliens Legislation in Scandinavia)*. Report NU 1970:16. Stockholm: The Nordic Council (1970); *Nordisk kommunal rösträtt och valbarhet (Voting Eligibility in Scandinavia)*. Report NU 1975:4. Oslo: The Nordic Council of Ministers (1975); *Yearbook of Nordic Statistics 1975*. NU 1975:38. Stockholm: The Nordic Council and the Nordic Statistical Secretariat (1976). NORDISKA ARBETSMARKNADSUTSKOTTET, *Arbetsmarknad och arbedmarknadspolitik in Norden. Report om utvecklingen 1975. (Employment Market and Policies in Scandinavia)*. Oslo: The Nordic Council (1975). NORWAY: NORGENS OFFENTLIGE UTREDNINGER, *Innvandringspolitikk*. Report No. 1973:17 by the Committee of October 16, 1970 on immigration of labor policies. Oslo: Universitetsforlaget (1973); Statement No. 39, 1973-74. The Parliament (1974); Statement No. 107, 1975-76. The Parliament (1976). OPSAND, OLE-PETTER, "Research on the Social and Educational Situation of Immigrant Children". Paper read before the Third Nordic Seminar on Migration Research, Espoo, Finland, May, 1976. Mimeo. PUNTERVOLD BOE, BENTE, "Foreigners in Norway". Paper read before the Third Nordic Seminar on Migration Research. Espoo, Finland, May, 1976 (1976). Mimeo. SWEDEN: COMMISSION ON IMMIGRATION, *Invandrarutredningen 3, Invandrarna och minoriteterna (Immigrants and Minorities)*. Report SOU 1974:69. Stockholm: Ministry of Labor (1974). SWEDEN: MINISTRY OF LABOR, *Immigrants in Sweden. A Summary of Swedish Immigration Policy*. Stockholm:

Ministry of Labor (1975). SWEDEN: NATIONAL CENTRAL BUREAU OF STATISTICS, *Population and Housing Census 1975*. Part 3:3. Population in Sweden and the administrative districts, alien and foreign born population. Stockholm: National Central Bureau of Statistics (1977). SWEDEN: THE NATIONAL IMMIGRATION AND NATURALIZATION BOARD, *Ny i Sverige (New in Sweden)*. Periodical. No. 5 (Norrköping). 1976. *SWEDEN: TJÄNSTEMÄNNENS CENTRALORGANISATION, Invandrings-och invandrarpolitik (Immigration and Policy)*. Report to the TCO (Salaried Employees Organization) Congress. Stockholm: TCO (1976). WIDGREN, JONAS, "Immigration in Sweden in 1972". In, *Migration Research in Scandinavia*. A Majava, ed. Helsinki: Ministry of Labor, Planning Division (1973); *The Position of Immigrants in Sweden*. Report for the UN Secretariat, May 26, 1974. Stockholm: Ministry of Labor. Mimeo; *The SOPEMI Report on Sweden*. Stockholm: Ministry of Labor and Paris: OECD Document SME/MI/76:12 (Sweden). 1976. Mimeo; *Memorandum on Swedish Immigration Policy, January 17, 1977*. Stockholm: Ministry of Labor (1977).

Chapter 11: Switzerland

ARBEITSGRUPPE FÜR DIE GESCHICHTE DER ARBEITERBEWEGUNG, *Schweizerische Arbeiterbewegung*. Zürich: Limmat Verlag (1975); *Verhandlung der schweizerischen Vereinigung für internationales Recht 1916*. Zurich: Orell Fussli (1917). BICKEL, WALTER, *Bevölkerungsgeschichte der Schweiz seit dem Ausgang des Mittelalters*. Zürich: Büchergilde Gutenberg (1947). BOHNENBLUST, ERNST, *Geschichte der Schweiz*. Erlenbach-Zürich: Rentsch (1974). BURCKHARDT, WALTHER, *Die Einbürgerung der Ausländer in der Schweiz*. *Schweizerisches Politisches Jahrbuch 1913*. Bern: K.J. Wyss (1913). DELAQUIS, ERNST, "Im Kempf gegen die Ueberfremdung". A speech before the Legal Society in Bern, *Zeitschrift des bernischen Juristenvereins*, 57:49-69. 1921. DE VALLIERE, P., *Treue und Ehre: Geschichte der Schweizer in fremden Diensten*. Lausanne: Les Editions d'art Suisse ancien (n.d.). FEHRLIN, WOLFRAM, "Die Rechtsgleichheit der Ausländer in der Schweiz". Dissertation. Faculty of Law. University of Bern: Stampfli (1952). FLEINER F. AND Z. GIACOMETTI, *Schweizerisches Bundesstaatsrecht*. Zürich: Polygraphischer Verlag (1949). Reprinted: (1965). FORSTMOSER, PETER AND ARTHUR MEIER-HAYOZ, *Einführung in das schweizerische Aktienrecht, Bern:* Stampfli (1976). GIACOMETTI, ZACCARIA, *Das Staatsrecht der schweizerischen Kantone*. Zürich: Polygraphischer Verlag (1941). GUGGENHEIM, PAUL, Niederlassungsverträge, Schweizerische Juristische Kartotek 662 (Genf 1943). n.d.; *Traité de droit international public*. Vol. 1. Geneva: Librairie de l'Université, Georg & Cie. S.A. (1953); *Repertoire suisse de droit international public . . . (1914-1939)*. Edited for the Bundesrat with L. Calfisch, C. Dominice, B. Dutoit, J.P. Ritter. Basel: Helbling and Lichtenhahn (1975). HAUSER, MATHILDE, "Die den Ausländern in der Schweiz garantierten Freiheitsrechte". Dissertation. Faculty of Law. University of Zurich. Winterthur: Hans Schellenberg (1961). In, *Historisch-Biographisches Lexicon der Schweiz. Vol. III*. Neuenburg (1926). HOFFMANN-NOWOTNY, HANS-JOACHIM, *Soziologie des Fremdarbeiterproblems: Eine theoretische und empirische Analyse am Beispiel der Schweiz*. Stuttgart: F. Enke (1973). ILG, ALFRED, "Die Einbürgerung kraft Geburt auf Schweizerboden (Das Ius soli)". Dissertation. Faculty of Law. University of Zurich. Vienna: Schöler (1922). KOLLER, ARNOLD, "Die unmittelbare Anwendbarkeit völkerrechtlicher Verträge und des EWG-Vertrages im innerstaatlichen Bereich", *Schweizerische Beiträge zum Europarecht*, vol. 8. Bern: Stampfli (1971). LANGHARD, J., *Das Niederlassungsrecht der Ausländer in der Schweiz*. Zürich: Orell Füssli (1913). LARGIADER, ANTON, *Geschichte von Stadt und Kanton Zürich*, Vol. 1. Erlenbach-Zürich: Rentsch (1945). LUDWIG, CARL, "Die Flüchtlingspolitik der Schweiz in den Jahren 1933 bis 1955". A report to the Bundesrat and the respective Local Council (Bundeskanzlei), n.d. MACHERET, AUGUSTIN, "L'immigration étrangère en Suisse à l'heure de l'integration européenne", *Schweizerische Beiträge zum Europarecht*, Vol. 2. 1969. MEIER-

HAYOZ, ARTHUR UND PETER FORSTMOSER, *Grundriss des schweizerischen Gesellschaftsrechts.* Bern: Stampfli (1974). MOSER, HANS PETER, "Die Rechtsstellung des Ausländers in der Schweiz. Referate und Mitteilungen des schweizerischen Juristenvereins", *Zeitschrift für Schweizerisches Recht,* Neue Folge 86 II, 101:327-488. 1967. NOHER, ERICH, "Die internationalen Verträge über Aus- und Einwanderung". Dissertation. Faculty of Law. University of Zurich: J. Weiss. (1937). PETITMERMET, P., "Les principes à la base du droit d'établissement des étrangers en Suisse", *Zeitschrift für Schweizerisches Recht,* Neue Folge 42:97a-185a. 1923. ROTH, ANDREAS HANS, "The Minimum Standard of International Law Applied to Aliens". Dissertation. Faculty of Law. University of Geneva. The Hague: Sijthoff (1949). RUTH, MAX, *Das Fremdenpolizeirecht der Schweiz.* Zürich: Polygraphischer Verlag (1934); "Das Schweizerbürgerrecht", *Zeitschrift für Schweizerisches Recht,* Neue Folge 56:1a-156a. 1937. SALIS UND W. BURKHARDT, *Schweizerisches Bundesrecht.* 6 Volumes. Frauenfeld: Huber Schlaepfer, Rudolf (1930); "Die Ausländerfrage in der Schweiz vor dem Ersten Weltkreig". Dissertation. Faculty of Philosophy I. University of Zürich. Zürich: Juvis Druck u. Verlag (1969). SCHMID, HANS, *Die Ortsgemeinden im Kanton St. Gallen . . .* Zürich and St. Gallen: Polygraphischer Verlag (1967). SODER, JOSEF, "Die Aus- and Eiwanderungsfreiheit". In, W. Schätzel u. Th. Veiter eds., *Handbuch des Internationalen Flüchtlingsrechts. Flüchtlingsrecht vol. 1,* edited by Furst Franz Josef von Liechtenstein-Stiftung. Wien u. Stuttgart: Braumüller (1960). VAUCHER, RENE FRANK, "Le statut des étrangers en Suisse", *Zeitschrift für Schweizerisches Recht,* Neue Folge, 86(2):489-643. 1967. VON WALDKIRCH, EDUARD, "Die Grundsätze des Niederlassungsrechts der Fremden in der Schweiz", *Zeitschrift für Schweizerisches Recht,* Neue Folge, 42:56a-95a. 1923. WILLI, VIKTOR, *Ueberfremdung — Schlagwort oder bittere Wahrheit?* Bern: Lang (1970).

Chapter 12: Greece

LIANOS, THEODORE P., "The Migration Processes and Time Lags", *Journal of Regional Science,* 12:425-33. 1972; "Flows of Greek Out-Migration and Return Migration", *International Migration,* 13:119-33. 1975; "Capital-Labor Substitution in a Developing Economy", *European Economic Review,* 6:129-41. 1975. MATZOURANIS, C., *Greek Workers in Germany* (in Greek). Athens: Gutenburg (1975). POLYZOS, N., *Report on Migration and Migration Policy* (in Greek). Athens: Center for Planning and Economic Research (n.d.). WERNER, H., "Freizügigkeit der Arbeitskräfte und Wanderungsbewegungen in den Länderns der Europäischen Gemeinschaft", *Mitteilungen aus der Arbeitsmarktund Berufsforschung,* 4:326-71. 1973. ZOLOTAS, X., *International Labor Migration and Economic Development.* Athens: Bank of Greece (1976).

Chapter 13: The Iberian Peninsula

ALMEIDA, CARLOS AND ANTONIO BARRETO, *Capitalismo e emigração.* Lisbon: Prelo (2nd Ed.) (1974). CASTLES, STEPHEN AND GODULA KOSACK, *Immigrant Workers and Class Structure in Western Europe.* London: Oxford University Press (1973). FERREIRA, EDUARDO SOUSA, *Origens e formas da emigração.* Lisbon: Iniciativas Editoriais (1974). FRANCO, ANTONIO DE SOUSA, *A emigração para a Europa no conjunto da emigração Portuguesa.* Lisbon: Livraria Editora Pax (1974). HERMET, GUY, *Les Espagnols en France.* Paris: Les Editions Ouvrières (1967). INSTITUTO ESPAÑOL DE EMIGRACIÓN, *IV congreso de la emigración Española.* Oviedo, Gijon y Santiago de Compostela. October, 1971 (Proceedings); *Emigración Española asistida.* Estadistica del Año 1974 e Estadistica del 1er Trimestre, Año 1975 (1975); *Boletín informativo.* No. 94, April, 1976. LEAL, A. SARAGGA, *L'évolution de l'émigration Portuaise.* Lisbon (1973). LOPEZ, FRANCISCO SANCHEZ,

Emigración Española a Europa. Madrid: Confederacion Española de Cajas de Ahorros (1969). MATEO, FELIPE VASQUEZ, *La nueva emigración a Iberoamerica.* Madrid: Instituto Español de Emigración (1968). MINCES, JULIETTE, *Les travailleurs étrangers en France.* Paris: Edition du Seuil (1972). PASSIGLI, G.G., "Report on Spanish Emigration". In, *Workshop on The Comparative Study of the Re-Integration Policy of Five European Labor Exporting Countries.* Berlin: Wissenschaftszentrum (1975). SERRÃO, JOEL, *A emigração Portuguesa.* Lisbon: Livros Horizonte (2nd Ed) (1974). TRINDADE, MARIA BEATRIZ, ROCHA, *Immigrés Portugais.* Lisbon: Instituto Superior de Ciencias Sociais e Politicas (1973); "Portuguese Rural Migrants in Industrialized Europe", *Iberian Studies,* 4:9-14. 1975; "Portuguese Migration Movements Inside Europe". In, *Workshop on The Comparative Study of the Re-Integration Policy of Five European Labor Exporting Countries.* Berlin: Wissenschaftszentrum (1975). Mimeo.

Chapter 14: Italy

BARBAGALLO, F., *Lavoro ed esodo nel Sud 1861-1971.* Naples: Guida (1973). BEI CLEMENTI, G., "Regioni ed emigrazione". In, *Regioni ed emigrazione, Quaderni.* Perugia: Regione dell'Umbria (1973). BERTELLI, L., G. CORCAGNANI AND G.F. ROSOLI, eds., *Migrazioni.* Catalogo della Biblioteca del Centro Studi Emgirazione di Roma. Rome: Centro Studi Emigrazione (1972). BRIANI, V., *Il lavoro italiano in Europa. Ieri ed oggi.* Rome: Ministero Affari Esteri (1972). CALVARUSO, C., *Sottoproletariato in Svizzera.* Rome: Coines (1971); *Sindacati ed emigrazione.* Rome: Coines (1974). CENTRO STUDI EMIGRAZIONE, *La Svizzera dopo Schwarzenbach.* Rome: Centro Studi Emigrazione (1970). CERASE, FRANCESCO P., *Sotto il dominio dei borghesi. Sottosviluppo ed emigrazione nell'Italia Meridionale 1860-1910.* Rome: Carucci (1975). CINNANI, P., "La scelta del governo italiano nel secondo dopoguerra", *Il Ponte,* 30:1342-1359. 1974. CONSIGLIO NAZIONALE DELL'ECONOMIA E DEL LAVORO, *Rapporto monografico sulle recenti tendenze dell'emigrazione italiana.* Rome: CNEL (1976). GOLINI, A. AND CASELLI, G., eds., *Bibliografia delle opere demografiche italiane (1966-1972).* Rome: Instituto de Demografia, University of Rome (1973). ISFOL, *Fondo sociale europeo. Quaderno di formazione.* Rome: ISFOL (1975). LENZI, R. AND A.M. BIRINDELLI, *Aspetti e problemi dell'emigrazione italiana con particolare riguardo a quella nell'ambito CEE.* Rome: CISP (in press). MINISTERO AFFARI ESTERI, *Aspetti e problemi dell'emigrazione italiana all'estero nel 1974.* Rome: Ministero Affari Esteri (1975); *Guida pratica delle norme statali e regionali applicabili sul territorio italiano nell'interesse del citadino emigrato.* Rome: Ministero Affari Esteri (1976). PITTAU, F., "Regioni ed emigrazione". In, *Dossier Europa. Emigrazione.* Rome: Centro Studi Emigrazione (1976). PUGLIESE, E. AND G. MOTTURA, "Mercato dell lavoro e caratteristiche dell'emigrazione italiana nell'ultimo quindicennio". In, *Agricoltura, mezzogiorno e mercato del lavoro.* Bologna: Il Mulino (1975). REGIONE DELL'UMBRIA, *La questione dell'emigrazione e la politica delle regioni per un nuovo ed alternativo modello di sviluppo in Italia.* Rome: Conferenza Nazionale dell'Emigrazione (1975). Mimeo. VERCELLINO, E., *Aspetti e problemi dell'emigrazione italiana.* Rome: Conferenza Nazionale dell'Emigrazione. Ministero degli Affari Esteri (1974).

Chapter 15: Turkey

ANDERSON, LEWIS S., *Turkey.* New York: The Population Council. Country Profile Series (January, 1970). BEYER, GUNTHER, "Migration from the Mediterranean Basin to Central, West and North Europe". In, *Emigration from Mediterranean Basin to Industrialized Europe.* F. Angelli, ed. Rome: University of Rome, Institute of Demography (1976). Pp. 13-19. ERDENTUG, N., "Köy topluluklari ile ilgili toplum kalkinmasinda *etnolojik* (sosyal antropolojik) calismalarin yeri" ("Ethnological Research and the Development of Rural Population"), *Antropoloji,* No. 3.

1965; "Türkiye geleneksel toplumlarinda (kültüründe) kültürdegismeri" ("Cultural Change and the Turkish Population"), *Antropoloji*, No. 4. 1969; *Türkiye Türk toplumlarinda kültürel entropolojik (etnolojik) incelemeler (Cultural Anthropological Studies of the Turkish Population)*, Ankara: Üniverzitesi Egitim Fakültesis Yayinlan, No. 29. 1972. KRAHENBUHL, R.E., *Emigration and the Labor Market in Turkey*. Report for the OECD Manpower and Social Affairs Committee: Paris: OECD (1969). PAINE, S., *Exporting Workers, the Turkish Case*. Cambridge: Cambridge University Press (1974). PFLEGERL, S., "Aetiologie und Veränderung des Migrationsmotivs als Grundlage des Reintegrationsproblems: Dargestellt am Beispiel der Türkei". Report before the International Workshop — Conference on Migration Policies; Research Committee on Migration of the International Sociological Association, in Vienna (1975). Mimeo; *Gastarbeiter zwischen Integration und Abstossung: Die Sozialisation der Gastarbeiter im Aufnahmeland*. Munich and Vienna: Jugend und Volk (1977). STATE PLANNING OFFICE (Ankara), *Yeni Strateji ve Kalpinma Plani. Unüncü Bes Yil 1973-1977* (Third Five-Year Plan). Ankara: Devlet Planlama Teskilate (n.d.); *Yurt disindan dönen iscilerin sosyo-skonomik egilimleri üzerinde bir calisma (Attitudes of Returnee Workers)*. DPT: 1372 - SPD: 264. Ankara: Devlet Planlama Teskilate (1974). TIMUR, T., *Türkiye'de aile yapisi (Turkish Family Structure)*. Ankara: Hacettepe Universitesi Yayini, No. 15. 1972. TÜMERTERKIN, E., *Türkiye'de ic göcler (Internal Migrations in Turkey)*. Istanbul: Istanbul Universitesi Yayinlare, No. 1371. 1968. WERTH, MANFRED, et al., *Türkische Arbeitnehmergesellschaften, Band II. Evaluierung von Betriebsgründungen in der Türkei*. Saarbrücken and Bonn: Report for the Bundesministerium für Wirtschaftliche Zusammenarbeit (1975). YASA, I., *Türkiye'nin toplumpsal yapisi ve temel sorunlari (Social Structure and Social Problems in Turkey)*. Ankara: Türkiye ve Orta Dogu Amme Idaresi Enstitüsi Yayinlar, No. 136. 1970.

Chapter 16: Yugoslavia

BAUČIĆ, IVO, *The Effects of Emigration from Yugoslavia and the Problems of Returning Emigrant Workers*. European Demographic Monographs, II. The Hague: Center of Population Studies (1972). Pp. 1-44; "Strukturen und Probleme der Wanderung Jugoslawischer Arbeitnehmer in das Ausland", *Münchener Studien zur Sozial — und Wirtschaftsgeographie*, 7:31-40. 1973; "Die Auswirkungen der Arbeitskräftewanderung in Jugoslawein". In, *Ausländerbeschäftigung und internationale Politik*. R. Lohrmann and K. Manfrass, eds. Munich and Vienna: Ouldenbourg (1974). Pp. 171-206; "Yugoslavia as a Country of Emigration". In, *International Migration*. Proceedings of a Seminar on Demographic Research in Relation to International Migration, Buenos Aires, March 5-11, 1974 (1974). Pp. 254-265; "Migration temporaire ou definitive: Le dilemme des migrants et les politiques de migration", *Studi Emigrazione*, 33:121-134. 1974; "Internationale Migration — ein Negativfaktor bei der wirtschaftlichen Integration", *Europäische Rundschau*, 3:105-112. 1975; "Some Economic Consequences of Yugoslav External Migration". In, *Les travailleurs étrangers en Europe occidentale*. Ph. Bernard, ed. Paris: The Hague: Mouton (1975). Pp. 87-104; "Die Jugoslawische Auswanderung im Lichte des Nord-Sud Konflikts", *Die Dritte Welt* (special issue) (1975). Pp. 286-301; "Social Aspects of External Migration of Workers and the Yugoslav Experience in the Social Protection of Migrants". In, *The Welfare of Migrant Workers and Their Families*. Report of a Conference, held in Hercegnovi, Yugoslavia, September 8-13, 1975, under the auspices of the European Social Development Program, United Nations (1976). Pp. 105-134. BÖHNING, W.R., "Some Thoughts on Emigration from the Mediterranean Basin", *International Labour Review*, 111:251-277. 1975. NIKOLINAKOS, M., *Politische Ökonomie der Gastarbeiterfrage*. Hamburg: Rowohlt (1973). PETROVIĆ, ZORAN, "Odanost i zapošljavanje", ("Plant Loyalty and Employment Abroad"). *Naše Teme*, 20:291-328. 1976. POLOVINA, SVETISLAW, "Migraciona kretania v Evropi i njihovo ekonomskodruŠteno znacenje", ("Migration Movements in Europe and Their Socioeconomic Impact"). *Naše Teme*, 13:1848-1966. 1969. RADLOVIC, OBRAD, *Normativno reguliranje privremenog zapošljavanja iugoslavenskih gradana u inozemstvu* ("Legislative Guidelines for Temporary Employment of Yugoslav Nationals Abroad"). Zagreb: Center for Migration Studies (Series Vol. 3. Pp. 1-41) (1977).

Index of Names

Index